The Church Across the Street

The Church

Across the Street

By

Reginald D. Manwell

and

Sophia Lyon Fahs

An Introduction to the Ways and
Beliefs of Fifteen Different Faiths

REVISED EDITION

BEACON PRESS   BOSTON

Preface

"Many years ago, sometime during the middle of the twentieth century . . ."

In this manner one of our descendants may begin writing of the times in which we now live. No doubt our times will seem as unreal to them as much of history now seems to us, yet the people who lived one or twenty centuries ago were real people like us. In spite of their strangeness of dress and customs, they looked, acted and felt much as we do. They helped to make the world we live in what it is, whether for good or for ill, just as we are making a world in which those who shall come after us must live. Looked at in this way, events and people of the past become as interesting and as vivid as current happenings and people in today's news. Fiction is not more fascinating.

The story of how the many different kinds of churches came to be is one of these true-to-life dramas. It is a saga of twenty centuries of tragedy and triumph. It is the tale of real men and women who had the insight and the daring to break with the traditions of their day and to venture forth along untrodden and dangerous paths. It is the story also of other real people who resisted change and who tried to perpetuate the old ways by destroying the books—and the men—that urged the reforms.

Our own church or denomination, whatever it may be, can be truly appreciated only when we understand how and why it came to be. Its significance in the society of today can be tested only when we have compared and judged the worth of that for which it stands alongside the worth of other churches that differ from it.

Most of us are very limited in our outlook and in our friendships. Our little worlds are much smaller than they need to be. How much more interesting our conversations with our friends in other churches might be if we knew enough to talk about the ways in which we differ, and if we understood how our several customs were first brought about! Intelligent understanding helps not only to keep old friends; it helps also in making new ones.

Many people yearn to travel widely about the world to gain an expanded outlook, sometimes without first becoming acquainted with the picturesque world that is almost on their doorsteps. They may make great sacrifices to see Palestine, and at the same time never attend a service in the Jewish synagogue only a few blocks away from their home. Visitors to France are often stirred by the ritual and music in the Russian Orthodox Cathedral in Paris, yet it may never have occurred to them that the same great choral music and the same kind of incense are offered in worship to the Creator in hundreds of Russian Orthodox churches in America.

Whether we live in large cities or in small towns, we may be sure that our churches are full of dramatic stories of the long ago. These stories lie hidden in stained-glass windows, in stone sculpture, in robes worn by priests or ministers, in ritual and music, and in the gospel message that is proclaimed. The stories are about us in abundance. They are being enacted over and over week by week. This book is written to help you know how to read these stories.

How many different kinds of churches can you name? Believe it or not, there are more than 250 different Protestant denominations in this country. Look it up in the federal census if you doubt it. There are some twenty-five kinds of Baptists and twenty kinds of Lutherans and ten kinds of Presbyterians! A few of these have recently merged, or are in the process of doing so, but not infrequently new religious groups are organized. There's a reason for every one, yet strangely enough many people belonging to these churches have no idea why they are different.

The leaders of the Protestant Christian churches of the world, after years of agitation and persuasion, have recently succeeded in uniting most of the denominations into one great World Council of Churches, which now includes 197 different religious bodies in sixty countries. To this Council even the Eastern Orthodox Church of Russia has just been admitted.

Yet some large Protestant groups still remain outside, and some indeed militantly oppose such union. In the United States thirty-three of the denominations, including nearly all the larger ones, have united to form the National Council of Churches. Yet how can we hope for a united mankind (without which peace among the races and nations is hardly possible), if churches believing in the brotherhood of man cannot get together?

In this book we have written stories of different kinds of religious bodies. We have included some of the best-known Protestant denominations, the Roman Catholics and the Jewish synagogues. We should like to have told of many more. The Adventists, for instance, who number almost three-quarters of a million and whose medical and humanitarian work in the remote corners of the world surpasses that of most other Protestant denominations, we have passed by with great reluctance; so it is also with a number of other interesting groups. On the other hand, we have included three rather small denominations—the Friends, the Unitarians and the Universalists—because it seemed to us that their significance far outweighs their numbers.

We warn those about to read this book against expecting to find in it an adequate history of any of the various religious groups considered. This is not a church history. It is merely an introduction to the larger study. In order to dramatize the issues at stake, we have centered the story of each denomination around a single pioneer who played an important part, but not necessarily a major part, in the establishment of the new church. In addition, we have given briefly a few of the most important or interesting facts regarding the present activities and beliefs of the groups chosen.

Instead of satisfying curiosities, we hope the book will arouse appetites for more understanding. When we hear a new church mentioned or see a "church across the street" with an unfamiliar name, let us accustom ourselves to ask: "Why is it here? What does it stand for? What is its story?"

REGINALD D. MANWELL
SOPHIA L. FAHS

Acknowledgments

In writing this book, the authors have been fortunate in being given the generous help of a number of notable scholars in Church history. We wish to express our great indebtedness to them all, for without their help the book would have failed in its purpose. At the same time we desire to free these friends of ours of all responsibility for any errors or lack of insight that may have crept into the writing of the book in spite of their scrutiny and their criticisms.

Merely to list their names suggests the richness of fellowship we have enjoyed. DR. CHARLES LYTTLE, Professor of Church History, Meadville Theological Seminary, and DR. MAX A. KAPP of St. Lawrence Theological School both read the entire first draft of the manuscript and made criticisms. Other professors have examined certain chapters when these were near their final form. PROF. WALTER RUSSELL BOWIE of Union Theological Seminary criticized the chapter on the Episcopalians. DR. ROBERT NICHOLS of the same Seminary read the chapter on the Presbyterians. PROF. ALFRED S. COLE, School of Religion of Tufts College and DR. CLINTON LEE SCOTT criticized the Universalist chapter. DR. FREDERICK MAY ELIOT, President of the American Unitarian Association, examined the chapter on the Unitarians. DR. JAMES R. JOY, Director of the Methodist Historical Society, criticized the Methodist chapter and furnished us with two photographs for it. DR. WILLIAM W. ROCKWELL, Professor (Emeritus) of Church History, Union Theological Seminary, gave many hours of painstaking, critical work on the chapters about the Lutherans, the Roman Catholics, the Eastern Orthodox Churches, and the Congregationalists.

MISS MARGUERITTE HALLOWELL, Office Secretary of the Philadelphia Meeting of Friends, criticized the chapter on the Friends. WILIAM D. K. KILPATRICK, Manager of Publications of the Church of Christ, Scientist, made valuable suggestions regarding the chapter on that church, and furnished us with two photographs. DR. LE ROI C. SNOW, Church Historian for the Church of Jesus Christ of Latter-day Saints, kindly sent us the two illustrations used for the chapter about that church. MR. JOSHUA LIEBERMAN, a liberal Jew of wide reading, helped with the writing of the chapter on the Jewish Synagogue, as did also RABBI H. PANITZ of Syracuse.

We are grateful also to all those who furnished us with illustrations.

The two authors of the book have shared almost equally the labor involved in writing all the chapters except the first, which is of an introductory nature. For this SOPHIA L. FAHS is primarily responsible.

Because of our desire to keep the book uncluttered with footnotes and with a long bibliography, we have not often given the sources of facts. Throughout our labor, however, we have been profoundly grateful for the written treasures made available to us through the painstaking work of many historical scholars.

During the years which have passed since the appearance of the first edition of this book it has benefited from the criticisms of many readers and friends throughout the country; to all of them the authors wish to express thanks.

Whatever virtues the book may have are in no small degree due to critics who have read with a kindly eye chapters of the manuscript dealing with various churches and offered suggestions, many of which have been incorporated into the text. Among them are Dr. Joseph B. Long, Secretary of the United Church of Canada, who not only read the chapter dealing with this great Church but put into the hands of the senior author much material not otherwise obtainable, and Dr. Joseph Smith, Professor of Church History at the Christian Theological Seminary in Indianapolis, who with several of his colleagues read the chapter dealing with the Disciples of Christ. Others who read new portions of the text dealing with their respective denominations include: Dr. Charles C. Noble, Dean of Hendricks Chapel, Syracuse University (Methodist);

Rev. Paul F. Bosch of the Hendricks Chapel Staff (Lutheran); Rev. Richard F. Manwell (Congregational), minister of the First United Church of Christ in Chelmsford, Massachusetts. Numerous others have been most cooperative in furnishing needed information, among them the Office of the First Presidency of the Church of Jesus Christ of Latter-day Saints in Salt Lake City, Utah, and Archbishop William H. Francis, of the Old Catholic Church, Woodstock, N. Y. The authors are grateful to all of them.

Contents

Illustrations

1. The Beginning

The Old Story of Salvation

Jesus did not found a new religion. He was Jewish in his faith throughout all his life. He was a reformer more than an initiator. He advocated a righteousness that exceeded legalism and a godliness more vital than that of ritual. Like the greatest Jewish prophets before him, he protested against turning piety into the saying of prayers and the offering of sacrifices in the temple. Like Rabbi Hillel, his older contemporary, Jesus emphasized the humble, contrite heart and the forgiving spirit.

Although Jesus won a large popular following, he failed to bring about the reforms he advocated. Formalized religion was promoted by many religious leaders of his generation. The elaborate rituals of the temple in Jerusalem were the glory of the nation. To maintain outward obedience to all the injunctions of the law, and to encourage all loyal Jews to make regular pilgrimages to Jerusalem to celebrate the festivals— these things were believed to be essential if the morale and faith of the people were to be maintained. These outward forms symbolized the national hope of future greatness when the longed-for Messiah would be sent from heaven to deliver the Jewish nation from its conquering enemies.

Jesus failed to win any large number of Jewish ecclesiastical leaders. His efforts were dramatically cut off by his tragic death at the hand of the Roman governor of Judea. Although Jesus himself had opposed rebellion against Rome, Pilate mistook him for a political agitator and inflicted upon him the punishment usually meted out to rebels—crucifixion.

This story of one of the great Jewish prophets, however, is not the story that was passed from man to man after Jesus died. It was not the story told by Paul or Peter or by the writers of the Gospels. It is, rather, the story of what the Christian Church early came to believe about Jesus.

The shock of Jesus' sudden and tragic martyrdom so stirred the hearts of his former friends and followers that their estimate of his significance began to change and grow to giant proportions. A great enthusiasm was awakened, not so much for the new ideas Jesus had set forth, as for Jesus himself as a unique person.

A strong conviction developed among Jesus' Jewish followers that he was not really dead after all. They believed they had actually seen him alive even after his body had been buried in the tomb. They thought of him as going back to heaven to prepare a place for them to come. They believed that his spirit returned to earth from time to time in invisible form to be present with them when they met together, to guide and to encourage them.

The result was that a new movement began. A new society was formed of people who worshiped this martyred hero. In spite of his death, they saw in him the fulfillment of their long thwarted hopes for a new world. Their old ideas of a national Messiah were completely changed. Their emotions were aflame. Their memories of Jesus were alight with the glory of their hopes.

So it came about, for these and other reasons, that the factual story of the unorthodox rabbi, who had taught in the synagogues and who had endeared himself as a friend of outcasts and sinners, became the story of a supernatural and divine being who had been sent especially to earth to save the world from sin. All the things he had done while with them in the flesh seemed wonderful to his followers. They were sure he would return to the earth, for his work was not finished. Then the world would see his glory and he would do greater wonders than before.

This was the story that was spread throughout the Greek and Roman world. Paul and Peter, two Jews, first conceived it. The writers of the Gospels enlarged upon it, and the church fathers filled in the story with more details. By means of this story they put their beliefs regarding the significance of Jesus

St. Augustine, from a fresco (1480) in Florence, Italy, after a paint-ing by Botticelli. (The Bettmann Archive)

within the framework of a stirring world drama. It was the story of the history of mankind as the early Christians conceived it. It represented a great cosmic plan originated by God himself. It began before the world was created and it was conceived as lasting beyond time into eternity. God's direct interventions into human history mark the great crises in the story. Jesus is the unique person in the drama, for he is God himself in human form. This was the gospel that Christians preached. This was the "good news," the great Story of Salvation.

In the fifth century Augustine immortalized the story by putting it into written form. In doing so he combined the old Jewish Bible with the gospel records and the Book of Revelation and made them altogether one great connected story. His genius conceived this inclusive story in the framework of seven great ages of time. In brief, this is the old story as Augustine wrote it.

The Seven Great Ages of Time

In the beginning was God and with him was his only Son and the blessed angels in heaven. Perfect happiness and peace prevailed.

Then God created the earth and sky, the sun, the moon and the stars. Everything He made was good, and God was pleased.

God created the first man and the first woman, forming them in the pattern of himself, and giving them the gift of immortality. These first people were good and God was pleased. He made for them a beautiful garden filled with fruit trees. He gave them all kinds of animals and birds and fishes to enjoy.

God forbade this first man and woman to eat the fruit of but one tree and that was the tree of the knowledge of good and evil, threatening them with the loss of immortality if they disobeyed.

Now one of the angels in heaven, Satan by name, had

already disobeyed God and had been cast out of heaven. In the form of a talking serpent he wandered through the beautiful garden and tempted the first man and woman to disobey also. With their disobedience came the first great tragedy in the history of the world. Pain, hard labor and death were their punishment. With this, their first sin, they lost the purity of their divine nature. The poison of sin began working within them. Not only did Adam and Eve die because of their disobedience, but all men have died and all men have inherited an evil nature.

Children were born. Generations passed away. Mankind became more and more wicked. God repented that he had ever created man. *So ended the First Great Age of Time.*

In justice all mankind should have been destroyed, yet God was long-suffering and full of kindness towards his creatures. He would give them another chance—at least he would give it to some. God, therefore, chose Noah and his family, who were living righteously and justly, to be the special objects of his protection. God commanded Noah to build an ark in which he and his family and a sampling of all the animals and birds might live for a while. When these chosen ones were safe within the ark, God sent a great flood that destroyed all other living things on the face of the earth.

When the storm had subsided and the earth was once more dry, human history again began. Since, however, even Noah and his family had inherited the evil nature passed on to them from Adam and Eve, Noah and his descendants grew more and more degenerate and wicked. They became proud of their strength, attempting to build a tower that would reach even to heaven, but God brought confusion among them, causing the workmen to speak each a different language, so that they were unable to achieve their dream of power. *So ended the Second Great Age of Time.*

From among all the men on the earth, God again chose one man who lived a life pleasing in his sight. This man's name was Abraham. God commanded Abraham to leave his homeland and to go with his family into a new country. There he was to found a new nation, a nation whom God would bless and make great, for they were to be His "chosen people," who would become an example and a light to all the rest of mankind.

Abraham did as God commanded. His descendants increased in number until they were in truth a great people, but even they became obstinate and rebellious. They, too, had to be punished. This God finally did by sending them into captivity in Egypt where they lived as slaves for several hundred years. *So ended the Third Great Age of Time.*

Again God raised up a deliverer in the hope that he might lift mankind back again to the standards of righteousness that had been man's at the beginning. This leader was Moses, who courageously defied the mighty Pharaoh, delivered his people from slavery and led them to the borders of a new land. God revealed to Moses the ten great commandments and other lesser laws by which the people should rule their lives— but, again, these "chosen people" were rebellious. Even Moses himself failed at a time of crisis. *So ended the Fourth Great Age of Time.*

Once more God provided a leader. His people were enabled to enter and conquer the land of Canaan. King David, a man after God's own heart, sat upon the throne and ruled his people in righteousness, but David's successors strayed from the path of obedience. They displeased God by worshiping lesser gods of stone and wood and following after wickedness. Again and again God sent prophets among them to speak in His name and to warn them of His wrath, but few there were who paid heed to their words. Finally God was obliged once more to punish. This He did by allowing certain neighboring nations to conquer his "chosen people." Their capital cities, Samaria and Jerusalem, were laid waste and the people scattered or killed or taken away to serve as captives in the lands of their conquerors. *So ended the Fifth Great Age of Time.*

The sinful nature of man was indeed desperately wicked. Again and again God had tried to help humanity by sending specially endowed leaders to teach them, but even his "chosen people" had forsaken His guidance. For five hundred years God allowed them to suffer.

A righteous God could not let man's sins go unpunished, yet His love for His creatures was unbounded. Man deserved everlasting punishment, yet God's mercy could not endure the prospect. So His great plan of salvation must still be worked out. Someone must be punished whose value would exceed the value of all humanity together. Such a one was God's beloved Son who had lived with the Father in heaven from all eternity. If this Son were sent to earth to live as a human being and if he were punished with death, then God could accept that punishment as a substitute for the punishment of all mankind.

So the great Son of God humbled himself and consented to be given human form. He left his beautiful heavenly home to live in poverty upon the earth. He was born as a babe in the womb of a pure woman, without the help of any man. This God-child, named Jesus, lived a perfect life, taught his people the truths they had forgotten or had been too blind to understand. He performed miraculous cures, even raising the dead, in order to show to all mankind that he was a Son of Heaven and had been sent by God to the earth.

God's "chosen people," however, rejected their Savior. Their leaders complained to Pilate and persuaded the Roman Pontiff to have him crucified. Thus the divine Son of God died on the cross as a ransom for the sins of all the world. Those who believed on Him, and were baptized and tried to live according to His teachings, would be saved from everlasting punishment. Though they died, they would live again with Christ in heaven.

As a final proof of His divine nature and mission, Jesus himself broke the bonds of death, came forth from the tomb and showed himself to his friends for forty days. Then he was lifted up again through the clouds into heaven where he now sits at the right hand of God. *So ended the Sixth Great Age of Time.*

The seventh great age is now passing. Mankind is waiting for the Son of God to return to the earth in glory. When he comes He shall rule all the nations of the world in righteousness. He shall be King of kings and Lord of lords. Righteousness shall fill the entire earth as the waters now cover the sea, and there shall be peace among men for a thousand years.

Finally the great Day of Judgment will come. All who have died will be brought back to life, and both the living and those who have died will stand before the throne of God and before His Son in heaven. Each one will be judged on the basis of his life on earth. If he has believed on Jesus as his Savior, has been baptized and thus has had his sins washed away and forgiven, he will be granted through God's great grace an eternal life of happiness with God and His Son in heaven.

Those others, however, who have been disobedient and who have not received the pardon of their sins through the sacrifice of Jesus, their Savior, will be sent to the place of everlasting punishment, where there will be weeping and gnashing of teeth forever. Thus on that Great Day of Judgment the *Seventh Great Age of Time* will come to an end, and eternity will begin.

Why This Story Is Important

This, then, is in outline form the Old Story of Salvation. To tell it so briefly in this manner seems inadequate and unfair, for when read in its details the story becomes much more impressive.[1] No story ever told has had so great an influence on the history of mankind as has this old story. Thousands of missionaries have left their homelands, have lived among strangers and have learned foreign languages in order to tell this story to those who have never heard it.

It should not be supposed, however, that all missionaries today are now proclaiming this gospel in these words, nor should we assume that all ministers who talk about Jesus as Savior are thinking in terms of this old story in this old form. Down through the years there have been many revisions made in the story. Certain parts have been refined. Many Christians have revised the old ideas of the atonement. Words such as

---

[1] It is told in detail in Sophia Lyon Fahs, *The Old Story of Salvation* (Boston: Beacon Press, 1955).

"divinity," "supernatural" and "miracle" have different meanings for different people. What is important for all of us to realize is that this story in its old form represents the religious foundation upon which the spiritual life of Europe and America has been building for fifteen hundred years. Before the progress of scientific discoveries had revolutionized man's outlook upon the universe and upon his own nature, this interpretation of life was convincing. It satisfied and inspired millions of people. The story has been loved and sung about as the "sweetest story ever told."

It is important, too, because many of the ideas expressed in this old story have become parts of our culture, our thinking and even of our language. Almost unconsciously we tend to conceive of nature and human affairs, even of our own conduct, as under the competitive control of two great supernatural powers, God and the Devil. God, if we pray, may perhaps be induced to alter events in our favor, even sometimes to the point of miracles like those the Gospels tell us were wrought by Jesus in Biblical times. Many people think of human nature as essentially evil, with sickness, suffering and even death as the continuing penalties for Adam and Eve's disobedience of the divine command in the Garden of Eden. This is the concept of Original Sin. Heaven and happiness, hell and misery, are often equated both in our thinking and in the dictionary. Men may be called by God to perform special tasks, or to devote their lives to fulfilling certain missions.

This Old Story, then, has influenced and continues to influence us all. Its ideas and concepts raise serious questions in our minds: "What is the real nature of God?" "Should we think of Jesus as God?" "Is it reasonable to think that he was born of a virgin?" "Do we need to believe in his virgin birth and his miracles as proof of his divine nature?" "Should we agree with St. Augustine that by his death Jesus made amends for the sins of all mankind?" "Is there a life after death, with eternal happiness or never-ending torment, depending on how we have lived on earth?" "Does God choose individuals (or peoples) to be his special instruments?" "Can we believe that

God answers prayer?" "Or that God ever suspends the operation of natural law and ordains miracles?" When millions of
people would answer such questions as these affirmatively, we
cannot afford to dismiss them without deep and honest
thought.

How this story has been changed is, in large measure, the
story of the development of the different churches. Revisions
in the story, as you will see, have come at a great price. Men
have suffered martyrdom because they denied some important
part of the story, while others have suffered with equal courage
to defend it in all its parts.

You will find scenes from the Story of Salvation embodied
in the art you will see in the churches you visit. The hymns
you sing will reflect it as well as the prayers that are said. No
one can really understand the culture of our Western world
who does not know this old story in its old form. It is so customary, however, to assume that everyone knows the old story that
it is now seldom told fully in its ancient form.

Even today you will find some leaders in our churches
afraid to speak plainly regarding the changes they have or have
not made in the old story. The issues involved still provoke
violent emotions. This, in itself, reveals the important meanings the story has had and still has for the Christian world.

A Spiritual Monarchy Founded,
Then Divided

The First Great Crisis

When the followers of Jesus were first called Christians,
most of them were Jews. Literally thousands of Jews, both in
Palestine and in many other countries in the Roman world,
became Christians. This meant that such Jews had revolutionized their idea of a Messiah. Jesus was not a national political

leader who would deliver his people from the hands of their enemies. To them he was, rather, a Savior from sin, from bondage to the law, from the wrath of God.

Greeks, Egyptians and foreigners from many lands also heard the glad news. Paul let them come into the Christian fellowship, and Peter also was finally persuaded to do so. They did not say that would-be Christians must first obey the Jewish laws, eat Jewish food cooked according to the Jewish codes. Those rules from the Torah were secondary. The important matters were things of the spirit.

But there were Jewish Christian leaders who did not agree with Paul and Peter. These others insisted that Jesus was a Jew in his religion and that any one who meant to follow him must also first become a Jew in the religious sense—he must take on the yoke of obedience to the Mosaic law.

Paul and Peter won in this first great crisis, with the result that Christianity became a religion for all peoples. Doubtless Paul said over and over what he wrote to the Christians in Galatia: "We are all sons of God, through faith, in Christ Jesus. . . . There can be neither Jew nor Greek, there can be neither bond nor free, there can be no male and female; for we are all one in Christ Jesus." (Gal. 3:26, 28.)

Antagonism from the Romans

There was another part of this new gospel preached by the first leaders, which also led to conflict, this time with the Roman rulers. As the movement grew in power and strength, Roman authorities became alarmed about this talk of a god-like person who would appear in the clouds and rule the world. Would not this mean the overthrow of the Roman empire? Furthermore, these Christians would not bow to the image of the emperor. They ceased to support the worship in the temples. They insisted on worshiping this Jesus whom they called their Lord.

So this new sect was suspected of disloyalty to Rome. They were watched as traitors, or ridiculed as fools. From time to time, they were hounded by local mobs. Later by orders from the emperor in Rome, some were crucified, burned at the stake, or thrown into the great Roman arena to be devoured by lions. In spite of these persecutions, however, the numbers of Greeks, Romans and Jews who called themselves Christians grew. Their hope of a heavenly reward was greater than their fear of death.

The Second Great Crisis

At last in A.D. 313, a great and permanent change came. Constantine became emperor in Rome, and at the same time he declared himself to be a Christian, to the amazement of the Roman world. It is reported that he saw a vision of Christ before entering his final battle for the throne. Constantine believed that by the Cross he had conquered. One of Constantine's first acts as emperor, therefore, was to sign his name to a law granting "both to Christians and to all others perfect freedom to practice the religion which each thought best for himself." The first great Magna Charta of religious freedom for the whole of the Roman Empire!

It was hard to believe. After nearly three hundred years of being treated with scorn and persecution, the Christians were free! They could worship openly wherever they pleased. The prestige of the emperor gave them respectability and much more. It gave them power. Soon their leaders began making friends with Roman nobles. Their bishops were entertained in court. These men who had been used to simple living, now began to love riches and the pomp of empire.

Up to this time the Christian churches scattered throughout the Roman Empire had been small groups of Jews and Gentiles who were banded together for mutual encouragement. They met in Jewish synagogues and in one another's homes. Master and slave, citizen and subject, rich and poor ate together. They put their money into a common purse so that none of their number suffered from lack of food or for the common comforts. They were very loosely organized, and those who became leaders lived as simply as the rest.

A Spiritual Monarchy

But when Christianity became popular even in the emperor's palace, things began to change. The simple democratic ways the Christians had been following seemed inappropriate for so great a religion. They began to love ceremony and pomp, and the elaborate organization of which the Romans had become masters. Slowly the churches lost the spirit of the humble Nazarene. They began to copy the organization of the Roman Empire, and the Church became an absolute spiritual monarchy, with cardinals, archbishops, bishops and priests— all as obedient assistant rulers to the one great bishop of the churches in Rome, namely, the pope.

To this pope was given absolute power in all spiritual matters, just as the emperor had absolute power in all temporal matters. The pope was called God's representative on earth. Later the pope's pronouncements on religious matters were held to be "infallible." On these he supposedly could make no mistakes, and his word could never be questioned.

In the earlier years, there were often differences of opinion among the leaders of the churches. Sometimes bitter feelings were expressed, but the conflicts were adjusted without division in the Christian society.

Now that the church had grown large and powerful, and its government had become like that of an absolute monarchy, the tendency developed to compel unity of belief by means of force. When conflicts seemed impossible to solve, it became customary for the emperor in Rome to call a council of all the bishops from all the provinces. There the issues were debated and a ruling decided upon. If the bishops could not agree, either the pope or the emperor would decide.

In addition, the Church Fathers expounded the faith more and more carefully. The council of bishops at Nicaea declared Jesus Christ to be "very God of very God." Men had to believe and accept this creed if they wished to be taken into the Church. The line of separation between the saved and unsaved was definitely drawn. All religious thought except that in harmony with the Story of Salvation or in accord with the pronouncements of the Church councils was stifled.

The free spiritual religion of Jesus which had once ac-
cented love of God and of one's neighbor equally with love of
oneself—a religion that appealed to the downtrodden and the
poor—was now ritualistic and pompous, a religion of creeds
and words, and outward rule and form; and the humble
teacher of Galilee was worshiped with all the rich pageantry
that the minds of men and the wealth of kings could muster.

The Holy Catholic Church Breaks in Two

Of course, dissensions continued. There were small
groups that stood out for independence, but if they refused
to obey they were "excommunicated," that is, expelled from
membership in the church; and sometimes they were driven
into exile and their writings burned. But on the whole, the
Roman pope held supreme power over the churches of all
Europe, Asia and Africa until the year 1054, when the bishop
of Constantinople excommunicated the pope, and the Roman
pope excommunicated the bishop of Constantinople. So the
two separate Catholic churches were established which exist
to the present day: the Greek Orthodox or Eastern Catholic
Church and the Roman Catholic Church.

As we look back today upon this first great schism, it
seems to have been caused more by general political rivalries
and by differences of temperament between the East and the
West than because of a fundamental cleavage in faith. Both
churches were ritualistic and formal, and both believed in the
essentials of the Story of Salvation. The East, however, refused
to accept the Roman pope as final authority, and built up
independently its own form of government and its own
customs. The Eastern churches banned all sculptures as idols
and substituted paintings, or *ikons* as they are called in Russia,
and they retained a different date for Easter.

The Protestors Were Called Protestants

Not until about A.D. 1500, or until nearly five hundred
more years had passed, was there any other major division

within the Roman Catholic Church. It is with the beginning of the sixteenth century that the story of the different Protestant denominations begins.

The men whose work necessitated the forming of new denominations and whose stories you will find in this book were all men who protested. Either they could no longer accept some part of the Old Story of Salvation or they protested against something in the form of government by which the life of the Church was controlled.

The men responsible for the rise of our many Protestant denominations, therefore, were all men who prized liberty of faith more than fellowship within the church, and sometimes even more than life itself. Some of the issues over which they fought may no longer seem to us to be worth dying for. If the issues on which our ancestors differed are no longer really important, or if the beliefs they held are now outmoded, should the churches and synagogues remain divided on the basis of the old scores? What beliefs do we hold today that really matter? At what price are we willing to sell our integrity?

Great men need not that we praise them; the need is ours that we know them. They are our common heritage. Whether we be of their faith or of another, whether our fathers fought with them or with their enemies, whether we stand where they stood or have traveled far on ways they dreamed not of, we are the richer that they lived.[2]

[2] Arthur Cushman McGiffert, "Martin Luther and His Work," *The Century Magazine*, LXXXI (December 1910) , 165.

2. Martin Luther
1483-1546

A Christian man is the most free lord of all, and subject to none: a Christian man is the most dutiful servant of all, and subject to everyone.

Now I would advise you, if you have any wish to pray, to fast, or to make foundations and churches, as they call it, take care not to do so with the object of gaining any advantage, either temporal or eternal.... What you give, give freely and without price, that others may prosper and have increase from you and from your goodness. Thus you will be a truly good man and a Christian.
—MARTIN LUTHER, *On the Liberty of a Christian Man*

"Here I Stand...!"

On a late spring morning in 1517 the townspeople of Jüterbog, Germany, crowded into the parish church to hear Friar Tetzel, a famous Dominican preacher. With awesome expectancy they sat through the service until the time came for the sermon, for they knew that Tetzel had come with an important commission from the Archbishop of Mainz.

Nor were they disappointed, for he said he had been authorized by the Pope to offer a "special indulgence." This everyone knew was a certificate with the seal of the church attached. If any one would pay the amount the Pope had set for such an "indulgence," a considerable part of the money would go toward the building of the great Cathedral of St. Peter in Rome. An "indulgence" would assure the holder of forgiveness for the penalties incurred for all the sins he had confessed to the priest. Or an "indulgence" might be used to secure forgiveness for friends and relatives who had already died and who might even then be suffering in purgatory.

"Do you not hear your dead parents crying out: 'Have mercy on us. We are in sore pain and you can set us free for a pittance. We gave you birth, we cared for you. We left you all our property, and yet you will be so hard-hearted that you will let us suffer on in purgatory!' " . . .

The audience was deeply stirred by the friar's vivid account of the miseries in purgatory. After the service, many pressed forward to purchase the papal pardon. To be sure, some of the buyers would have little money left for food and clothing, and the harvest was still months away. But what did these things matter, when the alternative might be suffering in purgatory until the Day of Judgment?

And who could doubt the efficacy of the pardon when he received from Friar Tetzel a certificate such as the following, issued to all purchasers?

INDULGENCE

In the Name of the Pope

For the entire life, I, by virtue of the apostolic power entrusted to me, do absolve thee from all ecclesiastical censures, judgments, and punishments which thou must have merited; besides this, from all excesses, sins and crimes thou mayest have committed, however great and shameful they may have been, and for whatever cause, even in those cases reserved for our most Holy Father the Pope. I obliterate every taint of unvirtues, all signs of infamy, which thou mayest have received. I release thee from all punishments which thou would have in Purgatory. I permit thee again to participate in the sacraments of the Church. I incorporate thee again in the community of the sanctified, and replace thee in the state of innocence and purity in which thou wert at the hour of thy baptism. So that in the moment of thy death the door through which the sinner enters the place of torture and punishment will be closed, and that will be open to thee which leads into

Portrait of Martin Luther. (Ewing Galloway)

the paradise of joys. If thou shouldest not soon die, so shall this grace remain unshakeable until the end of thy life. In the name of the Holy Father. Amen.[1]

JOHANN TETZEL
Apost. Commissarius

Tetzel himself had little cause for worry about the next world, for things were going well in this one. The Archbishop of Mainz was to have—after the payment of the expenses of Tetzel's sales campaign—half the remainder, and the other half was to go to Rome to build St. Peter's Cathedral. Business was good, not only in Jüterborg but in many other places visited by Tetzel. News of his preaching had brought people from the neighboring villages, and even from the university town of Wittenberg in Saxony.

Luther Is Stirred to Protest

Among those who heard stories of Tetzel's preaching was an Augustinian friar named Martin Luther, a young professor in the University of Wittenberg. Luther was angered by the things he heard and saw. He was sure that certain of the habitual sinners in Wittenberg, who had confessed their sins to him, were getting off too easily. Some poor widows were actually taking food out of the mouths of hungry children to give money for "indulgences." Luther knew full well how little of the money ever reached Rome. He openly denounced Tetzel's methods, but words seemed to have little effect.

Finally, in the fall of that same year, Luther determined to make his protest felt. On October 31, the eve of All Saints' Day, he walked up the hill to the castle church and nailed on the door, where all could see, three sheets of parchment, covered with writing. He had numbered each statement. There were 95 points in all.

"Out of love for the truth and from a desire to elucidate

---

[1] Translation quoted from William Dallman, *Martin Luther, His Life and Works* (St. Louis: Concordia Publishing House, 1917).

it," so the document began, "the Reverend Father Martin Luther, Master of Arts and Doctor in Sacred Theology, and ordinary lecturer therein at Wittenberg, intends to defend the following statements and to dispute them at this place."

The next morning, those who passed by and read the challenge were amazed at the young friar's audacity. He called the selling of "indulgences," "a grave and public error." He said they were like nets for gathering in money and hindered the proclamation of the gospel. Repentance is a matter of the heart. Forgiveness is from God alone.

Someone who could read the Latin in which Luther had written the protests, would translate for those who knew no Latin.

"Thesis No. 23!" he would call. "It is certain that avarice is fostered by money clinking in the chest, but to answer the prayers of the church is in the power of God alone."

"Thesis No. 36! Every Christian who feels true repentance has by right remission of punishment and guilt without letters of indulgence."

"Thesis No. 37! Every true Christian, whether living or dead, has a share in all the benefits of Christ and the Church, given him by God, even without such letters."

Some few stayed to hear all the challenges even till the ninety-fifth had been read. Others were satisfied with hearing only a few. In one way or another the whole list had to do with indulgences.

How did the young man dare to say such things? Had not the Pope authorized the sale of "indulgences?" Had not Christ given the Pope the keys to purgatory as well as to heaven? The people knew no other way to gain happiness in the world to come except by following the rules laid down by the church. The fear of being excluded from heaven hung daily over their heads. How could anyone afford to risk eternal disaster by refusing to pay money when the Pope urged it?

News of this bold challenge to debate spread quickly, not only through the town of Wittenberg, but also copies of the protests were made and sent to members of the clergy in many cities. Almost over night the name of the young professor at Wittenberg became known throughout Germany.

All Germany Hears the News

Some of Luther's fellow friars became alarmed for the reputation of their order. Others feared for Luther's personal safety; yet there were many others who were loud in their praise of the courageous friar. Luther had the quiet approval of the Elector of Saxony, who in later years proved a life-saving friend. The feudal lords had long been irked by the vast sums of money that were being drained from Germany into Italy. And the common folk everywhere, who had been feeling themselves caught in a burdensome system, were given hope. At last the man for whom they had been waiting had appeared. Luther quickly became their popular leader.

It was too much to expect silence from the Church when one of its lucrative sources of income was threatened. Luther's courageous stand seriously reduced that share of the proceeds allotted to Albert, Archbishop of Mainz. He soon complained to Pope Leo X. At first the Holy Father regarded the matter as simply a monks' squabble. He appealed to the other friars of the Augustinian order.

Luther, however, was not so easily frightened. Devout Catholic though he was, he was sure of his ground. He would take nothing back. Instead he publicly denounced the "indulgence" sellers from his pulpit in the castle church with even more vigor than before. His students were aroused and proud of their professor. Later Tetzel published some theses intended to refute those of the teacher of Wittenberg, but Luther's students secured copies and made a public bonfire of them.

Pope Leo X Acts

News of these happenings soon reached Leo X, who could no longer overlook so open a challenge to his own authority. He summoned Luther to Rome to stand trial for heresy. Had the trial been held, conviction would have been a foregone conclusion; but during the sixty days given Luther to make the trip, the Pope learned of Luther's large and popular fol-

lowing among the ruling princes of Germany. Leo decided
caution was to be desired.

Finally he sent his chamberlain, a Saxon nobleman
named Miltitz, a man of great tact, to negotiate with Luther.
Since the Pope wished to retain the support of the Elector of
Saxony, he authorized Miltitz to win the Elector by offering
him the papal decoration called the Golden Rose, an honor
the Elector had long desired. To the troublemaking professor
Miltitz might offer a bishopric, if necessary. Although the
Elector accepted the Golden Rose, the most that Miltitz could
get from Luther was a promise to keep silent on the matter of
"indulgences" if his opponents would do the same.

The Public Debate in Leipzig

Thus matters stood for over a year when in the winter of
1519 Luther received a letter from John Eck, the famous
theologian, challenging him to a public debate on a set of
theses, "aimed ... at your teachings ... which seem to my
feeble judgment false and erroneous." Although Luther was
still bound by his promise of silence, yet this had been con-
ditioned on the silence of his opponents. He considered that
Eck's move released him from his agreement. Luther, therefore, made arrangements to meet the great theologian at
Leipzig.

It was a picturesque and truly epochal event. The universities of Leipzig and Wittenberg were rivals, Leipzig being
keenly jealous of the prestige Luther was bringing its Saxon
neighbor. Students of both institutions were there in force
and they kept the city well stirred up. The debate was held in
the great hall of the duke's palace, not only with students and
townspeople, but also with many dignitaries in attendance.
Excitement was at a high pitch. The city fathers were taking
no chances, and had extra police on duty throughout the entire
two weeks the debate lasted.

Luther was a good debater, but Eck was even more skillful. He finally drove Luther to admit that John Hus, the

In a dramatic renunciation of the Pope's authority, Luther burned the papal bull before the city of Wittenberg's east gate, December 10, 1520. (Ewing Galloway)

Bohemian reformer, who had been burned at the stake, was not wholly wrong. This was equivalent to saying that the Council of Constance, which had condemned Hus, had made a mistake. According to the medieval belief, these duly convened world-wide councils were infallible. "If you believe this," said Eck, "you are to me as a heathen and a publican."

The debate, therefore, had settled at least one thing. It made a break with the Pope inevitable and this was not long in coming. In May 1520, the Pope issued a bull (an official order) directing that all Luther's books be burned and giving him sixty days to recant. Since Luther did nothing of the sort, a bull of excommunication followed in January of the next year.

Trial Before Emperor Charles in Worms

The next scene in this rapidly moving drama followed soon. Luther was summoned to defend himself in the city of Worms before the annual meeting or "Diet" of the princes of Germany. The journey from his monastery in Wittenberg to Worms was more like a triumphal procession than the journey of a condemned man. The city of Wittenberg raised a fund for a wagon in which Luther might travel in comfort, and he was accompanied by a delegation of friends.

Everywhere the populace turned out to greet him. At Erfurt the faculty and students of the old university organized a procession to escort him into the town. A picturesque sight it was, with Luther and his companions riding in a wagon half-filled with straw. Heading the parade was the imperial herald, carrying the royal standard, "a square yellow banner, with a black, two-headed eagle." In the procession also were many of Luther's fellow townsmen, and both students and faculty from his own university. Some were on horseback, others on foot. Luther himself frequently played the lute as the company sang, for he loved music and took the instrument with him to help pass the long hours. A great dinner in Luther's honor, given by the city fathers of Worms, climaxed the celebration.

Also making the trip to Worms was Aleander, the papal representative. But his experience was very different from that of his heretical fellow churchman. Innkeepers refused to put him up, bystanders cursed as he passed. He saw caricatures representing himself hanging head downwards from a scaffold. It was very clear that the German people supported Luther.

When the watchman in the tower by the city gates announced Luther's approach, about two thousand townspeople hurriedly left their breakfast tables and crowded into the streets to see the friar who had become a national hero. It seemed almost true, as someone has said, that "every stone and every tree cried out 'Luther.' "

On the afternoon of the next day, April 17, 1521, Luther appeared before this Diet. There sat the princes of the Empire, including Emperor Charles V himself; and, of course, the papal representative, Aleander. The imperial marshal led Luther into the great hall. Facing him was the Emperor, and on a table near by was a pile of books, which Luther easily recognized as his own. The silence was soon broken by a very dignified looking official who formally arraigned Luther, saying:

"Martin Luther, His Imperial Majesty, Sacred and Victorious, on the advice of all the Estates of the Holy Roman Empire, has ordered that you be summoned here to the throne of his Majesty. . . . First, I ask you to confess that these books exhibited in your presence . . . which have been circulated with your name on the title page, are yours, and do you acknowledge them to be yours? Secondly, do you wish to retract and recall them and their contents, or do you mean to adhere to them and reassert them?"

A solemn moment it was for Luther. If he retracted, he might save his life. If he did not, it was almost certain that he would be burned alive at the stake. To admit error would have been easy. But Luther believed God was on his side. He had no choice but to obey his conscience.

In a clear and deliberate voice he answered:

"I cannot deny that the books named are mine, and I will never deny any of them: . . . But as to what follows, whether I shall reaffirm ... or shall retract.... I beg, with all respect, that your Imperial Majesty give me time to deliberate that I may answer the question without injury to the Word of God, and without peril to my own soul."

After some deliberation, Luther was given twenty-four hours to make his final decision. The imperial herald escorted him from the council chamber.

"Without Horns and Without Teeth"

The next day the crowd in the great hall was even greater than the day before. The air was close and the smoke from many torches made it worse.

After a sharp and vindictive speech by John Eck, it was Luther's turn. Mistakes, he said, were human. No doubt he had made his own share of them. If such were proved, he would willingly recant.

"If his Imperial Majesty desires a plain answer, I will give him one without horns and without teeth, and it is this: It is impossible for me to recant unless I am proved to be in the wrong by the testimony of the Scriptures or by evident reasoning; I cannot trust either the decisions of Councils or Popes, for it is plain that they have not only erred, but have contradicted each other. My conscience is chained to the Word of God, and it is neither safe nor honest to act against one's conscience. God help me!"

Here the Emperor interrupted. He had heard enough. There was great confusion in the court. Luther was adamant. "Here I stand," he said. "I cannot do otherwise."

Strange to say, Martin Luther was not condemned to be burned at the stake. Instead he waited a week in Worms, and to his surprise he finally received permission to start for home.

Twenty-Five Years Unmolested

Something happened then which kept all Germany guessing for a year thereafter. As Luther and two companions were riding through a dark forest toward Gotha, suddenly a party of armed men appeared and carried him off. Actually the arrest was due to a plan made by his old friend, Elector Frederick, to insure Luther's safety; for as Frederick had foreseen, the Diet soon placed the heretical friar under the "ban of the Empire." So Luther was spirited off to the picturesque Castle of the Wartburg, in which he became an involuntary guest.

While confined to the castle, Luther wrote many pamphlets and books which were freely circulated throughout Germany. His greatest achievement was his translation of the New Testament into German. Later he completed the Old Testament also. Although his translation of the Bible into German was not the first to be made, yet it had much more influence than any other, for Luther knew how to use the robust, vigorous language of the people. Luther's Bible helped more than any one thing to unify the Reformation in Germany.

After a year in hiding at Wartburg Castle, Luther broke away from his place of refuge, against the advice of his old friend, the Elector Frederick, and went back to live again as a professor in the University of Wittenberg. Since a number of the princes of the country openly became Protestants, the reform movement grew rapidly. Luther was never again brought to trial. He lived and worked for nearly twenty-five more years.

What Was the Reformation About?

What, then, was this Reformation which Martin Luther started? Why did it take such a strong hold upon the people of Germany and spread so rapidly? Just what was it that Luther was protesting against? Was it merely the evils of "indulgences"? Or was something even more significant happening?

The truth is that in the beginning, Luther had never intended to start a new movement. He had not meant to break with the Pope. But one step taken led to another. His own thinking changed and matured as a result of the reactions that were made to his protests. Luther was not against "works," such as celebrating the sacraments, offering prayers, giving alms, doing penance. But he was against doing such "works" *in order to be saved*. Luther insisted that men cannot *earn* salvation through "works." It is a free gift. God's forgiveness once given is complete. It covers every sin. After a person is once accepted of God, he has nothing to fear. God has chosen or "elected" him for heaven and God will see that he gets there. All that one does to gain this assurance is to have "faith." Living a good life after that is the natural expression of gratitude to God.

Luther said also that every man is his own priest. Each has direct access to God. Luther did not propose doing away with priests, but he insisted that men are not completely helpless without priestly aid. To Luther the central fact in the gospel is "faith"; by "faith" we are saved and not by "works."

The Roman Catholic church, however, had made the religious life a matter of faithfulness in prayer, attending the mass, receiving the sacraments, making confession to the priests, performing penance, doing deeds of charity—all of which were regarded as "good works." The fear of not having done enough to merit heaven followed the people continually. An unforgiven sin might result in a stay in purgatory, and even one unforgiven "mortal" sin deserved eternal damnation. Luther saw the people so absorbed in accumulating merit in order to save themselves from the wrath to come, that many had no leisure to be happy.

Luther's gospel was a wonderful message to preach to such fear-bound subjects of the Pope. Luther not only preached this "good news," he also wrote hymns that the people could sing. Even yet many of them are sung, such as "Away in a manger" and the magnificent *"Ein' feste Burg ist unser Gott"* ("A mighty fortress is our God").

Luther's gospel brought also a new view of one's daily work. Luther, who had renounced a promising career in law and had for years been a pious friar, came to the conclusion:

It is not necessary that he who would serve God should undertake some special kind of an occupation.... It looks like a great thing when a monk renounces everything and goes into a cloister, carries on a life of asceticism, fasts, watches, prays, etc. On the other hand, it looks like a small thing when a maid cooks and cleans and does other housework. But because God's command is there, even such a small work must be praised as a service of God far surpassing the holiness and asceticism of all monks and nuns.[2]

As others came to accept Luther's estimate of the worth of all kinds of work, monks began to abandon their monasteries. Many of them married, did work as other men and ceased their begging. Luther himself married a nun who had been converted to his point of view. Luther liked to call her "My Lord Kathe" because she managed his affairs so well and much to his profit. To them were born six children. Some of Luther's letters to them are models of tenderness and humor.

Luther Turns Against the Peasants

During his later years, Luther's inconsistencies became increasingly apparent. In the beginning he was the idol of the poor. As a result of the new hope which Luther's Reformation inspired, the peasants organized and began to protest against the treatment given them by their landlords. At first Luther encouraged them. He showed interest in the Twelve Articles which they put into what they called their charter. Luther warned the landlords of their danger if they did not lessen the hardships of their peasants. But the landlords turned deaf ears to Luther's warnings. Finally, Luther begged the peasants to yield to what was for the time inevitable.

The peasants refused. Without skilled leadership, their organization got out of control. Small groups, led by fanatical leaders, fought with scythes and axes as well as with swords. Before long the peasant revolt became a bloody class war. Luther had to side with the princes, for they were the men who were protecting the Reformation movement and were

[2] Arthur Cushman McGiffert, "Luther and the Unfinished Reformation," Union Theological Seminary Bulletin, I (January 1918), 22.

soon to establish his Protestant churches. Furthermore, Luther believed that the princes had been given their authority directly by God. Both sides were angry and determined to fight it out. Finally in desperation, Luther wrote a scathing pamphlet in which he called upon the princes to slay the rebellious peasants as if they were mad dogs. Fearful atrocities occurred on both sides. About 100,000 peasants are said to have been killed. From that time on Luther became fearful of all social revolutionary movements.

As a result, the Reformation, started by a man who was himself a miner's son, became controlled by the ruling classes. It was decided that the religion of a given territory, such as that belonging to Luther's prince, the Elector of Saxony, should be the religion of its prince. As a result perhaps two-thirds of the total area of the Holy Roman Empire became Protestant though not all of these territories remained so. This turn of events ended the persecution of the Lutherans in these territories; but it led also to a growing conservatism in the Lutheran movement.

An Unfinished Reformation

The Protestant revolt in Germany affected all of Europe and England as well. News of the success of the movement spread from country to country. Some men were frightened and as Roman Catholics led in the persecution of "heretics." Others were emboldened to join in the Protestant revolt. It would have been of inestimable advantage to the Protestants had they been able to present a united front to the ancient and powerful Roman Catholic Church. But Luther grew too dogmatic in the positions he took to be able to cooperate with the leaders in southwestern Germany and in parts of Switzerland when they disagreed with him, even on matters that now seem to us to be unimportant.

Luther is rightly remembered as one of the great men of history. He started a religious reformation that had in it the possibilities of a further development in freedom of thought, but neither Luther nor his generation were prepared to face the hazards of a larger freedom. In the midst of political turmoil and disunity in Europe, Luther and his colleagues sensed keenly the need to keep the Protestant movement united. Having rejected the strong monarchical type of Roman Catholic church government, the Lutheran churches attempted to secure unity by agreement on doctrine. Their leaders struggled painstakingly and long to secure agreement on every theological issue that seemed important to their generation. The authority on which doctrine was based was that of the Scriptures. The early Lutherans, therefore, stressed orthodoxy, and prepared the longest creedal statement for common acceptance that any Protestant Church has ever produced. ". . . [Luther] dominated more than half the western world, and the whole of it is changed because he lived. . . . He was of titanic stature, and our common standards fail adequately to measure him."[3]

The Lutherans in America

Lutheran Beginnings in America

It was not until the early part of the eighteenth century that German and Scandinavian immigrants began coming to the New World in large numbers. Most of these immigrants came to improve their economic status rather than to escape religious persecutions. Because of their poverty, their migrations and their lack of ministers, their churches grew slowly.

Realizing their need of help from outside, these Lutherans appealed to their home churches in Germany for a leader. Fortunately, in 1742 their German brethren sent Rev. Henry Melchior Muhlenberg, a young minister from the University of Halle in Germany. After a hazardous voyage, in which only

[3] McGiffert, *Martin Luther: The Man and His Work* (New York, 1911), p. 388.

the fortunate meeting with two British warships saved all on board from dying from thirst, Muhlenberg and his wife landed in Charleston, South Carolina.

He made his headquarters, however, in Pennsylvania, and set about at once to use his strength and genius to help bring the scattered Lutheran settlers into a unified church. He traveled from settlement to settlement. Sometimes he rode on horseback over Indian trails. Sometimes he made his way laboriously on foot through country that still was a primeval wilderness. Sleeping under the stars and fording rivers were for him common occurrences. When, in some settlements, he could find no one who could teach the children, he would organize classes himself and teach, spending perhaps a week in each settlement.

With all his traveling, preaching and teaching, Muhlenberg and his wife found time to bring up a family of six sons and five daughters so successfully that all the sons in their turn became Lutheran ministers, and most of them achieved considerable reputation. One served as a general in Washington's army, another was the first speaker of the House of Representatives, and still a third was a famous botanist. But the Muhlenberg story does not end there, for some of his grandsons also earned eminence. Few American families have contributed as much to the nation as these pioneer Lutheran Muhlenbergs.

Eminent Lutherans of Today

In more recent times other Lutherans have achieved reknown for their nobility and courage. No story of World War II would be complete without mention of Pastor Martin Niemoeller, the stouthearted minister of the fashionable Jesus Christus Kirche (church) of Berlin, who dared to defy the Nazis and was rewarded for his courage by imprisonment in a concentration camp for eight years. And there was the late Dag Hammarskjold, servant of all mankind as Secretary of the United Nations, whose greatest goal was peace among all nations.

How Many Lutherans Are There?

In the United States at the present time there are approximately 8 ½ million Lutherans. They outnumber every other Protestant body in Michigan, Minnesota, Montana, Nebraska, North and South Dakota, Wisconsin and Pennsylvania. Lutherans are most numerous where immigrants from Germany, Scandinavia, Finland and Denmark have settled. They are the largest Protestant body in many American cities, including Buffalo, Milwaukee, Minneapolis, St. Paul, Detroit, Toledo and Chicago. Lutherans are also numerous in Canada, where there are nearly half a million.

In the Scandinavian countries the Lutheran Church is the established or state church, although there is religious freedom and others are tolerated. It is therefore difficult to know just how many people are actually Lutheran in belief. Lutherans are also numerous in West Germany, although in East Germany the Lutheran Church has encountered the same strong opposition from the Communists as has every other form of organized religion. This opposition has been directed most strongly against Lutheran youth.

The present membership of Lutheran churches the world over is said to be just under 75,000,000. They are thus the largest Protestant denomination, and are exceeded only by the Roman Catholic and Eastern Orthodox churches.

Lutheran Services

No matter what kind of Lutheran church you may visit, you are likely to find a prayer book and a ritualistic type of service. Like the Episcopalians, the Lutherans observe the special days of the Christian calendar.

When you attend a Lutheran service, however, you may find that the prayers, readings and even the sermon are all in a foreign tongue, but this is much less common today than formerly. If you can decide whether you are hearing German, Finnish, Danish, Swedish, Norwegian or Icelandic, you will know the country from which the original members of the church emigrated. One marked characteristic of these Lutheran churches is the tenacity with which they have clung to the use of their native languages in their services of worship. In some places one service on Sunday may be in a foreign language, for the special benefit of the older people, and another service may be in English to please the young people. Slowly all the churches are introducing the English language.

Kinds of Lutherans

Although Luther himself, like many another religious reformer, wished only to purify his own church and had no intention of starting a new one, his followers today, especially in the United States, are split into sixteen or more sects. Some, like the Suomi (Finnish) Synod, are based on the country of origin, but others have to do with minor differences of belief. In recent years, however, such differences have tended to fade and there has been a strong tendency toward union. Three of these churches (Evangelical, American, and United Evangelical) have already united under the name of the American Lutheran Church, which, with its more than 2 million members, will be one of the larger denominations; it may become even larger should the Lutheran Free Church also join, as seems likely. Four other Lutheran bodies, with a total membership exceeding 3 million, have also voted in favor of a merger. These are the Suomi, United Lutheran Church in America, the Augustana Synod and the American Evangelical Lutheran Church.

Lutheran Beliefs

Many of the dissensions over the creeds which rent the Lutheran churches in Europe apart, have been carried over into the New World. In their beliefs Lutherans are conservative, and most of them still loyal to the Augsburg Confession.

This was a long and careful statement made, after consultation with Luther, by Melanchthon and other experts and presented at a session of the Diet held in Augsburg in 1530. Most Lutherans still accept the Old and New Testaments as the divinely inspired rule of faith and practice.

The most conservative Lutheran group in the United States, now usually called the Missouri Synod, organized in 1872, is centered in St. Louis, but has strong organizations also in adjoining states. It has a membership of about 2½ million.

In some Lutheran churches the children are still being taught the Smaller Catechism, which Luther wrote for the children of his day. By question and answer, the little book sets forth the interpretation of the gospel as skillfully phrased by Luther. In some churches the children learn to repeat the answers word for word and so become grounded in the faith.

Lutheran Church Organization

Lutheran churches are organized into synods, to which in many ways each church is subject; yet each congregation is left quite free to choose its own minister and to govern its own affairs. For young people there are societies, such as the Luther League and the Walther League, both of which have many thousands of members. There are also Lutheran chaplains and student centers on many college and university campuses.

Although there are no Lutheran bishops in the United States, the Lutheran state churches of the Scandinavian countries have an episcopal form of government. The bishops of Norway and Sweden are considered to be the direct successors of the Roman Catholic prelates of Reformation times who were converted to the reformed faith.

Lutheran Community Activities

Ever since Luther's day, his followers have been zealous for education. He has sometimes been called the "father of the public school," because he urged the German princes to establish schools in their territories which would be open to all alike. Luther even advocated that girls go to school for an hour a day.

The Lutherans in some American communities, particularly in the Midwest where the church is strongest, have founded parochial schools of their own in which religious instruction is made part of general education. They have also established many colleges; among them are Gettysburg, Muhlenberg, Wittenberg, St. Olaf's, Capitol University, Susquehanna University and more than forty others.

This is not all. For Negroes in the South, schools have been started. There are Lutheran schools for the deaf, many orphanages, homes for the aged and hospitals for the sick.

3. John Calvin
1509-1564

He who commands us to use this world as though we used it not, prohibits not only all intemperance in eating and drinking, excessive delicacy, ambition, pride, haughtiness, and fastidiousness in our furniture, our habitations, and our apparel, but every care and affection which would either seduce or disturb us from thoughts of the heavenly life, and attention to the improvement of our souls.

—JOHN CALVIN, *Opera*, III

The Ruler of "a City of God" on Earth

Two years after Luther was tried before the emperor in the city of Worms, a young Frenchman, named Jean Cauvin (later known as John Calvin), was beginning his studies at the University of Paris, with the expectation of becoming a Roman Catholic priest.

He was tall and thin of build. His piercing dark eyes and his black hair lent a severity to his thin face. His light eating habits and his long hours of study until midnight had already induced a tendency to poor digestion. Even in his youth he had what his biographers have described as "an iron spirit incased in a frail body." He condemned the drinking, gambling and loose living of his fellow students, with outspoken frankness.

Calvin—the Restless Student

John Calvin had begun his college life in Paris with a view to entering the Roman Catholic priesthood. By so doing, he was able to secure a much-needed scholarship. Later his father ordered him to study law instead, since the profession promised more lucrative employment in the end. So John Calvin left the University of Paris and for several years studied in Orleans and Bourges. His interests were divided between a study of law and a study of the Latin and Greek classical literatures.

Again Calvin returned to the University of Paris. His interest in religion was being awakened as his knowledge grew regarding the Protestant Reformation in Germany. Some of his professors had strong Protestant leanings, although they were very guarded in their expressions of sympathy with the movement. France was a strong Roman Catholic country, and the Church had its observers everywhere who were spying upon all possible heretics. One of Calvin's fellow students, Nicholas Cop, was becoming secretly enthusiastic over the Protestant movement. Calvin began reading whatever he could lay his hands on of the writings of Martin Luther.

Finally, the crisis came for John Calvin when he had what he called a "sudden conversion," which he believed had come to him through God's direct guidance. Just what it was that happened, Calvin never described. All we know is that on that day he began his stormy career as a Protestant reformer.

Later, when he was about to graduate from the department of theology, his friend Nicholas Cop was to be installed as rector of the University of Paris. Calvin, out of kindness, so the story goes, helped Cop write his inaugural address. According to the conservative professors who heard the address, however, it contained too many Lutheran ideas. The result was that both Cop and Calvin saw that they must flee at once from Paris. Calvin returned to his home in Noyon, but even there he was unable to refrain from speaking out. As a result he was soon imprisoned for having made "an uproar in the church." His release came quickly, however, and this time Calvin found refuge in Basel, Switzerland, where he lived for several years in quiet seclusion.

Calvin's First Great Book

Calvin's experience with persecution merely spurred him to harder study and to clearer thinking. Hours at a time he worked alone in a rented room, his Bible beside him. His logical mind was struggling with one big idea after another. It was the Word of God he was trying to set forth. He wanted to include all the important doctrines essential to salvation and to a sound faith. As he worked, his thoughts grew into a book. It came to have six chapters. He expounded the nature of God—his sovereign will, his predestination before the foundation of the world of certain people to salvation and others to damnation. He wrote of the sinful nature of man, the authority of the Bible as setting forth God's will and the rules of right living. He explained the church and the sacraments. As Calvin wrote, the truth seemed to become clear. He felt that he had written things that should be made known. He would publish them as a book and he would call it *The Institutes of the Christian Religion.* (The word *"institutes"* means textbook.)

Finally, one morning in 1536 at an appointed hour, he left his room and walked briskly down the cobbled street to the little printing house where he had committed his pages to the printer's ink. When he again came out on the street he was carrying a copy of the book in his hand. No wonder he was excited, this young man of twenty-six years. Would the book sell? Who would read it? What would happen to him for writing it?

During the remaining years of his dramatic life, although he wrote many other books and preached thousands of sermons, Calvin never changed the fundamental positions which he set forth in his first religious book. Later he added other chapters. He took up certain subjects in more detail, but he never revised his points of view.

Nothing else that Calvin ever did, important as was his rule of the city of Geneva, had such a lasting influence as this one book. The ideas in *The Institutes* were not only Calvin's own guide throughout his life, they have comprised the fundamental beliefs that have prevailed for four centuries in many churches. The Presbyterians, many of the Reformed churches and the Puritans were all deeply influenced by Calvin's theology.

Beginning the Great Experiment

Shortly after finishing his book, Calvin set out once again for his home in Noyon, but because of a war which was then raging, he had to detour through Geneva, Switzerland. There he met a young Protestant minister named William Farel, who was trying to make the thirteen thousand people of that city into loyal and good Protestants. The highest council governing the city had sometime before proclaimed that Geneva was a Protestant city. The Roman Catholic Mass was no longer observed in the churches. The four monasteries and the one nunnery had been closed. A religion, however, which had endured for centuries could not be destroyed over night. There were still many who preferred to remain Catholic. There were others, called "Libertines," who frequented the taverns to drink, dance and gamble; and they were not at all hankering after any strait-laced righteousness.

William Farel was an eloquent Protestant preacher, but tactless. He had neither a broad education nor the ability to organize and discipline. He did have, however, an uncanny ability to sense genius and he thought he had found it in Calvin.

So, in July 1536, when only twenty-seven years of age, John Calvin began the great Protestant experiment of trying to transform the city of Geneva into a City of God on earth.

He set to work at once along two lines, first to establish purity of doctrine, and second to require purity of conduct.

He came armed for his task with the belief that the Old and New Testaments contain "the perfect rule of faith and practice." He came also with the inner conviction that he had been commissioned by God to proclaim His sovereign will as revealed in the Holy Scriptures. He believed that those whom God had foreordained to salvation from the foundation of the world would listen and obey. Those who refused obedience would thereby show that they had been foreordained to sin and punishment.

Purity of Conduct

Calvin's training in the school of law made him skillful in turning the Christian life into a set of rules to be followed. He declared that failure to attend all regular services held in the church would be fined. All shops must be closed on Sunday. Gambling, drunkenness, card playing were all forbidden.

In order that these laws might be enforced, Calvin had representatives chosen from among the members of the various congregations to act as councils. These men were responsible for spying on their neighbors and for reporting all forms of misconduct. At all hours homes could be entered without warning on the assumption that one should never do anything he was ashamed to have known.

Geneva already had well-organized city councils who administered the government. They were not permitted to decide what acts were criminal. They could not make the church laws, but they could participate in deciding the punishments, and they could act as police to make arrests and to gather fines. Although Calvin believed that the Church should be free of all state control, he did not believe that the state should be free of control by the Church.

Purity of Faith and Worship

Calvin began changing also the character of the church services, introducing into them a plain, even austere solemnity. He had all images and works of art removed from the churches. He introduced congregational singing as a substitute for the gowned choirs and the elaborate music of the Roman Catholic services. He forbade the use of all musical instruments in the church. Later he had the pipes of the organ in the Geneva cathedral melted down, and the material used to make cups for Communion wine.

Calvin also set for himself the task of stating the beliefs that all Protestants should hold. He prepared a Catechism for the instruction of old and young. He wrote also a Confession of Faith, to be used in the services of worship. The Catechism was taught and expounded at special gatherings during the week.

From our modern outlook, Calvin's rule in Geneva seems perhaps more like a reign of terror than like the beginning of a "City of God" on earth. But during the sixteenth century the people of Europe were accustomed to dictatorship and rough discipline, and Calvin's rule was not maintained for the sake of any personal gain. He believed he was acting in the name of the God of righteousness. There were wealthy, liberty-loving families, however, and red-light districts and theaters in Geneva which even the Roman Catholic priests had secretly aided. These Libertines resented Calvin's stern efforts to prohibit their pleasures. At first they showed their resentment by making him the butt of their jokes whenever he walked the street. In the darkness of the night, they serenaded him with lewd songs.

Crisis and Banishment

Matters finally came to a head over an issue which to us today scarcely seems worth fighting over. Calvin and Farel, when performing the sacrament of the Lord's Supper, had been accustomed to use leavened (or yeast) bread. The city council, however, who were determined that things in Geneva should be done as they were being done in the Protestant city of Berne, ruled that only unleavened bread should be used. Although it was not of great importance to Calvin which kind

John Calvin preaching his farewell sermon in Geneva, Switzerland, in expectation of his banishment from that city. (The Bettmann Archive)

of bread was used, he was determined that the civil authorities should not make rules for the Church.

Heated discussions day after day led nowhere. Angry feelings were at their height on Sunday morning, April 21, 1537. The great church of St. James was filled with worshipers. The time came for the observance of the Sacrament, and John Calvin refused to serve the bread and wine of the Communion. He said that altogether they were in no proper spirit to receive the Sacrament.

No further match was needed to kindle the flame of antagonism against Calvin and Farel. The very next day, the city council voted to banish them both from the city of Geneva.

The two men promptly left for Strassburg in Germany (now the French city of Strasbourg) where Calvin was soon invited to become minister of a Protestant church there and to become a professor of theology at the local university. Calvin used this time of exile for further writing. He revised and expanded *The Institutes of the Christian Religion*. He compiled a hymnbook for congregational singing, setting some of the old Psalms to familiar tunes.

The opportunity for quiet work of this type, however, did not last long. After two years, the people of Geneva, repenting their having banished their great leader, appealed to him to return. Without him the "City of God" on earth could not survive.

The Second Experiment

After long consideration Calvin reluctantly accepted. With renewed assurance he took up his work where he had left off. Again he organized the churches, defining carefully the different responsibilities for pastors, elders and deacons. The pastors were to form the Venerable Company, a body charged with meeting periodically for the study of the Bible and for mutual self-criticism. Out of the several congregations, a council of twelve elders was chosen and known as the "Consistory." To these elders fell the scarcely pleasant duty of watching over faith and morals, especially of those who seemed to "err and lead a disorderly life."

The church Consistory had no power to compel obedience to the laws, but they could recommend to the city council the punishments to be meted out for violations, and such recommendations were usually followed. They could threaten public exposure of offenses, and could excommunicate the offenders. Since excommunication was regarded as proof that the victim was not one of the elect, and hence doomed to eternal punishment in the hereafter, it was a very potent penalty.

The list of misdemeanors was enlarged. It included such matters as having one's fortune told by gypsies, all forms of idolatry, such as having images or sacred relics of any kind in home or church, or saying that the pope was a good man. Calvin even made a list of names which should not be given to children. He tried to turn the taverns into places where men would give thanks to God before drinking, and where Bibles were prominently displayed in the hope that thus the conversation would be turned to serious subjects.

Banishment, imprisonment, in some cases drowning, were penalties inflicted on unchastity. To sing or even to have in one's possession lewd songs was a crime: to laugh at Calvin's sermons, or to have spoken hot words of him in the street, was a crime: to wear clothes of forbidden stuff or make was a crime: to give a feast to too many guests or of too many dishes was a crime: to dance at a wedding was a crime:—to all of which, with many others of like sort, appropriate punishments were meted out. Everybody was obliged to attend public worship: everybody was required to partake of the Lord's Supper: no sick man might lie in bed for three days without sending for the minister of the parish.[1]

Calvin should be given credit, however, for certain practical items in his code, such as requiring garbage and filth to be disposed of in sewers rather than in the streets. He also made laws regarding the lighting of fires in certain unsafe places.

[1] Charles Beard, *The Reformation* (London, 1883), p. 250.

He established a hospital for victims of the plague, and encouraged the Protestant refugees, who flocked to Geneva from other countries of Europe, to develop a first-class weaving industry.

Development of Education

Calvin was also definitely interested in educating the people. He and Farel had long been attempting to carry on a program of free compulsory education. In 1558, Calvin persuaded the city council to enlarge the inefficient little school which they had and to provide for instruction from the primary grades through college. He insisted on securing the best available teachers and made careful provision for instruction in religion. From such a beginning the famous University of Geneva has grown, a memorial to the educational interest of John Calvin and to his wise foresight.

The Significance of the Experimenter

For twenty-three successive years Calvin dominated the City of Geneva. Finally, unremitting labor, combined with little sleep, a too frugal diet, and frequent indigestion exacted their toll. Tuberculosis, that for years had been burning in his frail frame, finally completely overwhelmed him at the early age of fifty-five. On May 28, 1564, his outworn body was buried without pomp or ceremony. According to his own expressed wish, no stone was placed above it to mark his last resting place.

In his farewell talk to his ministerial colleagues, Calvin uttered these words which reveal the spirit of this significant man.

I have lived in marvelous combats here. I have been saluted in mockery of an evening by fifty or sixty gun-shots before my door. Fancy how that could shock a poor student, timid as I am and as I confess I have always been. After that, I was hunted from this city and betook myself to Strassburg. Having dwelt there for some time, I was recalled, but I had not less trouble than before in the discharge of my duty. They set dogs on me, and these gripped me by my coat and legs. They cried "scoundrel, scoundrel" after me. . . . Yes, I have been in combats, and you will have more of them, not less but greater. . . .

Although I am nothing, I know that I have suppressed three thousand tumults in Geneva. Be strong and of good courage, for God will preserve this church and defend it. I assure you God will keep it.[2]

However we may judge the severity of Calvin's rule over "the City of God" that he established, or however much we may decry the autocratic methods he used, it is a fact that within the city "the drunkard, the harlot, the blasphemer, and the idler had been driven under cover," and that outwardly, at least, "Geneva was morally the cleanest city of all Europe."[3]

Weighed in the balance of modern ethical insight, some may regard his influence as containing more of evil than of good. Nevertheless, it must be admitted that both as an ecclesiastical statesman and as a theological thinker, John Calvin ranks among the Protestant reformers as the man who has had the greatest and the longest influence.

The Presbyterians

Just as the Lutherans are the descendants of the Reformation led by Luther, so the Presbyterians are the inheritors of

[2] *Joannis Calvin; Opera Quæ Supersunt Omnia,* ix, 891 ff., quoted by Georgia Harkness, *John Calvin: The Man and His Ethics* (Nashville: Abingdon Press, 1931) , p. 58.

[3] *Ibid.,* pp. 59, 60.

the work of John Calvin. Today in the United States, Presbyterian Church members of all varieties number about 4 million, and there are nearly a million more in Canada.

The Spread of Calvin's Doctrines

During Calvin's lifetime his ideas won adherents far beyond the boundaries of Switzerland. Many Protestants in other parts of the continent of Europe followed his leadership. This was true especially in France and Holland.The Calvinists made advances as minority groups also in many parts of present-day Germany, in Austria, Bohemia, Hungary and Poland. Many of these gains were lost as a result of Jesuit missions and of terrible civil wars. Today in Europe, Calvinistic churches are strong chiefly in Switzerland, France, Holland and Hungary, and in Germany in the region centering about Heidelberg. Presbyterian or Calvinistic churches in Hungary, like others, have suffered from Communist opposition.

In England the Calvinist doctrine and theory of church government were particularly strong during the latter part of the reign of Queen Elizabeth and the period when Oliver Cromwell established his Commonwealth. The Stuart kings, however, became increasingly hostile to it.

During Calvin's lifetime his most ardent and energetic disciple, John Knox, lived in Scotland. Since Protestants were then being cruelly persecuted in Scotland, John Knox fled to Switzerland and spent three years in Geneva. There he became thoroughly imbued with Calvin's gospel. He grew so enthusiastic over the way "the City of God" was ruled that he called it "the most perfect school of Christ that ever was on earth since the days of the Apostles."[4] When freedom for Protestants was again established in Scotland, therefore, Knox returned with the burning ambition to make not only one community a City of God on earth, but to make over all Scotland according

[4] John Knox, letter of December 9, 1556, to Mrs. Locke, quoted by Harkness, *op. cit.*, p. 59.

From his pulpit John Knox thundered against the religion of Scotland's Catholic queen, Mary Stuart. (Keystone View Co.)

to Calvinist faith and practice. His success is shown by the fact that the Presbyterian Church became the state Church of Scotland.

The Scotch-Irish Presbyterians

In the sixteenth century, when England and Scotland declared their independence of the Church of Rome, the great majority of Irishmen resented the attempts of the English Crown to compel them to accept Protestantism and to require the use of the prayer book in the English language.

The conflict grew acute during the reigns of James I and II. By order of the Crown, Roman Catholic landholders in Ireland were driven off their lands, and Scottish Presbyterian settlers were brought in to occupy the country. These Scotsmen were called Scotch-Irish.

During the seventeenth century these new Scottish settlers were kept in continual uncertainty and danger because of two strong rebellions which the Irish initiated. Finally, because of the continued hostility of the Irish toward them, many of these Scotch-Irish fled to America. Many of the Presbyterian churches founded in Ireland in those years still endure, however, especially in the northern part of the country, which, largely because of its rugged Protestantism, elected to remain a part of the British Commonwealth rather than accept domination by the Catholic-oriented Republic of Eire. Those who migrated came by the thousands every year for several decades during the eighteenth century and settled in every American colony. Wherever they went they organized Presbyterian churches. The prophet who had inspired them was John Knox, but the gospel they spread and the pattern of church life which they followed had come first from the mind of Calvin.

How Presbyterian Churches Are Organized

The government of churches according to the Presbyterian pattern is neither as monarchical as that of Episcopal churches, with their bishops, nor is it as democratic as that of the Congregational and Baptist churches, where each congregation is self-governing. The very name, Presbyterian, suggests a government by a chosen few, for the word *presbyter* comes from the Greek word *presbyteros*, often used in the New Testament meaning *elder*.

In a local church there is the minister and a board of ruling elders, called the session. Both are elected by vote of the members of the congregation. A second elected governing body is the board of deacons, who usually distribute the funds for the charities of the church. There is also a board of trustees, required by state law, to manage all business matters.

Anyone wishing to join the church is asked to appear before the session to be examined orally regarding his faith. The session inquires also into his character and habits of life. On the basis of their findings the session decides whether or not the person is fitted to become a member of the church.

The churches in a given district are ruled by what is called the presbytery. This is composed of the ministers of the district, with at least one elder representing each church session. Three or more presbyteries may unite to form a synod. The synods, in turn, come under the rule of the general assembly which is the highest national body. Its presiding officer is called the moderator. This highest governing body is composed of an equal number of ministers and laymen chosen by the presbyteries.

Such a system furnishes a well-knit and efficient organization in which, at each level, power is vested in groups of chosen men rather than in single individuals.

What Do Presbyterians Believe?

On the whole Presbyterian churches have "a conservative habit of mind." They demand that their ministers and elders give assent to the Presbyterian statement of faith, called the Westminster Confession. This document was drawn up in 1647, in famous Westminster Abbey, at the time when Puritanism was in power in England. This Confession intends to set forth the "system of doctrine taught in the Holy Scriptures." "It proclaims the complete sovereignty of God in the universe, the complete sovereignty of Christ in salvation, the sovereignty of the Scriptures and the sovereignty of the individual conscience in the interpretation of the Word of God."[5] As an oft-sung hymn puts it, "God is his own interpreter, and He will make it plain."

The essentials of this Confession of Faith are more simply set forth in the Shorter Westminster Catechism, which used to be committed to memory by all young people who were regarded as properly prepared for admission into the Church. Although today in most Presbyterian church schools this catechism is no longer taught to the children, yet the essential doctrines found in that ancient catechism still influence the attitudes of many who write and teach for the church schools.

"No Protestant church has stood more staunchly by its doctrines than has the Presbyterian, which accounts for the fact that the most famous of modern heresy trials have taken place within the Presbyterian Church. In this twentieth century we are accustomed to say that doctrine and creed do not count, that it makes very little difference what a man believes; but the Presbyterian Church has always said that it does make a difference."[6]

Presbyterian Varieties in the United States

In Scotland, where the Presbyterian Church had become the state church, there arose a number of divisions. Certain conscientious objectors arose who refused to sign oaths of citizenship required or statements of creed to which they could not subscribe. Most of these small divisions were transplanted

[5] William N. Sweet, *Our American Churches* (New York: Methodist Book Concern, 1924) , p. 106.
[6] *Ibid.*, p. 106.

to America, and many of them have survived to the present. A process of unification has been going on, however, for over a century.

The most recent merger (1958) was that of the Presbyterian Church in the United States of America and the United Presbyterian Church of North America, to form the United Presbyterian Church in the United States of America, a denomination numbering more than 3 million members and having close to 9,500 churches. Yet unity is still something more to be hoped for than an accomplished fact, as is shown by the names given to the two largest remaining divisions of the Presbyterian Church. The Northern Presbyterians represent the great merged group just referred to, while the Southern Presbyterians, with almost a million members, call themselves the Presbyterian Church in the United States. The smallest group of all is the Associate Presbyterian Church of North America with only seven churches and some 500 members.

Presbyterian Philanthropy

At the present time over forty North American colleges owe their existence to Presbyterian philanthropy, including several in Canada. There are also a number of excellent Presbyterian hospitals that serve the public without regard for creed, color or financial status. The most famous of these are in the great medical centers in New York and Chicago. Presbyterian work for the American Indians, for Negroes, for migrant workers, and for children and families crowded in tenements in our large cities has been notable.

The Presbyterians have long been active also in missionary work in foreign lands. Their primary schools and colleges, their homes for orphans and famine refugees, their institutions of healing are to be found on every continent. In cooperation in world-wide tasks, the Presbyterian Church has shown high qualities of Christian statesmanship.

High Educational Standards

Calvin's concern for popular education and for the education of the church's ministers still characterizes the Presbyterian denomination. The public school system of which our nation is proud is in no small measure an outgrowth of the town schools demanded by Calvinistic standards.

The first Presbyterian ministers in this country were brought over largely from Scotland and Ireland. Relatively few came from England. Many had degrees from Edinburgh, St. Andrews or Aberdeen. As New England Puritans migrated westward, many became Presbyterian. Not a few ministers among them were graduates of Yale and Harvard. Schools for the education of ministers in America were early begun, the first having been established in Pennsylvania. It was called The Log College, because it was held in a log cabin. In 1746 it was succeeded by the College of New Jersey, situated at Princeton. In 1896 this became Princeton University. Although this great university no longer trains ministers, one of the larger Presbyterian seminaries is still located in Princeton.

From the very beginning the Presbyterians have held to high educational standards for their ministers. While other denominations often used preachers in the western outposts who did not have even a grammar school education, the Presbyterians usually insisted that all their ministers should have had a college education and should have studied Greek and Hebrew, since these were the languages in which the earliest manuscripts of the Bible were written. Now Presbyterian ministers must also take a theological course. This emphasis upon education perhaps accounts for the fact that so many Biblical scholars have arisen in the Presbyterian ranks.

4. *Michael Servetus*
1511-1553

For my own part I neither agree nor disagree in every particular with either Catholic or Reformer. Both of them seem to me to have something of truth and something of error in their views; and whilst each sees the other's shortcomings, neither sees his own. God in his goodness give us all to understand our errors and incline us to put them away. It would be easy enough, indeed, to judge dispassionately of everything, were we but suffered without molestation by the Churches freely to speak our minds.

—MICHAEL SERVETUS

He Tried to Reform the Reformers

The year 1492 is a memorable one for all the Americas. The Spanish monarch, King Ferdinand, and his Queen Isabella, have long been honored because of the help they gave to Christopher Columbus.

And 1492 is also remembered because of an almost unbelievable tragedy that came that year to thousands of Spanish subjects. It all came about because of the accepted practice of that day in almost every European country of requiring the people to accept the religion of their rulers. Since King Ferdinand and Queen Isabella were loyal Catholics, they believed it to be their duty to force the Roman Catholic religion upon all their subjects.

Tragedy for Jews and Mohammedans

In Spain at that time, however, there were thousands of Jews and Mohammedans, both of whom were ardently loyal to their own religions. Although there were many reasons why neither Jews nor Mohammedans cared to become Christians, there was one big reason that seemed to make it utterly impossible for them to change their religion to Christianity. This insuperable stumbling block was the belief in God as Trinity. Both Roman Catholics and Protestants regarded this as an essential cornerstone of their faith, the belief in God the Father, God the Son and God the Holy Ghost (or Spirit). Each of the three was declared to be equal to the others and all were eternal, yet the three were but one God. To Jews and Mohammedans this belief in the Trinity had one meaning, namely, that there were three gods. Being staunchly monotheistic in their faith, these people refused to renounce their allegiance to their own religions.

For the Jews the climax of their troubles came in the famous year 1492, when King Ferdinand and Isabella ordered eight hundred thousand Jews to be banished from the realm. During the next score of years, thousands of Mohammedans were also banished. What is even more tragic, among those who refused to bow the knee to a God in whom they could not believe, were twenty thousand people who were burned at the stake.

A Spanish Student's Discovery

During these years of barbarous persecution, a young Spanish lad was growing up in the town of Villaneuva in Aragon. Like all other Spanish boys, he first attended a Roman Catholic school where he was taught the important principles and rituals of the Catholic faith. Often on street corners and at play he heard derogatory comments regarding Jews and Mohammedans. Michael Servetus was a sensitive, sympathetic lad, and his heart was torn by the tales of suffering he heard. Perhaps he even witnessed a burning at the stake, and was puzzled to understand why anyone should prefer such a death to saying the Christian creed: "I believe in God the Father, God the Son and God the Holy Ghost." What did three gods in one mean anyway? But such questions were never asked at school. Michael probably scarcely even thought them clearly in his mind.

When he was seventeen years of age, Michael left home and crossed the Pyrenees Mountains into France to attend the University of Toulouse in order to study law. During his first year of study there he made a great discovery. He found a copy of the Bible, and for the first time he began reading it for himself. In all his years in the Roman Catholic school at home, he had never been allowed to read the Bible. Now it was like a new and wonderful book to him; and he was deeply impressed by the story of Jesus that he found given in the Gospels, one so different from the God Jesus Christ who was worshipped in the church. As Michael read on, his surprise grew because nowhere could he find the Trinity even mentioned.

When he had finished the book, he decided that the belief that Jesus Christ was equal and co-eternal with God was not based on the Scriptures, but was an error that the church had promoted in order to add power to its preaching. Servetus now saw Jesus as divine in a more natural sort of way, perhaps more as other good men may also become divine. He could no longer believe that Jesus was God himself, born before the foundation of the world.

So, at the ripe age of eighteen, knowing full well that heretics and unbelievers both in Spain and in France had met death by the thousands at the hands of spying inquisitors, this spirited and optimistic young fellow determined to devote his life in an effort to expose the error of the Trinity, believing there was something better and more inspiring for Christians to believe if they could but be led to see that Jesus was more nearly like themselves and that he *became* the Son of God because of the quality of his life and because God so rewarded him. Servetus believed he had the Scriptures back of his position.

Another Chance to Learn

By the end of his first year, being in need of funds, Servetus took a position as a kind of secretary to a Catholic monk,

Juan de Quintana, who a little later became Father Confessor to the Emperor Charles V himself.

This employment brought Servetus another great experience. He and Juan de Quintana journeyed to Rome in the Emperor's suite in order to be present at his coronation by the Pope. There young Servetus saw the supreme pontiff treated as if he were God himself. The impression made upon Servetus was still so vivid even years later that he could write:

> With these very eyes I saw him [the pope] borne with pomp on the shoulders of princes, and in the public streets adored by the whole people kneeling, to such a point that those that succeeded even in kissing his feet or his shoes deemed themselves happy beyond the rest. Oh, beast of beasts the most wicked! Most shameless of harlots!

And the reason for this revulsion was understandable:

> ... on the other hand, behind the scenes, he [Servetus] saw among the highest dignitaries of the Church sickening evidences of worldliness, selfish ambition, cynical skepticism, and unconcealed immorality. Henceforth the official religion of the Church seemed to him but a hollow mockery, and the Pope became for him the very Antichrist predicted in the New Testament.[1]

Again when Servetus traveled in the Emperor's suite he had another remarkable opportunity. This time he attended the famous Diet at Augsburg, where the leaders of the Protestant Reformation in Germany worked out the statement of their faith which for years afterwards became the standard by which heretical beliefs were measured.

He Tried to Reform the Reformers

Soon after this event, Servetus gave up his position with the monk Quintana and ventured on his own to work out his

---

[1] Earl Morse Wilbur, *Our Unitarian Heritage* (Boston: Beacon Press, 1925), pp. 55-56 and n.l.

great ambition. Surely, he thought, the Protestant Reformers would listen. It was fundamental with them to base their faith on the Scriptures.

Though but nineteen years of age, Servetus sought out the Protestant leaders in Strassburg and Basel, some of whom were men twice his age. He set before them his views about the Trinity in the hope that he might persuade them to revise their gospel or else convince him of his error. Although the reformers treated Servetus with courtesy and patience, they were not easily persuaded to revise this most important article of the Christian faith.

Refusing to be discouraged, however, Servetus decided to write his views and publish them, believing that, if people only understood, they would agree with him. The little book was called *De Trinitatis Erroribus Libri Septem,* meaning *Seven Books on the Errors of the Trinity.* No publisher in Strassburg, however, would print the book for him. Still Servetus persisted and finally found a publisher in Alsace who was willing to run the risk.

He Hides Under an Assumed Name

The book aroused a great deal of attention. It was read by all the leading reformers. Servetus naively thought it would surely win acceptance, but instead the reformers, one and all, denounced it vigorously. Luther called it "an abominably wicked book." Its sale was forbidden in Basel and Strassburg, and soon it was suppressed throughout the whole empire. Opposition became so violent that Servetus soon found himself penniless and without a friend in Germany. He left Strassburg, assumed the name of Michel de Villeneuve, and for twenty-one years Michael Servetus was as a dead man to all who had known him.

What he actually did was to go to Paris where he again became a student, this time finally pursuing a course in medicine. While studying in Paris he met John Calvin, and he used to engage in arguments with him. Later he established himself as a practicing physician near Lyons. Soon he achieved such a reputation that the Archbishop of Vienna invited him to become his private physician, and for ten or twelve years Dr. Michel de Villeneuve lived in the midst of the comforts of a palace.

He Ventures on Another Book

Having many leisure hours, the young physician again became ambitious to write. Quietly for four years he worked on another book. Under his assumed name he began corresponding with Calvin who was then in Geneva. Servetus still naively thought he might convert the Protestant leader to his point of view. He even sent a part of his new manuscript for Calvin to read and comment upon. The correspondence began politely, but ended with abusive epithets from both sides.

Of course, Calvin soon realized who this Dr. Michel de Villeneuve really was, and wrote his friend Farel that if Servetus ever came to Geneva, and John Calvin had any influence, the heretic would not get away alive.

Undaunted by Calvin's attitude, and unmindful of the danger of again exposing his identity, Servetus finished his book. The title he gave it was *Christianismi Restitutio,* meaning *The Restoration of Christianity.* Again it was with the greatest difficulty that he found a publisher. Only by the enticement of a large fee was Servetus able to lure an unknown printer who could work secretly in a vacant house to take the risk. Even then the printer refrained from placing his name on the title page.

He Escapes from Jail

But Michael Servetus boldly signed his own real name to the book. As he might have himself predicted, as soon as the

Portrait of Michael Servetus

book began to circulate, the Roman Catholic inquisitors searched out the author and put him in jail to await trial for heresy.

In some mysterious way, no one knows just how, Servetus escaped by night from his captors. The next morning, even though the prisoner was absent from the courtroom, he was tried and condemned to be burned to death by a slow fire. The following day in the public square of Vienne he was hanged in effigy and then burned in the same fire with all the copies of the book which could be found.

The agents of the French court did such a thorough job in ferreting out copies of this *Restoration of Christianity* that today only three are known to exist. These are prized not only because of their high value for the history of Christianity, but also for another quite surprising reason. This brilliant young physician had, quite casually, introduced an illustration into the text of his book. This was an account of his own discovery of the circulation of the blood through the lungs. In this discovery Michael Servetus was seventy-five years ahead of the great Englishman, William Harvey, who first conclusively demonstrated the course of the blood through the entire body.

His Arrest and Trial in Geneva

Again Dr. Michel de Villeneuve was a fugitive. For four months he wandered in the general direction of Naples. Unfortunately, he had to pass through Geneva and arrived on a Sunday. Since the law of the city required attendance at church, he went with the crowd to hear Calvin preach. Even before the sermon began, he was recognized, perhaps by Calvin himself. At any rate, Servetus was arrested then and there. So once more he found himself languishing in prison, awaiting trial for heresy, this time by Protestants.

At first, Servetus did not worry overmuch for he still believed he could defend his position in such a way as to be convincing. He knew also that Calvin was having other troubles of his own, for with a large and vocal minority Calvin was very unpopular. Some of them openly sided with Servetus.

The trial dragged on for weeks. Some of Calvin's staunchest supporters brought charges against Servetus and others of Calvin's opponents took up the cudgels in the prisoner's behalf. Calvin's authority seemed to be challenged. He came himself into the court and brought his charges directly. He had a copy of the *Restoration of Christianity* introduced and read. Calvin called Servetus' ideas, "Partly impious blasphemies, partly profane and insane errors, and all wholly foreign to the Word of God and the orthodox faith." Calvin spared no effort to bring about the heretic's conviction.

In the end Calvin had to make one compromise. The court decided to lay the whole matter before the other Swiss churches before coming to a decision. There were, therefore, more weeks of waiting. The jail was a filthy place. Servetus became ill and wrote a letter to the city council complaining that the vermin were eating him alive and that he had had no change of clothing since his confinement.

His Painful Death

Finally, the replies came back from the churches. Due partly perhaps to propaganda from Geneva, the unanimous verdict was *guilty*. In the face of these reports, excommunication or death were the only possible outcomes. Still Servetus was hopeful that his Protestant brethren would be more lenient than the Roman Catholics in France had been. When, therefore, he heard the verdict that he should be burned at the stake, the weary man broke down. But it was not for having to die that his heart failed him. It was rather the fear that in the agony of suffering he might recant, and not prove himself a true "disciple like his Master."

The last morning, William Farel went to jail and begged the prisoner to renounce his errors and so save himself. Instead, October 27, 1553, outside the city of Geneva, in the presence of both friends and enemies, Michael Servetus was bound to a stake with two of his books tied to his waist and a crown of straw and brimstone on his head. Then the fagots were lighted.

The Unquenchable Flame

Almost immediately the news of Servetus' martyrdom brought bitter criticism upon Calvin's head. As for discussions on the truth of the Trinity, these continued. It took men a long time to learn that flames kindled by burning men along with their books are not easily quenched. The human voices are stilled, but the issues are not consumed. Servetus was by no means the first or the only man in his time who was protesting against belief in the Trinity, or who was trying to persuade the Reformers to honor greater freedom of expression, and his martyrdom tended to incite more interest in the issue rather than to dull it.

It is not known just when the word "Unitarian" was first applied to those who opposed the Trinitarian belief; it is known that during this sixteenth century the movement by that name spread into a number of countries of Europe. Although after Servetus' death Protestants seldom condemned heretics to the stake, there were many heretics who were exiled. Because of this persecution, the seeds of the movement were scattered. For a time in Poland, Unitarians were in the majority. In Transylvania, which then included Hungary and Rumania, Francis David became an able champion of the cause. Through his influence, King Sigismund was converted and Unitarianism became the state religion of Transylvania and continued as such until recent times.

Whatever our own convictions may be, all believers in freedom of religion owe a debt to these courageous men. What they were willing to purchase with so great a price of blood and treasure was not simply freedom to deny certain ancient beliefs. They were affirming with all their minds and hearts the right of men to believe in a religion consistent with reason and with the Holy Scriptures, untrammeled by the tyranny of higher ecclesiastical authority. Theirs was a faith in man himself, as well as in God.

The Unitarians

Channing's Famous Sermon

To most dwellers in Baltimore in the year 1819, it was just another quiet Sunday morning in May when William Ellery Channing, the famous Boston minister, was to preach and to share in the ordination of young Mr. Jared Sparks as minister in the recently organized First Independent Church of that city. Those who heard the great Dr. Channing, however, were well aware that they were witnessing a significant event. For some years the liberals and the orthodox in the Congregational churches of New England had been growing apart. Dr. Channing and those of like belief had been the objects of much public and bitter criticism. Although on most occasions, he was a gentle, peace-loving character, in his sermon that morning he became the champion of the liberal movement.

Taking up one by one the distinguishing beliefs of Unitarians, he showed how they were supported both by reason and by the Scriptures. The Trinity he said was difficult to understand and without foundation in the Bible. He denounced in eloquent language the Calvinistic belief in a God who would "bring us to life wholly depraved . . . [so that] the child [endowed with] a ceaseless tendency to unmingled crime [would be subject] to . . . everlasting damnation." Likewise he condemned the idea of predestination, the belief that God "selects from this corrupt mass of mankind a number to be saved," all the rest of humanity being "born under the blighting curse" of future everlasting torment in hell. Such a God, Channing said, would be "a being whom we cannot love if we would, and whom we ought not to love if we could." Such beliefs he declared were creations of the theologians and not to be gotten from the Bible. What the Bible taught could be understood only by the use of the same intelligence we apply to other matters.

Unitarians Declare Their Independence

Reports of this sermon were published far and wide. Probably no sermon preached in America up to that time had so many readers and so great an influence. It has often been called "the Unitarian Declaration of Independence." It precipitated a break in the Congregational churches of New England, between the orthodox and the liberal or Unitarian churches.

The seeds of Unitarianism had been in the Mayflower Compact, and were nourished in the democratic atmosphere pervading the autonomous individual Congregational churches. With the end of the American Revolution, free religious thinking had begun to flourish.

Strangely enough, the first church in America to become Unitarian was the oldest Episcopalian Church in New England—King's Chapel in Boston. As early as 1782 this church called the Rev. James Freeman to be its pastor, a man openly holding the Unitarian belief. Under his leadership, the church eliminated from its Book of Common Prayer all references to the Trinity and all prayers to Christ.

A few years later, the first churches to be called by the name Unitarian were organized in Northumberland, Pennsylvania, and in Philadelphia. Dr. Joseph Priestley, noted discoverer of oxygen and a Unitarian minister in England, became their leader. After a number of years of distinguished and unmolested service in England as minister in two large churches, Dr. Priestley had been attacked by a mob that had burned his meetinghouse, his home, his laboratory, and had destroyed all his books and manuscripts. Dr. Priestley, knowing that the mob had been secretly encouraged by high author-

The Old Ship Church meetinghouse in Hingham, Massachusetts, was built in 1681 as a Congregational church. In 1718 it turned Unitarian when Ebenezer Gay became its minister. Note the "widow's walk" around the small bell tower. (Ewing Galloway)

ities in the Church of England, realized that imprisonment might be the next step; and to save his life he found refuge in America. With the same heroism with which he had faced persecution in his native land, Dr. Priestley faced in this country the more intangible but none-the-less intense fires of fanatical prejudice.

About this same time, the oldest Church of the Pilgrims in Plymouth and its parish voted overwhelmingly for a Unitarian ministry. Year by year other Congregational churches began taking similar steps, and so the movement gathered momentum. Within a score of years over one-third of the Congregational churches in Massachusetts had become Unitarian. Many other churches in other parts of New England joined the seceders. Only in Connecticut was the secession stemmed, and that was accomplished by disciplinary measures used by higher regional authorities.

Serious as the loss of ministers and members was to the Congregational churches, the loss of church property to many liberal groups added greatly to the bitterness. When the Rev. Henry Ware, Unitarian minister in Hingham, was elected to the chair of divinity at Harvard University, the storm burst. Dr. Jedidiah Morse, father of Samuel Morse, inventor of the telegraph, began organizing the orthodox ministers for a fight. In his magazine, called the *Panoplist,* he incessantly attacked the anti-Trinitarians and challenged them to open debate. As the liberals in turn became bolder and expressed their views openly in their pulpits, the conflict raged with increased ill feelings.

Channing Champions Social Causes

Channing's fight, however, was not merely against Calvinistic theology. He never hesitated to take a vigorous stand against all forms of selfish exploitation, because to him the spirit of man was of infinite worth. Slavery inspired him with horror, for as a youth in Virginia he had seen it in operation. His courageous statements from his Boston pulpit caused considerable furore, since New England cotton mills were at that time dependent on slave labor.

War to Channing was the greatest of human follies, and he did all he could to advance the cause of peace, yet he was no pacifist, and once remarked heatedly, ". . . sometimes we *must* fight." Intemperance also he believed debased the human spirit, and he stoutly opposed it. Education was a forge in which nobler and more useful characters might be hammered out; so he did what he could to improve the schools and the training of teachers. He had great hopes for the French Revolution of 1830. He passionately desired the liberation of mankind from all kinds of tyranny. When a young Harvard student, noting Channing's unquenchable enthusiasms, remarked, "You seem to be the only young man I know," the older man replied warmly, "Always young for liberty!"

Unitarianism in Europe and in England

Although Channing was one of the great pioneers of the Unitarian Church in America, he was by no means the only one. The development of the movement in Europe and in England antedated him by three and a half centuries.

In Switzerland there was Michael Servetus, whose martyrdom in 1553 lit a flame for freedom that persecution has never extinguished. A few years later came two Italians, Laelius Socinus and his nephew Faustus Socinus, who so influenced the development of anti-trinitarian thought in Poland that a strong Unitarian church was established there which flourished for nearly a hundred years until it was ruthlessly blotted out by the bitter persecution of the Jesuits. In Transylvania was the great Francis David, who was the means of converting the king of the country to the Unitarian faith and who made the Unitarian Church the state Church of his land, but who also proclaimed freedom of worship to other sects.

Even in England the growth of Unitarian beliefs has had its coterie of martyrs. John Biddle, sometimes called "the Father of English Unitarianism," spent more than six years

in prison because of his faith. For many years those who made
known their belief in one God rather than in the Trinity were
ostracized by both Roman Catholics and Protestants. Until
1813 the Blasphemy Act made it impossible for one who denied the Trinity to hold any civil office. The struggle for civil,
mental and spiritual freedom made by such seventeenth-cen-
tury reformers as John Robinson, pastor of the Pilgrims who
fled to the Netherlands, fed directly into Unitarianism.

Unitarian National Organizations

The year 1825, by an unintentional coincidence, became
a red-letter year for Unitarians on both sides of the Atlantic,
for in that year both in England and in America, national
Unitarian organizations were formed. In both countries
these organizations are democratic societies representing the
churches and supported by them. They also lead in movements
regarded as important to the cause of liberal religion.

Until the merger of Unitarians and Universalists, finally
accomplished in May 1961, the American Unitarian Association had its headquarters in Boston. Now its functions are
continued by the Unitarian Universalist Association, also in
Boston. The elected president of this association, its officers
and committees, respond to the will of the united denominations, and care for those matters which are of common concern.
They assist young churches, plan for the education of ministers, guide the educational work of the churches, and prepare
literature of many kinds.

The Unitarians and Universalists together number about
800 churches in the United States and Canada, and there are
also several hundred fellowships. The latter are led by laymen
and are not yet eligible to assume church status, since they are
not large enough to be self-supporting. The combined membership of the two denominations is about 180,000. Unitarians
in Great Britain claim about 400 churches, but their churches
tend to be smaller than those in America. Nevertheless, there
have been many eminent English Unitarians.

What Do Unitarians Now Believe?

Just as the Trinitarians gained their name from a belief in the Trinity, so Unitarians were given their name because of their insistence on the unity of God. This belief has had as its natural corollary, a belief in the humanity of Jesus. In different times and with different Unitarians this belief in Jesus' humanity has been expressed in different ways, some of which do not differ in actual meaning from beliefs held by many ministers and members of other Protestant churches.

This one original protest, however, has now become but a symbol of the attitude of mind out of which this protest developed. It is usually described as the "free spirit" which refuses to be checked in its search for truth by the demand for adherence to a creed stated by an ecclesiastical authority as necessary to membership in the church. Consequently, the bond that unites Unitarians is not a statement of a common faith, but rather the spiritual fellowship that is found in the sincere use of reason and the scientific attitude in the quest for truth, and in the consciousness of a common purpose to live for "the ennoblement and enrichment of human life."

This accent on the use of reason has been so strong that Unitarians have often been accused of being intellectual and cold. Their refusal to form a common creedal statement has laid them open to the charge that they have no beliefs to support and strengthen them, and that there is nothing inspiring for which the church stands. These charges, however, do not adequately represent the character of the Unitarian fellowship. Unitarians have as strong beliefs as others, but they do not insist that they have found "final" truth. Uniformity in beliefs they do not regard as essential, and some indeed go so far as to assert that God exists only as a kind of Supreme Good in the hearts of men. Such Unitarians are usually known as "Humanists." Worship and the traditional practices of religion interest them much less than religion as a force in human progress. But all Unitarians vigorously reject the old orthodox belief in man's natural sinful nature.

Had he realized it, Abraham Lincoln might have found

himself at home in a Unitarian church,[2] for he said: "When any church will inscribe over its altar, as the sole qualification for membership the Saviour's condensed statement of the substance of both Law and Gospel, 'Thou shalt love the Lord thy God with all thy heart and with all thy soul and with all thy mind, and thy neighbor as thyself' that church will I join with all my heart and with all my soul."

Influential Character of the Unitarian Movement

Although the Unitarian Church has not been a large denomination either in England or in America, yet it has had in its membership a disproportionately large number of educated and famous people in the fields of letters, politics, social reform, education and science. Consequently, the Unitarian Church has influenced cultural change more strongly than its numerical size would suggest. The combined Protestant denominations in the United States have nearly 70 per cent of the total membership of the Christian churches, while the Unitarians have less than 1 per cent of the total. Yet in the American Hall of Fame at New York University, a score of the seventy-two statues are of Unitarians.

Among noted American writers and poets have been the following Unitarians: Henry W. Longfellow, Nathaniel Hawthorne, James Russell Lowell, Ralph Waldo Emerson, Henry Thoreau, Julia Ward Howe, Louisa May Alcott and William Cullen Bryant. Thomas Jefferson hoped that some day everybody would be Unitarian. A few of the most noted American scientists who have felt able to worship in Unitarian Churches have been Charles Steinmetz, Louis Agassiz and Robert Millikan. Among the educators and social reformers have been some of the greatest Unitarian names—Horace Mann, Ezra Cornell, Charles W. Eliot, Peter Cooper, Dorothea Dix, Susan B. Anthony and Elizabeth Peabody.

---

[2] It is known that Lincoln was a close friend of a number of the men who founded the Unitarian Church of Bloomington, Illinois, and that he often attended its services.

Most of the social reforms and philanthropic movements that have been started or carried forward by Unitarians have not been given names to indicate their church connections, so that the source of their inspiration is often unknown. There are no Unitarian hospitals or colleges, although there are two theological schools, Starr King on the Pacific Coast and Meadville, originally in Pennsylvania, but now on the campus of the University of Chicago. Harvard Divinity School, founded by Unitarians, has a number of Unitarian professors and students.

There has been an outstanding benevolent organization, however, at work during the last two world wars and denominationally set up. It is called the Unitarian Service Committee, Inc. Its aim has been whenever possible to help people help themselves. Teams of doctors have been sent out to train native medical workers, medical personnel from abroad have been brought to the United States for further study, institutes to train social workers have been sponsored in postwar Germany, Italy and Greece, and an educational program for native teachers has been set up in Cambodia. For several years the Committee administered all homes for displaced children in the British Zone in occupied Germany. Emergency help has been given in Hungary and Korea, and aid has been given a hospital in the Peruvian jungles, operated by a physician disciple of Albert Schweitzer. In the United States much work has been done for the Navaho Indians in New Mexico. Thus, throughout the world, this organization has given thousands of men and women a new opportunity and thousands of children have been fed, clothed and given the encouragement of loving care.

The World-Wide Spread of Unitarianism

Although Unitarianism has never been a proselyting religion, the number of Unitarian churches has been steadily increasing and Unitarians can be found in many lands, including Australia, New Zealand, South Africa, and India. A few years ago a Congregational Church in Samoa asked, on its own initiative, for membership in the American Unitarian Association.

Liberal groups in Europe are scattered but steadily growing stronger. Churches have been springing up, particularly in Denmark, the Netherlands, Italy and Switzerland. Numerous churches dot Rumania and Hungary. The Unitarian movement in Czechoslovakia, founded as recently as 1921, has been vigorous and growing.

"Unitarianism is, today, the second most powerful religion in Iceland, a one time Lutheran stronghold. . . . Bringing into closer union and co-ordinating into one great movement the efforts of these and other liberal churches throughout the world is the International Association for Liberal Christianity and Religious Freedom. The churches affiliated with it represent some twenty million people."[3]

[3] John Nicholls Booth, *Introducing Unitarianism* (pamphlet of the American Unitarian Association, No. 375, Boston, 1945), pp. 23-24.

5. Ignatius Loyola
1491-1556

I, Ignatius Loyola, promise to Almighty God and to the Pope, His Vicar upon earth, before His Virgin Mother and the whole court of Heaven, and in the presence of the Society, perpetual poverty, chastity and obedience, according to the manner of life set forth in the Bull of the Society of Our Lord Jesus, and in the Constitutions declared or to be promulgated, of the same Society. Moreover, I promise special obedience to the Supreme Pontiff with regard to the missions mentioned in the Bull, and likewise to be diligent to see that children are taught the rudiments of the faith, according to the same Bull and Constitutions.
—Vow taken by Ignatius Loyola and all the Company of Jesus

"Onward, Christian Soldier!"

When Knighthood Was in Flower

Another Spaniard, who later became significant in Christian history, was living his boyhood while Columbus was sailing the seas. Inigo de Loyola, born, it is thought, in 1491 near the village of Aspeitia in northern Spain, was given his early education in the court school of Queen Isabella. There he learned the routines of reading and writing and the fundamentals of the Catholic faith. The Duke and Duchess of the Castle of Loyola little dreamed of the kind of fame their youngest son would eventually achieve.

In the daily regimes of the castle they were training him, as all his brothers had been trained, to be a brave knight. Inigo enjoyed the thrill of horseback riding, of charging with drawn sword against an imaginary enemy, of practice fighting in a coat of armor. He also enjoyed gambling, feasting, rowdy drinking. His greatest ambition was to become a dashing cavalier for a certain lovely lady of the Queen's court. He dreamed of himself as a chivalrous knight of great renown.

Opportunities were at hand for just such a life. France and Spain were at war. The city of Pamplona, only fifty miles away from Loyola, became the place of battle. A small garrison was trying to hold the castle there, and Inigo became one of their young captains. The Spaniards were ill prepared; his superiors finally advised surrender. Inigo's Spanish blood was hot, and his honor was at stake. From the ramparts where he stood under fire beside his men, he called back, "We fight on!" The wall was breached. A cannon ball shattered Captain Loyola's right leg. He collapsed. The castle was taken.

For ten days as a prisoner of war, Loyola was nursed by his enemies. By litter they carried him back to his father's castle. The setting of the bones was bungled. With no anesthetics the leg was twice reset; a piece of the bone had to be sawed off. It was a matter of pride with Inigo not to flinch or cry out. He lay helpless in bed for many months.

New Dreams Replace the Old

During the tedious days of slow recovery, he asked for books to read about knights and ladies, but the only books that were to be found in the castle were religious. One was a life of Christ and the other had the quaint title, *Flowers of the Saints.* At first, Inigo had little interest. He preferred to daydream of knights and ladies, but slowly the books conquered his dreams. He began to picture another kind of courage, such as he found in Jesus and in the lives of the saints. Inigo began to wonder, "How would it be if I were ever to become like St. Francis or St. Dominic?" In his dreaming, Inigo saw two flags, one belonging to Christ and the other belonging to the Devil. In his

*Ignatius Loyola, as seen in a painting by the great Flemish artist,
Peter Paul Rubens. (The Bettmann Archive)*

heart, he finally enlisted under the banner of Christ. Inigo would "do great things" not for the love of his lady fair, but "for the love of God." He would be a soldier of Jesus.

But how? He was already thirty years old. He had but little education. He could not read Latin. It seemed late to begin something entirely new—but not too late. He would try. Perhaps he might go on a pilgrimage to Jerusalem, convert the Mohammedans, and visit places Jesus had made holy by his presence.

A Knight for Christ

His family were out of sympathy with Inigo's new ambitions. He could not speak with them about his new dreams. He made his plans in secret. When his leg was finally well enough so that he could walk about, he said good-by, giving his family the impression that he was leaving for a short visit with friends. Dressed in his knightly cape and short breeches, and with sword and dagger at his side, he rode out the castle gate on the back of a mule.

At the town of Montserrat, he bought some rough cloth, the kind from which sacks are made. He had a tailor sew him a plain garment that could be tied about his waist with a rope girdle. He bought also a staff, a calabash and a pair of sandals.

With this strange new outfit in a bundle on his shoulders, the young knight climbed the hill to the Benedictine monastery where for a number of days the monks gave him hospitality. There he opened up his heart to the Abbot and sought for his wisdom. With the other monks and also alone in his room, he spent many hours in prayer. With great earnestness he made confession of his sins to the Abbot. Finally he spent three whole days in writing down all the sins he could remember that he had ever committed. He was determined to start anew the book of his life with pages made clean by God's forgiveness. At last he was at peace and prepared to come before the Holy Mother herself whose famous image stood beside the altar in the little chapel of the monastery.

His Vows Before the Holy Mother

He ordered his mule taken away. He clothed himself in the sackcloth garment and sandals. At dusk on March 24, 1522, he went alone to the chapel, carrying his sword and dagger in one hand, and his former blue mantle and breeches and yellow stockings and knightly cap over his other arm. In front of the chapel he gave an astonished tramp the knightly clothes no longer needed. Entering the chapel, Inigo hung his sword and dagger alongside the statue of the Virgin, as another symbol of the life he was determined to renounce. All night long standing or on his knees, he paid homage to the Queen of Heaven, seeking her blessing. At daybreak, this newly enlisted soldier of Jesus, stole quietly away in the direction of Barcelona. Limping on his still tender foot, he began his pilgrimage, hoping some day to reach the Holy Land.

As Inigo walked along over the hills, he made yet another decision. He would change his name to that of one of the Christian martyrs of whom he had read while convalescing in the castle. It would no longer be Inigo Loyola, son of a duke of the Basque country. It would be Ignatius Loyola, the pilgrim, who had embraced "poverty with Jesus Christ poor, rather than riches; shame and insults with Jesus Christ reproached and insulted, rather than honours; the reputation of a fool with Jesus Christ mocked and scorned, rather than a great name for wisdom among men."[1]

For ten months Ignatius Loyola lived as an unknown beggar in the town of Manresa, not being able to go on toward Barcelona because of the plague. By turns he lived in the poorhouse, in a cell given him by the Benedictine monks, and in a cave on the hillside. He begged his bread in the streets, giving away to the sick and hungry whatever was beyond his own simple needs. In penance he scourged himself three times a day. He spent eight hours a day in prayer. This once fastidious knight even let his fingernails grow long and his hair remain uncut and uncombed.

[1] James Brodrick, *The Origin of the Jesuits* (London, 1940), pp. 21-22.

His Spiritual Exercises

With all his striving, however, Ignatius failed to find peace of heart. His long hours of devotion and his privations brought him twice to the gates of death. Later, however, he learned more wisdom, and abandoned these extremes in asceticism. Although he always lived simply and begged his food, his love of order and cleanliness prevailed. Once more he cut his hair and nails. He did not feel obliged to rise in the middle of the night for prayers. He found his own soul blessed while nursing the sick and while teaching children and peasant women, as well as when he knelt in prayer. He learned that true self-denial is not to be found in externals of dress and ritual. He would live for the love of Christ with people and not separate himself from them.

Ignatius, however, did not abandon his devotions. He became a skilled and practical technician in the promotion of the soul's inner resources. During these early months of his new life, he wrote down for himself and for others, detailed directions so that hours spent in prayer might yield the most in repentance, peace and strength. These directions were later published in a book called *Spiritual Exercises*. To follow them meant a rigorous and exacting regime lasting a month, and became a kind of initiation into the way of life for other soldiers of Jesus, who followed Ignatius' leadership.

On leaving Manresa, Ignatius begged his way to Barcelona, to Rome, to Venice. By galley ship and sailing vessel and over land on foot, he wended his way until after six long months "with more than mortal joy" he beheld Jerusalem.

His dream of remaining there the rest of his life in order to convert the Mohammedans came to naught, however, for the Franciscan monks refused to allow him to stay. So the disappointed crusader turned his back on his hopes and begged his return passage to Spain.

Ignatius Goes to School

Ignatius now realized that if he were to become a worthy soldier of Christ, fitted to teach others the way of life, he should be better educated. So even though already thirty-two years old, this irrepressible Spaniard started to school and sat on benches alongside boys in their early teens and tried to repeat the Latin declensions. For the next ten years he studied in several colleges in succession, going finally to the University of Paris where in 1535 he received the degree of Master of Arts.

Out of class hours, he begged bread or money as before. In the evenings, he would often seek out people in the slums of Paris, those poorer than himself, and too timid to beg. He would "press on them sweetly and humbly the coins he had collected in the streets."[2] At other spare times, he would have informal classes of his own when he discussed with his fellow students the Christian way of life and taught the *Spiritual Exercises*. In changing his own way of life, Ignatius apparently did not forfeit his knightly charms. One of his disciples writing of how Loyola won friends said:

> By I know not what means he so much became their friend, so imperceptibly stole into their souls, that by his example and his slow pleasant speech he kindled in them all a vehement love of God.[3]

His Virtue a Weakness

Sometimes, however, his trust in others was greater than his wisdom. On one occasion, when a student at Montaigu College in Paris, he loaned all his money to a fellow student, who speedily spent it and failed to repay anything. So Ignatius had to move to the poorhouse, which was so far from college that he frequently missed his first classes, which came at five in the morning.

But such things as early classes and unpaid loans were not all Ignatius had to worry about. Students there were di-

---

[2] *Ibid.*, p. 27.
[3] Simon Rodriguez, *Epistolae Broëti, Monumenta Historica Societatis Jesu,* quoted in *ibid.*, pp. 38-39.

vided into two groups, the rich and the poor. Life was not easy for either, but for the poor it was especially hard. In the winter all they were given was "a morsel of bread . . . and as for their drink, they must draw out of a well of bad water. . . . Nor shall I take notice how many rotten eggs were eaten nor how much sour wine was drunk."[4]

Since Loyola was completely orthodox in his faith, it seems strange that he should have had trouble with the inquisitors. But his excess of zeal (which was indeed sometimes almost fanatic), and his unconventional manner of dress, and the fact that without being ordained as a priest he presumed to teach other people, awakened suspicion. Some of his accusers may have been jealous of his success. Since on examination, no one could ever find anything unorthodox in his beliefs, Loyola was always acquitted and after a brief confinement freed from prison.

The First Company of Jesus

During his ten years as a student, Loyola won a group of devoted disciples, who like himself, took the vows of lifelong poverty and chastity. There were nine of these disciples by the time he completed his university studies. These men thought of themselves as soldiers of Jesus, who had enlisted for life in his service. They chose the name *Company of Jesus*. As soon as all had finished their studies, they planned to go to Rome to seek permission of the Pope to go to Jerusalem as missionaries to the Turks. But if His Holiness decided they were more needed elsewhere, they resolved to be willing to go anywhere in the world the Vicar of Christ might command them to go.

When studies were finished, however, Loyola was ill and was ordered by his doctor to convalesce in the balmy air of his native Spain. So he bade good-by to his nine disciples, presumably to return to his brother's castle, where it was hoped he

---

[4] Desiderius Erasmus, *Colloquies,* quoted by Paul Van Dyke in his *Ignatius Loyola* (New York, 1926) , p. 79.

At the left, Loyola kneels before Pope Paul III. At the right, he is shown writing his Religious Exercises *and sending forth his missionaries. (The Bettmann Archive)*

might regain his health. Meanwhile the other nine, as soon as they were ready, were to move on toward Rome where Loyola hoped to meet them in a few months.

Instead of going to live in the comfort of the family castle, however, Loyola, to his brother's consternation, sought lodgings in the poorhouse of the village of Aspitia. But Ignatius had a reason. He wanted to do something to better the lives of the villagers and so to make amends for the dissolute life he had lived there as a young man.

He announced early in his stay he would teach classes for the children and for any others, men and women, who cared to come. "Nobody will come to your classes," said his brother Martin in scorn. "One is enough for me," answered Ignatius. Scores came. Being a little man like Zacchaeus, Ignatius would sometimes climb a tree and sit on a branch above the people so that all could see him. In practical ways also he helped to improve the life of the village. He organized a kind of cooperative and regular system of relief for those who were unable to work.

A New Order Is Sanctioned

Many more months passed before Loyola joined his nine disciples in the city of Rome. They sought the Pope's permission to found a new society, dedicated to the service of Jesus and the Church, whatever that service might be. This permission was obtained with difficulty, since some of the cardinals who advised the Pope thought there were already too many monastic orders, and others were jealous of the success which Loyola and his companions were having with the common people.

The influence and power of the society grew. Money was often hard to find, yet somehow gifts always came in when they were most needed. Wherever these soldiers of Christ went they sought out those sick and in distress. They nursed men with leprosy and others smitten with the plague. They found food for the hungry and clothes for those who were cold. Those whom they taught were for the most part people whom the church, with its wealth and power, seemed to have forgotten. So the poor and humble heard these sixteenth-century disciples of Jesus gladly, as they had heard Jesus himself fifteen hundred years before.

As the new order found friends, so also it found recruits. At first the papal charter had limited membership to sixty, but this restriction was soon lifted when the usefulness of the society to the church became evident. Standards of admission were set high. No one younger than fourteen nor older than twenty-five was considered for admission. The order was officially named The Society of Jesus.

Conditions of Membership

Nor was it easy to qualify for full membership. Two years of probation were required, and eight years of work in a college or university. Before taking the final vows, candidates were obliged to give up all their property, for Loyola knew that "where a man's treasure is, there will his heart be also." Like all priests and nuns of the Roman Catholic church, Jesuits were sworn to chastity.

To Loyola it seemed that members of other monastic orders were limited in their usefulness by the rigid requirements of a special garb, and that by withdrawing from the affairs of the world, and by leading sheltered lives within their cloisters, they lessened their usefulness. Complete poverty and austere self-denial were a part of their monastic vows, yet not a few of them soon became lax and soft in their manner of living. Worse than that, many led lives of vice, and the common people knew it. In some orders the chief interest seems to have been to collect their rents, for many became wealthy landowners.

Loyola realized that the greatest dangers which threatened the church came from the evils within, rather than from its enemies without. He, therefore, prepared the Constitution of the Company of Jesus with great care. Members, either individually or collectively, were forbidden to hold property, or to accept honors (such as bishoprics) within the church, or to accept fees for anything they did.[5] He bade them "avoid any sort of avarice." They could not even have collection boxes in their churches. He wished them to be as free as possible to go anywhere at any time, on missions for the church.

The vow of absolute and unquestioning obedience to their superior in the Company and to the Pope, as the "Vicar of Christ" on earth, was taken with great seriousness. Obedience should be "perinde cadaver," meaning "with as little objection as a dead man would make." If the church should officially say that black is white, said Loyola, members of the Company of Jesus were bound to believe it. For to Loyola, the soldier, obedience was as necessary in the ranks of those who fought the church's battles as for those in the armies of any earthly monarch.

The Growth of the Order

Loyola intended also that the Jesuits should be a missionary order. The work of teaching was to him of equal importance with that of benevolence and care of the sick. As a result these Soldiers of Jesus have gone to the far corners of the earth. One of Loyola's earliest disciples, Francis Xavier, traveled to the Orient and baptized converts in many parts of India and in the Malay Islands. He even did some work in China and Japan.

The Company of Jesus, which in time numbered its soldiers by the thousands, was a body of well educated, able and devoted men under a military leadership, which was always at the disposal of the church.

They founded many colleges and universities in Europe. Since many of the students studying in these institutions were often of noble birth, the support they later gave to the work of

[5] The prohibition of property-holding did not extend to Jesuit *institutions,* although the property they hold must be administered by lay trustees.

the order was of great value. Other Jesuits became influential in the courts of kings and princes, and thus gained power in determining the policies of governments toward the church.

It Becomes a Counter Reformation

These devoted Jesuits perhaps did more than any other group or organization to check the rising tide of the Reformation, which threatened to sweep most of Europe into the Protestant fold. Because of their influence, Unitarianism in Poland was utterly wiped out, and relentless persecution left the Protestant movement much weakened throughout the whole of Central Europe.

Thus Ignatius Loyola became significant as the leader of a powerful counter-reformation which checked the spread of the Protestant Reformation by strengthening the missionary zeal and effectiveness of the Roman Catholic Church and by cleansing it of some of its grossest moral abuses.

Its Weakness and Its Power

Success and power, however, often bring disaster, and thus it has been with the Company of Jesus. The Jesuits came to believe that the end justified the means, even though the means were evil. The Order as a result became deeply involved in political schemes and intrigue, although such activities were opposed to the teachings of their founder. Some of the Jesuits quarreled with other Roman Catholic orders, and so brought on themselves the dislike of many within the church. Their worst mistake was to engage in commercial trading on a large scale in violation of their own constitutional rule. This eventually brought financial loss to many investors, and finally feeling against the Jesuits became so bitter that the Pope himself suppressed the Order in 1773, although the ban was lifted in 1814.

Even during the period of suppression, the Society of

Jesus refused to die, and it is still strong. It has a number of colleges and universities in the United States, and the number is growing. Marquette, St. Louis and Fordham universities, as well as a number of institutions which bear Loyola's name, are examples. LeMoyne is one of the newest and, unlike most Jesuit colleges, is coeducational. The initials S.J. after the name of a priest or university teacher, stand for Society of Jesus. There have been Jesuit scholars of note in many fields. They have excelled in mathematics and astronomy particularly, yet as a Society, they have resisted the impact of new ideas on the accepted beliefs of the church. Religion which was so dynamic a force in their living, became a shackling one to their thinking.

Of Loyola, one of his pupils said that few great men have had so few ideas, but fewer still have been as thoroughly earnest in their realization. Without the work of Ignatius Loyola and his Society the great Roman Catholic Church might have fallen apart, and Protestantism might have gathered more strength. Because he lived the ancient church remains a powerful and world-wide institution, but one in which liberty of religious thought is circumscribed within the framework of creeds and traditions, and the declarations of the Pope.

The Roman Catholic Church

Two Meanings of the Word Catholic

The majority of Protestants repeat the so-called Apostles' Creed in their church services. In this creed there is the phrase: "I believe . . . in the holy catholic church." In this statement, the words "catholic church" are used in their original meaning, namely world-wide or universal church, one that is inclusive of all true Christians.

Roman Catholics, however, claim that only the subjects

of the pope have the right to call themselves "Catholic." They alone are regarded as "true" Christians. All Protestants who repeat the Apostles' Creed or the Nicene Creed thereby assert that they also belong to the world-wide church, and thus definitely reject the claim of the Roman Catholics to a monopoly of the adjective "catholic."

The Authority of the Pope

Roman Catholics teach that Jesus founded their church, and appointed St. Peter the supreme lawgiver and ruler over all "true" Christians. This claim is based on a statement found only in the gospel of Matthew (Matt. 16:17-19). There Jesus is said to have made a pun on Peter's name, which in Greek means rock (petros). Peter has just declared emphatically his belief that Jesus is the Messiah (Christ), the Son of the living God. Jesus is reported as responding with deep satisfaction, saying that Peter has had a direct revelation from God. Then Jesus is said to have added these words: "Thou art Peter (petros) and upon this rock I will build my church. . . . I will give unto thee the keys of the kingdom of heaven; and whatsoever thou shalt bind on earth shall be bound in heaven; and whatsoever thou shalt loose on earth shall be loosed in heaven."

There has been disagreement as to the meaning of this conversation, and indeed certain outstanding scholars regard Jesus' reply, given by Matthew alone, as not historical: yet the Roman Catholics have built their entire church structure upon this foundation. In other words, they assert that Jesus gave Peter the keys to heaven and hell and, therefore, the power to decide what is right and what is wrong, and the power to forgive or not to forgive sins. It is this belief that led medieval artists to picture St. Peter as holding two keys in his hands.

To Roman Catholics, therefore, St. Peter was the first pope, and all subsequent popes are believed to have succeeded to his powers. This means that the pope claims to be the supreme earthly ruler, lawgiver and judge of all true Christians, and Christ's vicar on earth so that to disobey the pope's authority is to disobey God.

Although the pope is thus regarded as an absolute spiritual monarch, he is himself very definitely bound. He must not issue orders that contradict the commands of Christ or the teachings of the Bible or the dogmas already adopted by duly called councils of the entire Church.

But this still leaves much room for uncertainty. What exactly are the commands of Christ or the teachings of the Bible? How are they to be interpreted? Formerly when such questions seemed important enough they were laid before "Ecumenical Councils" of bishops of the Church.The problem of what books should be included in the Bible was settled in this way. However, since the Vatican Council of 1870 decreed that decisions of the pope bearing on "matters of faith and morals" are infallible, there has been little need for such conclaves. But this decree met with such opposition at the time that some of the dissenters seceded and formed what has since been known as the "Old Catholic Church." Though never large, this church has branches in Poland, France and elsewhere in Europe. In the United States it claims about 90,000 members. Its beliefs are essentially those of Roman Catholicism except that it refuses to recognize the pope and is in communion with the Eastern Orthodox Church. The American Old Catholic Church is governed by an archbishop whose seat is in Woodstock, N. Y.

In 1917, Pope Benedict XIV issued a detailed and very carefully prepared law book, called *The Code of Canon Law*. Although these laws are not enforceable in civil courts in the United States, they are binding in the courts of the Roman Catholic Church.

In order to exercise his authority in all countries, the pope has delegated powers and duties to others. Named in order of precedence, these include cardinals, patriarchs, archbishops, bishops, priests, deacons, sub-deacons, and other lower orders of servants of the church.

Mixed Marriages and the Education of Children

The points at which the average non-Catholic is apt to come in conflict with this *Code of Canon Law* are in its legislation regarding mixed marriages and regarding the education of children. First of all, the Roman Catholic Church forbids Christians who have been baptized in the name of the Trinity to become divorced. It considers the remarriage of such divorced persons to be sinful. The Roman Catholic Church also forbids all artificial methods of birth control. As a result, many Roman Catholic families are large.

If a Roman Catholic wishes to marry a Protestant, for example, the church refuses to recognize the ceremony performed by a Protestant minister as a true marriage. The couple so married is regarded as living in sin. The Roman church requires that the parties go through a second ceremony before a Roman Catholic priest.

The priest in turn is forbidden to perform the marriage ceremony unless the Protestant party signs two promises. First, he or she must agree not to interfere with the Roman Catholic party's going regularly to church and confession. All children born to the couple must be brought up from their earliest days as Roman Catholics. The Roman Catholic spouse must make a third promise, namely, that he will pray perseveringly for the conversion of the Protestant party to the Roman Catholic faith.

No Church has attached more importance to the instruction of children in its own faith than has the Roman Catholic Church. Even in a country where the state provides free education for all children, the Roman Catholic Church has established its own parochial schools in a vast number of towns in the country, and new ones continue to be built. The cost of maintaining these schools places a heavy financial burden on Catholic families and parishes, even though monks and nuns do the teaching and are not paid. Hundreds of thousands of children receive their entire education in these church-controlled schools where religious instruction is of supreme importance. In marked contrast to the public schools, neither the parents nor the public have any voice in their control. Even the ownership of the school property may be vested in the hands of the local bishop or archbishop, who then operates legally as a one-man corporation. The ownership of these schools is never in the hands of the Roman Catholic people of America, although they pay for them and their children are pupils. Some of the Roman Catholic institutions of higher learning, such as Notre Dame and the Catholic University of America, are well known. Many of them are controlled by religious orders; for instance, the Jesuits control Holy Cross in Massachusetts and Loyola University in Chicago, as well as the University of Detroit. Manhattan College in New York City is run by the Christian Brothers. There are also numerous colleges for women, such as the College of St. Elizabeth in New Jersey, conducted by the Sisters of Charity.

Roman Catholic Hospitals

Few cities are without hospitals founded and supported by the Church; they are found in smaller communities as well. More than a thousand such hospitals exist in the United States, some of them with many beds and treating hundreds of patients each year. Although patients are usually admitted without regard to their religion, the majority of the doctors on the staff are likely to be Catholic, and many of the nurses are nuns. Often direct control is in the hands of some nursing order of nuns.

Vatican City

Although the popes once governed a large part of central and northern Italy, now their temporal power is confined to one-sixth of a square mile called Vatican City. This beautiful enclosure situated on a hillside above the Tiber River, has about a thousand inhabitants over whom the pope actually rules; but if any serious disorders should arise he may call in the Italian police.

In this Vatican kingdom is the papal palace, called the Vatican. It is a cluster of large and impressive buildings with landscaped courts between them. In one section of the palace live the pope and a few of his highest officials. Here is the famous throne room where especially privileged visitors are received. Here are many well-staffed offices where ecclesiastical diplomats and other functionaries maintain close contacts with all parts of the world. Here also are museums with priceless treasures of sculpture, painting and tapestries, also a large library containing priceless old manuscripts. Within Vatican City are a half-dozen beautiful chapels, the most famous of which is the Sistine Chapel. Besides buildings there are the famous Vatican Gardens, made beautiful with flowers, shrubs and trees of many varieties.

Inside Vatican City is also the vast Cathedral of St. Peter, with its magnificent dome, the largest and most renowned church building in the world.

Roman Catholics and the Bible

The Church of Rome regards the Bible as infallible. It also denies to the individual the right to a private interpretation of any passage in the Bible on which the pope or the Church has declared the meaning. Consequently, most Roman Catholics are not encouraged to study the Bible directly themselves. Instead, they are instructed in the teachings of the Church. Since World War I, however, the pope has permitted the circulation of certain approved translations of the Bible from the Latin into several modern languages, including Italian, French and English. The standard English translation is called the Douay Bible, so named from the town in France where in 1610 the first Roman Catholic English translation was completed.

The Roman Catholic Sacraments

To Roman Catholics, there are seven sacraments. Five of these, baptism, confirmation, the Eucharist (Holy Communion), penance and extreme unction are for everybody. These sacraments are intended to dignify and to make sacred the important crises of life from the cradle to the grave. The other two sacraments are holy matrimony and holy orders. Matrimony is intended to give divine sanction to marriage and to the propagation of the human race. Holy orders (ordination) hallows and safeguards the supplying of ministers of the Church.

Roman Catholics teach that all these sacraments were instituted or arranged for by Christ himself. In performing them, certain words must be said exactly as they are given in the service book and certain visible acts must accompany the words. Otherwise the sacrament will be of no avail.

Each sacrament is intended to bring a special benefit to the person receiving it. In the language of the Church, the sacraments "confer grace." The word "grace" is defined as "a supernatural help from God which enlightens our mind and strengthens our will to do good and to avoid evil."[6]

The Sacrament of Baptism

For example, the sacrament of baptism is said to wash off the guilt of one's original sinful nature, which it is believed even innocent babies have inherited because of Adam's sin in the Garden of Eden. This does not mean, however, that baptism makes one perfect. By no means; the tendency to sin still remains. Consequently, new sinful acts sprout again like weeds in a flower bed and will need forgiveness.

The Roman Catholic Church teaches that, since the time of Christ, no unbaptized person will be admitted to heaven. It is believed that babies, who through no fault of their own

[6] *A Catechism of Christian Doctrine,* rev. ed. of the Baltimore Catechism, no. 2. 1941.

die unbaptized, cannot go to heaven, but live forever in a comfortable and beautiful region (called the limbo of infants), a place especially reserved for them.

The Sacrament of Confirmation

Confirmation is defined as a sacrament that imparts to one the sevenfold spiritual gifts that the Holy Spirit bestows. This strengthens a person and prepares him to face the difficulties of the Christian life. In modern times in America, many children are confirmed between the ages of nine and twelve. Usually only a bishop is permitted to administer this sacrament. After making the sign of the Cross on the child's forehead with fragrant sacred oil, the bishop gives the child a gentle slap on the cheek to suggest that he must be prepared to endure all affronts for the sake of the faith.

The Sacrament of the Eucharist

Protestant churches celebrate the sacrament of the Lord's Supper, often called the Communion, in remembrance of the farewell meal of Christ and the twelve disciples just before his trial and crucifixion. In the Roman Catholic Church this sacrament is called the Eucharist, a Greek word used in the Old Testament to mean "thank offering."

The service at which the Eucharist is celebrated is called the "Mass." This word comes from the Latin *missa,* meaning "the dismissal." It is so called because in the early Church unbelievers or other unbaptized persons were dismissed at the close of the first portion of the service, the Eucharist being considered too sacred a mystery for them to witness. For a baptized person who has reached the age of responsibility, not to attend Mass at least once a week is a "mortal" sin.

In this sacrament the "elements," which are bread and wine, when consecrated by the priest are believed to have been converted into the actual body and blood of Christ. The

Roman Catholic Church teaches that these elements have become more than mere symbols; that they have been actually
changed into the *substance* of the body and the *substance* of
the blood of Christ. This doctrine is called by the long name,
transubstantiation. In this sacrament, two miracles are alleged
to take place at the same instant. The first is the conversion
of the bread and wine into the substance of the real body and
blood of Christ. The second is the fact that this changed substance still looks, tastes and smells like bread and wine.

After the consecration of the bread and of the wine and
before he takes Communion himself, the priest performs a
ceremony known as the *Elevation*. With an appropriate
prayer, he lifts one consecrated wafer high above his head as
a sign that he is offering to God the body of Christ. A moment
later, he elevates the chalice containing the wine. In celebrating Mass the priest believes he is repeating in a "bloodless"
fashion the sacrifice made by Christ when he was crucified.
This repetition of the infinite sacrifice of God's Son is said to
benefit all who partake afterwards of the Communion. In
Roman Catholic churches today, in the United States and
almost everywhere, lay members are not allowed to drink the
wine; only a priest may do that.

Every Roman Catholic is required, unless illness pre-
vents, to confess his sins to a priest and to receive Communion
(that is to have the priest place a consecrated wafer on his
tongue) at the altar rail at least once a year. This is one reason
why Roman Catholic churches are so crowded at the Easter
season.

At the Sunday afternoon services in Roman Catholic
churches, no Masses are celebrated. Instead in a very impressive ceremony, called the Benediction of the Blessed Sacrament, a consecrated wafer is exhibited in a sparkling gilded
frame, called a *Monstrance*. When it is looked upon, all
Roman Catholics present kneel and make the sign of the cross.

Famous composers have written music to accompany the
Mass and the Benediction of the Blessed Sacrament. Protestant
Church music has been greatly enriched by selections from
the works of Roman Catholic musicians.

The Sacrament of Penance

The sacrament of penance is believed to be the means ordained by Christ by which the guilt of sins committed *after* baptism may be removed. Penance involves confessing one's serious (or "mortal") sins to a priest, naming the sins to him and expressing repentance and the purpose not to repeat them. Coveting a neighbor's wife or even his material possessions is one of the "mortal" sins. It is not enough to confess one's mortal sins to another person who is not a priest, or even to the person who has been wronged; nor is it sufficient to confess one's mortal sins in private prayer to God. The priest claims to represent Christ as judge, on the theory that God has given the priest the power to forgive sins or to leave them .unforgiven. He may also prescribe certain tasks to be performed as a penalty to satisfy God's justice. The priest, however, is in duty bound to keep secret all knowledge gained through confessions made to him. It is taught that if one commits even one mortal sin and dies before making confession to a priest when the means for confession are accessible, that person is liable to the penalty of eternal damnation. Soldiers and others dying suddenly are excused from such strict requirements.

The Sacrament of Extreme Unction

This sacrament is performed on those about to die. It offers forgiveness of the last sins which may have been committed. In this sacrament, the priest usually touches with consecrated oil the eyes, nose, mouth, hands and feet of the dying person and prays for forgiveness for all sins of which these different parts of the body may have been guilty. If the person should recover, the sacrament may be repeated when the need again arises.

The Saints and the Festivals

The Roman Catholic Church takes pride in a very considerable number of good men and women who have been "heroically" faithful to Christ and the Church. After the death of such persons, if they are thought to be desirable candidates for sainthood, prolonged and costly investigations will be made of their lives and the results of the study will be presented to the pope. If he judges that, although not 100 per cent sinless, the persons when living were really saints, and if he finds proof that two miracles have been performed by them since their death, the pope will add their names to the approved list. An elaborate ceremony of "canonization" will then take place in Rome.

From that time on, those who come to a church to pray may beg the newly canonized saint to intercede with the heavenly Father to grant special grace or favor. Answers to such prayers are often publicly acknowledged by placing stone placques in the churches, bearing such inscriptions as: "Thanks be to St. Agnes for help in passing an examination," or for "recovery from a serious illness." In some churches, worshipers express their gratitude for cures for which they have prayed by getting the sexton to hang discarded crutches on the inside wall of the church, or a wax model of a leg or arm.

Some shrines have become very famous for the cures said to have taken place there. Such a one is that of St. Anne de Beaupré in Quebec, Canada. To this shrine many pilgrims flock from all over North America, hoping for the miracle that will cure them.

How Many Roman Catholics Are There?

There are said to be about 45 million Roman Catholics in the United States. It should be noted, however, that in making their statistics the Roman Catholics include all who have been baptized in infancy and are not known to have died, even though many of these are children or may have neglected Communion or lost touch with their priest through moving to some other town. Once one is a member of the Catholic Church, one becomes a permanent member in the eyes of the Church. Thus this figure of 45 million is not entirely comparable with the membership figures of Protestant churches, although these too are not entirely accurate. In addition to the Roman Catholics, there is also the membership of the dissident Old Catholic Church, numbering somewhat less than a hundred thousand, and itself split into several smaller groups.

The Power of the Church

In spite of all that may seem outmoded in Roman Catholicism, in spite of its exaltation of the authority of the Church above what may seem to others as the authority of truth, there is a power in this ancient institution which deserves profound respect.

One who as a child attended Mass regularly with his parents and who later left the Church, describes in these words the elements of value which it had for him. "I got an impression of mighty wonder and the feeling that this worship possessed an awful and final authority. We were there not because we had nothing else to do, nor because we were going to be entertained; we were there because tremendous things surrounded us and mighty things awaited us and prodigious things were above us." The Church dramatized—"man's loftiest concern, which is the winning of help from the Unseen, and his deepest hunger, which is for sublimity and ecstasy and awe."[7]

The Eastern Orthodox Churches

Eastern Orthodox churches can usually be recognized by their distinctive architecture, the most striking features of which are their onion-shaped domes. These churches stem

[7] William L. Sullivan, *Under Orders* (Richard R. Smith, 1945), p. 31.

from that group of churches which in the eleventh century ceased to be in communion with Rome. They are sometimes called Greek Orthodox churches because the earliest liturgies were in the Greek language, whereas the Roman Catholics from the third century onward used Latin. From the ninth century onward the Slavic nations, such as Bulgaria, Serbia and Russia, have used a translation from the Greek into an ancient tongue called Old Church Slavonic. Some of the Orthodox churches still use Syriac in their liturgy, an ancient language very similar to the Aramaic which Jesus spoke.

These churches are divided into sixteen different organizations, each bearing a national name. These branches are quite independent of each other, yet they are in communion with one another, each recognizing all the others as genuine Orthodox churches. They all agree in doctrine and use in their services ancient liturgies. They regard themselves as the successors of the apostolic churches in Asia Minor and lay great stress on orthodoxy. They have now some of the leading Christian churches in Jerusalem.

The Russian Orthodox Church

Before World War I, these Eastern Orthodox churches had a membership estimated at 121 million. Eight times as many of these were in Russia as in all other countries put together. As early as 997, Czar Vladimir, whose chief city was Kiev, had made Christianity the state religion. As it grew in power and wealth the Russian Church became very subservient to the state, and deserved some of the abuse heaped upon it by Lenin and his followers. With the overthrow of the czarist empire by the Union of Socialist Soviet Republics, the Church as such was separated from the state and persecuted, and deprived of its great wealth. No one outside Russia can estimate the present strength of the Church there, nor can one prophesy what the future may bring.

The oldest icon of the Virgin in Russia is found in the Cathedral of St. Sophia, in the ancient city of Novgorod. (The Bettmann Archive)

The Missionary Work of the Russian Church

With the expansion of the Russian empire into eastern Europe, Siberia and the Caucasus, the Orthodox Church also spread. It established churches in Alaska as well. When Poles, Russians, Syrians, Albanians, Greeks, Bulgarians and Rumanians began emigrating to America, the Orthodox churches followed them. Thus it happens that there are about twenty branches of the Eastern Church, most of them having a different national origin and each largely independent of the rest. The largest in North America is the Greek archdiocese; with its South American membership included, it has a membership of more than a million. The next largest is the Russian Orthodox Greek Catholic Church of America with a membership of about 760,000. The combined membership of all the Eastern Orthodox churches in North America is nearly 3 million, which makes this ancient Church far from the smallest of religious bodies in the New World. Like the Roman Catholics, the Eastern Orthodox Catholics tend to be concentrated in cities. There are many of them in San Francisco, Chicago, Detroit, Pittsburgh and New York.

Their Forms of Worship

To attend a service in one of the Eastern churches is a most interesting experience. Worshipers may purchase candles as they enter. Instead of images there are on the walls many paintings, called *ikons,* before which worshippers place their lighted candles and kneel in prayer. Some even kiss the *ikons.* The air is filled with the odor of burning incense.

In the United States the language of the liturgy is usually Old Church Slavonic or Greek. Worshipers may stand throughout the service, which may last two or three hours. The vestments of the priests are very colorful but different from those worn in the Roman Catholic services.

In no church is the choral music more beautiful than that heard in the Eastern Orthodox churches, their music having been developed to a fine art through many centuries. No musical instruments are used, but remarkable effects are obtained by the skillful blending of male and female voices. Music composed by Russians has greatly enriched church music in many denominations.

Their Organization

There are three orders of the ministry. Beginning with the lowest they are deacons, priests and bishops. Certain of the bishops of the large sees are called "metropolitans" and a very few are called "patriarchs." The parish priests are called "popes," which is equivalent to "father." Some of the priests become monks. The vows of all monks are alike and bind them to obedience, chastity, prayer and poverty. The parish priests are allowed to marry before ordination, but if the wife dies, there can be no second marriage. The monks must be celibate. Only monks may be elected bishops.

Their Beliefs

In belief, the Eastern Orthodox churches resemble the Roman Catholic Church. They accept the seven sacraments, except extreme unction. Baptism is by immersion. They do not usually practice confession to the priests. In most countries the date for Easter is different from that in the Western world. They permit divorce by lay members.

The division of the Western and Eastern churches was not due primarily to differences in doctrine. It came about rather because of the political situation in Europe during the period of Christian expansion. Both churches have a complex system of church government, in the West headed in Rome by the pope, and in the East by his rival the patriarch of Constantinople. Their elaborate liturgies are utterly unlike anything known in the early days of the churches founded by the apostles. Both seem far removed from the free and spiritual religion of Jesus.

The Eastern Catholic Churches

The Crusaders, and later the Roman Catholics in Poland and France, made many efforts to induce the Eastern churches to recognize the pope as their only lawful head. They achieved their greatest success in Poland, where several million such converts to Rome were made. These converts submitted to the pope, but were allowed to retain almost unchanged their litanies in Old Church Slavonic. Called "Uniats" by the Russians, they are coming to prefer to be called Eastern Catholics. These Uniats are increasing in the United States. They pray for the pope and he chooses their bishops.

6. Thomas Cranmer
1489- 1556

Will you not understand what the priest prayeth for you? Had you rather be like pies and parrots, that be taught to speak and yet understand not one word what they say, than be true Christian men, that pray unto God in heart and faith?... Be you such enemies to your country that you will not suffer us to laud God, to thank Him, and to use His sacraments in our own tongues?

—THOMAS CRANMER

"This Hand Hath Offended"

If only Henry VIII had married someone else instead of his brother's widow, if only she had borne him a male child; if only she had not been Catharine of Aragon, the daughter of Ferdinand and Isabella, the greatest sovereigns of Europe; if only Henry VIII had not become so passionately enamored of Anne Boleyn; if only the pope had been willing to compromise and say that Henry's first marriage had been unlawful, and, therefore, no marriage at all; if only—then how long would England have remained a Roman Catholic country? Who can say? Life is full of just such "ifs," and no one can predict which *if* is going to add just the extra weight needed to change the balance of destiny.

Henry VIII Finds His Man

Henry VIII cared supremely for but one thing and that was to marry the beautiful Anne Boleyn. But his people were

the spiritual subjects of the Roman pontiff, and belonged to
the Holy Catholic Church; and the Church meant the words
used in the marriage ceremony: "What God hath joined let
no man put asunder." So Henry VIII had to choose. It was
either the pope or Anne Boleyn; Henry chose the woman he
loved, and in so doing he himself became the head of the
Church in his kingdom.

To Henry VIII it seemed a long time between the day
in 1527 when he openly announced his desire to find another
queen who might bear him a royal son and heir to the throne,
and the day seven years later when he actually achieved his
desire. He could flout the pope, but his conscience would not
allow him to flout the Christian Church in his own land. So
until he could find a churchman who would be willing and
able to assist him toward his goal, Henry was helpless. He
needed a man learned in the canon law, a priest well trained
in holy orders, a suave, unassuming gentleman, who would be
subservient to the royal will.

It was the king's good fortune to find just such a man, but
Thomas Cranmer was more than all this. He was already
secretly inclined toward some of the Protestant beliefs. In his
own heart he had rejected the miracle of the change of the
bread and wine at Communion to the substance of the body
and blood of Christ. Secretly he yearned to change the Roman
Catholic rituals at a number of points. He believed in allowing
priests to marry, for he himself was both a Catholic priest and
a married man, but he dared not live openly with his wife.
Thomas Cranmer was no Luther or Calvin or Knox. Cranmer
was too timid and too politic to risk his life by boldly initiating
a new movement; yet he was willing to go as far as his Royal
Highness cared to go.

Henry's discovery of Cranmer seems almost a matter of
chance. A royal representative came one day to the same home
in which this young professor from Oxford was visiting. The
conversation turned about "the king's matter." "Why not sub-
mit the question to the university faculties?" suggested Thomas Cranmer. "If they rule favorably the king will have good
cause, no matter what the pope may decide." Simple though

the idea sounds, it was passed on to the king who promptly sent word to Cranmer to write out a case for him which might be presented to the faculties of Oxford and Cambridge.

The King Becomes Supreme Head of the Church

From then on Cranmer's advancement was rapid. He was sent as a special emissary to Rome, but to no avail. On his return the king made him chaplain to the household of Anne Boleyn, and finally his Royal Highness appointed him as Archbishop of Canterbury, the highest ecclesiastical office in the land.

Through Cranmer's adroit exposition of canon law and of the so-called facts in the case, a favorable verdict was handed down by the faculties and concurred in by Parliament, who even passed a law forbidding appeal to any authority outside England. Archbishop Cranmer pronounced the marriage with Catharine of Aragon null and void, and proclaimed Henry VIII and Anne Boleyn to be man and wife. At Henry's command, Parliament announced its recognition of the king as "the Supreme Head of the Church of England." From that day to this (with the exception of about six short years), the national Church of England has been a Protestant Church.

Other Reasons for the Reformation

But how, one asks, could such a tremendous change, affecting the religious life of a whole nation, be brought about through the mere annulment of a royal marriage? Why has not the Reformation been rescinded during all these four hundred years since 1534?

The answer is in part that the Roman Catholic Church, in acquiring wealth and power, had lost its soul. In its zeal for power it had removed itself from the common people. Furthermore, many of the clergy were grossly immoral and most of them were ignorant.

Once the break with Rome was made, Henry VIII began wantonly to dismantle and to destroy the monasteries where, it is said, over a fourth of the wealth of the nation had been concentrated. These lands, buildings and priceless works of art Henry seized and distributed widely among the smaller and greater manorial lords of the land; and, of course, he appropriated a bounteous portion for the Crown. Through this campaign against the monasteries Henry VIII made the Reformation a profitable venture. Thousands of Englishmen were given a financial stake in its maintenance.

It is also true that Englishmen have long resisted infringement of their liberties by any foreign authority. The Roman pope seemed far away. The spirit of nationalism had been spreading and with it came a weakening of the power of the pope. Many Englishmen had long resented papal attempts to collect revenues in England and the control exercised by Rome in the matter of marriage.

There were other and deeper causes, however, for the success of the reformation, even though it was occasioned by the love affairs of a sensuous king. To understand these, one must search the annals of the fourteenth and fifteenth centuries in England to find the real, though often forgotten men who had been leavening the thought of English churchmen with Protestant heresies, and so had been secretly undermining the power of the Holy Catholic faith.

The Significance of John Wycliffe

One of these men died almost one hundred and fifty years before Henry proclaimed himself the head of the Church. John Wycliffe is often called "the morning star of the Reformation in England." And why? Because it was John Wycliffe who first persuaded an English king to refuse to pay a certain part of the tribute demanded by the Holy See, saying that it was wrong for the pope to be rich if he were the representative of Christ on earth. It was John Wycliffe who protested against the rich estates held by the monasteries and against the profligate living to which even friars sworn to poverty had succumbed. It was John Wycliffe who organized a band of "poor preachers" and who sent them from village to village throughout central England, to teach the people the spiritual lessons of the gospel in words they could understand. It was these "poor preachers" who held services, using the English language in their prayers and readings, while all the Roman Catholic clergy were chanting Latin. It was John Wycliffe who first, with the help of his associates, translated the entire Bible into the English language. It was John Wycliffe who had proclaimed every man his own priest and so able to approach God directly, and who asserted that even the pope might make a mistake, and if he did wrong he should not be obeyed.

Although this same John Wycliffe escaped being burned at the stake, he and a half-dozen of his followers were dropped from their professorships at Oxford. Some recanted; others fled the country. Had it not been for a stroke of paralysis, John Wycliffe would have had to obey the Pope's summons to Rome to be tried. Even thirty years after Wycliffe's death, fear of the further spread of his doctrines was so intense that by command of the Pope the Bishop of Lincoln required that Wycliffe's body should be exhumed and burned at the stake and the ashes thrown into the river.

William Tyndale and His English Bible

Then came the fortuitous invention of movable type which, by the end of the fifteenth century, made possible the distribution of the printed page throughout England. This meant that the Bible, instead of being laboriously copied by hand, could now be duplicated by the hundred. A Bible, previously sold for two hundred pounds, could now be obtained for ten pounds. Families of moderate means could have copies in their own homes.

There was also a man, named William Tyndale, a contemporary of Thomas Cranmer, who became fired with a zeal

to make a better translation of the New Testament, by working it out from the original Greek text. "If God spare my life,"
he said to a churchman of rank, "ere many years I will cause
the boy that driveth the plough to know more of the Scripture
than thou dost."

Some years before this, however, Arundel, the Archbishop of Canterbury, caused a law to be enacted forbidding
any one under threat of excommunication to make a translation of the Scripture without a license. Tyndale was unable to
secure this license. He therefore sought safety in another
country. He went to Germany, consulted Martin Luther, and
worked in secrecy for many years. Finally on a German press
in Worms, his English New Testament was printed.

In this great work William Tyndale showed his power
of beautiful and forceful expression. The rhythms that char-
acterize the language in our King James Version of the Bible,
rhythms so pleasing to the ear and so harmonious with the
thought, are in large measure the rhythmic words created by
Tyndale's skill and devotion.

Tyndale was equally adept in writing thought-provoking
comments on the Biblical texts and adding them to the
chapters. Many of these had anti-Catholic implications, and
when copies of his New Testament began to trickle into England, one fell into the hands of Henry VIII. The comments
so offended his Majesty that he had all copies banned from
the country.

In other ways William Tyndale proved himself to be
neither suave nor politic. He expressed himself vigorously
against the king's plan to marry Anne Boleyn. As a result, Tyndale was not safe even in Germany. He worked secretly, moving apparently from time to time to avoid spies Henry sent out
to hunt him down and kidnap him wherever he might be. But
with the help of his friend Coverdale, Tyndale finally succeeded after nearly ten years of quiet work in translating and
printing the entire Bible.

Then he fled to Antwerp, hoping to be able to live quietly in a Protestant country. But on the sixth of October 1536,

spies sent by the Roman Catholic emperor in France, lured him out of his hostelry by trickery, strangled him and burned his body.

An English Bible in Every Church

The Bible that Tyndale and Coverdale had translated was not so easily destroyed. In fact, it was but one year after Tyndale's murder that Cranmer induced Parliament to order a large volume of this translation to be placed in every church in the land, and the clergy were enjoined "expressly to provoke, stir, and exhort every person to read the same." But another name than Tyndale's had been substituted on the title page, and all his comments had been omitted. Only by so doing could Henry have been persuaded to accept the innovation as appropriate. When this act had been finally decreed, Cranmer wrote the prime minister saying, "You have showed me more pleasure herein, than if you had given me a thousand pounds."

All through the lifetime of Henry VIII, Thomas Cranmer fretted inwardly for opportunities to initiate more changes in the Roman Catholic forms of worship, but outwardly he held himself in willing conformity to his master's will. Others in favor in the king's court, officers, ministers, queens, one by one fell under his wrath and one by one they were put away; but Thomas Cranmer stood by the king unto death and the king trusted Cranmer as he did no other man. From the day of the king's death to Cranmer's own tragic end, he let his beard grow uncut as a sign of his loyalty.

Cranmer Is at Last Free

At last, in 1547 when the old king died, Thomas Cranmer was free. In spite of all six marriages, Henry VIII had but one son who survived him. Edward VI he was called, a sickly ten-year-old lad, completely under the control of Cranmer and the

Three English churchmen joined the ranks of Protestant martyrs: Bishops Nicholas Ridley (left) and Hugh Latimer (right) were burned at the stake in 1555, Archbishop Thomas Cranmer (center) in 1556. From the painting by Lejeune. (Keystone View Co.)

ministers of the court. Thomas Cranmer, Archbishop of Canterbury, was now the real head of the Church of England, and he was free to lead the people forward toward as thoroughgoing a reformation as he desired.

He set about to bring to completion three important changes, on which he had been working quietly for years. The first was to prepare and promulgate a series of services in English which could replace the Latin rituals that were still being used throughout England. The second change was to state in creedal form the beliefs of the new Church, and the third was to state the laws by which the new Church and the morals of the people should be governed.

The Book of Common Prayer

It was in what Cranmer did to bring about the first of these changes that he made his most lasting and important contribution to the Protestant Church in England. If he had merely translated the Latin prayers and readings into English, without making any changes at all in the ideas, many would have been shocked to hear prayers said in the common language of daily speech. But to make radical changes in the ideas besides—to eliminate all prayers for the dead in purgatory, to cut out all words of address to the Holy Mother of God, to change the Communion ritual so that the people partook of the bread and wine merely in remembrance that Christ died for them—to make such changes meant changing everything important.

And with the changes in words went more spectacular changes. Altars were removed from the churches and simple Communion tables substituted. The minister stood at the head of the table facing the congregation instead of turning his back and kneeling before the altar. All partook of both the bread and wine, instead of the priest's drinking the wine for all.

Although the new prayer book was not appreciated by the people of Cranmer's generation, his part in the prepara-

tion of this Book of Common Prayer represents the most lasting and important contribution which he made to the Reformation. Like William Tyndale, Thomas Cranmer had a
remarkable gift of expression through the written word.

Although the edition now used is not just as Cranmer
composed it, many of the prayers, litanies and collects are as
he penned them. They are English prose at its best. They
"provided a substitute for the noble Latin rhythms on which
the soul of Europe had been formed for more than a thousand
years, and he gave to the Church of England a treasure by the
aesthetic effect of which more than by anything else her spirit
has remained alive and she has attached herself to the hearts
of men."[1]

Catholic Mary Becomes Queen

Cranmer's steps toward reform, however, had scarcely
more than begun when the boy king died. At the age of sixteen,
in 1553, he was succeeded on the throne by Mary, the eldest
child of Henry VIII and Catharine of Aragon. Mary was a
devout, even a fanatical Roman Catholic. So the tables were
turned: those who had plotted to keep her from the throne, in
order to give her Protestant sister Elizabeth the crown instead,
were executed as traitors. Those who had been supporting the
Reformation either fled or recanted or were imprisoned and
sent to the stake. In one month's time fifty Protestant martyrs
were burned at the stake. Even the politic and powerful Archbishop of Canterbury found himself in mortal peril.

With two of his most faithful bishops, Ridley and Latimer, he was imprisoned in the Tower of London. Later all
three were removed to the Bocardo prison in Oxford, hard by
the city wall. For a while the three shared a common room;
later Ridley and Latimer were removed. Sometime later Cranmer stood at his window, watching a milling and shouting
crowd outside the wall, and saw his two friends tied to two
stakes and burned to death.

[1] Hilaire Belloc, *Cranmer* (London: Cassell, 1931), pp. 245-246.

For the true confession of his faith in St. Mary's Church, Oxford, Cranmer was pulled from the platform by friars and papists and led immediately to the stake. (The Bettmann Archive)

Archbishop Cranmer Is Unfrocked

Still Cranmer himself was spared. Without the command of the Pope, Queen Mary could not burn for heresy a man who once had held the highest office in the Church of England. He must be put through the ceremony of debasing. When the Pope's condemnation finally came, messengers arrived at Cranmer's prison. They clothed him in all the official vestments, suitable to the highest of the seven orders of rank in the church, including those of the Archbishop of Canterbury. Thus adorned, and with staff in hand and the sacred mitre on his head, Cranmer was conducted to the cathedral. There in a mocking ceremony, they stripped from him one after another all the vestments of office. In their stead, they gave him a yeoman's plain and much-worn gown. To make his degradation complete, a barber shaved his head.

Cranmer's Struggle with Conscience

Still Thomas Cranmer waited in prison not knowing what his fate might be. Men were sent to plead with him to recant. It was not too late to gain a reprieve. Finally the old man began to weaken. He had always believed it right to be obedient to the throne. Many a time he had yielded to Henry VIII when his conscience would have led him by a different road. Perhaps now his fidelity to the queen should supersede his loyalty to the faith. He wrote a letter to her Majesty expressing his loyalty to her. This was not acceptable. He wrote again and yet again. Each assertion became stronger than the one preceding until he had written six different recantations, until he had denied all the important things for which he had stood during the previous twenty years. He pronounced himself a loyal Roman Catholic on every count.

Still there was no response from the throne. Instead, the hour was set for his final appearance in St. Mary's Church. It was a rainy spring morning. A crowd of villagers waited outside the church as a procession headed by two black-gowned friars, with a white-bearded old man between them, entered the house of worship. Voices were hushed as the beautiful, yet plaintive, strains of *"Nunc dimittis"* issued from the great organ. It was the music which for years untold has sanctified the passing of a man from this life into the hoped-for life eternal.

The friars escorted the old man to a platform opposite the pulpit. Soon a priest stepped to the pulpit and began to preach. "He made a recital of all Cranmer's enormous misdeeds." For years Cranmer had set forth heresy after heresy. These he had openly preached and many he had written down in books. It was only during his last days in prison that the grace of God had moved him to recant—but "never had evils so enormous been excused, never had a man continuing so long in them been pardoned, *and for the sake of example, pardon could not now be granted: the Queen and the Council had taken their decision and Cranmer was to die."*[2]

The Final Recantation

When the priest had finished his sermon, he asked the congregation to pray for the condemned man. Thomas Cranmer knelt with the rest. He prayed aloud in a pitiful cry for forgiveness. "Oh, Father of Heaven, Son of God, Redeemer of the world . . . have mercy upon me. . . . I have offended more grievously than any can express. . . . Oh, Lord God, my sins are great, yet have mercy upon me for Thy great mercy. Oh, God the Son, Thou wast not made Man for few nor small offences. . . . Although my sins be great, yet Thy mercy is greater."

He rose. A solemn quiet filled the church. From a downcast and pitiable figure, Cranmer became transformed. Uprightness and resolve were manifest in the way he stood. His voice was calm and clear.

And now, forasmuch as I have come to the last end of my life, whereupon hangeth all my life past and my life to come,

2 *Ibid.*, p. 309.

either to live with my Saviour Christ forever in joy, or else to be
in pains forever with the wicked devils in hell; and I see before
mine eyes presently either heaven to receive me, or else hell ready
to swallow me up: . . .

The great thing that so troubleth my conscience, more than
any other thing that I ever said or did in my life . . . is my setting
abroad of writings contrary to the truth, which here now I renounce and refuse as things written with my hand contrary to the
truth which I thought in my heart, and written for fear of death,
and to save my life if it might be; and that is all such bills which
I have written or signed with my hand since my degradation;
wherein I have written many things untrue. And forasmuch as my
hand offendeth in writing contrary to my heart, it shall be first
burned. And as for the Pope, I refuse him as Christ's enemy and
anti-Christ, with all his false doctrine. And as for the sacraments....

The Noble End

With these words a great clamor arose. There were shouts
of "Stop the heretic's mouth!" "Take him away!" Thomas
Cranmer was dragged from the platform and hurried down
the aisle, out of the church, through the village lane toward
the north gate, and out beyond the wall to the spot where, but
a short while before, he had seen his friends Ridley and Latimer, meet their death. The people from the church crowded
about the upright stake around which fagots had been piled.
They watched as he was bound to the stake with a steel band.
Those who were nearby wondered that there was no trace of
fear on his face. He even shook hands with a few of the people.
At the final moment he stood triumphant, at peace with his
Maker, of whose mercy he was now sure.

As the flames rose, the people saw him hold his right hand
out into the fire, and they heard him cry with a loud voice,
"This hand hath offended, let it first be burned!" And there
he held it till the flames destroyed his power to command.

Thus died Thomas Cranmer, the man, unfrocked and
penitent.

The Episcopalians

"What a beautiful church this is!" How often that remark is heard! In New England the white church spire and the pillared porch are almost as much a feature of the landscape as are the lovely green hills. Such churches are frequently Congregational (now United Church of Christ), or Unitarian (now Unitarian Universalist). Elsewhere, as for example in Virginia, quaint brick churches are more often seen, reminiscent of the little village churches of old England, with their ivy-covered walls and adjacent churchyard. Often these are Episcopal, and they are in a sense as truly monuments of Archbishop Cranmer as if they had been built with his own hand. In them each Sunday are read those beautiful litanies and prayers which he helped to prepare four centuries ago.

Although the Episcopal Church is today one of the strongest denominations in the United States, with somewhat less than $3\frac{1}{2}$ million members, it was not always so. During the American Revolution, churches linked with the Church of England almost ceased to exist. This was true even in Virginia, where the first Episcopal (then called Anglican) church on this continent was founded in 1607 at Jamestown. This was true despite the fact that two-thirds of the signers of the Declaration of Independence were Anglican. George Washington himself was an Anglican.

The Tory record of some of the Anglican Church members, however, was not the only handicap from which the Church of post-Revolutionary days suffered. Prior to the Revolution, the Anglican Church in America had been under the jurisdiction of the bishop of London. Its ministers were obliged to cross the Atlantic for ordination. All church affairs were handled in England, except when they were of purely local concern. After the thirteen colonies broke away from the mother country, the Anglican churches found themselves without bishops and without the means of getting any, for any new bishop, in order to be consecrated, had to take the oath of allegiance to the king of England.

The Independent Protestant Episcopal Church

Samuel Seabury was finally elected by the Anglicans of Connecticut as their bishop, and was sent to England for consecration. After a year of waiting, he found the English bishops still unwilling to consecrate him. Seabury, therefore, went to the small and independent Episcopal Church of Scotland. Their bishop willingly acceded to the request of the Connecticut church, and consecrated Samuel Seabury to his holy office on November 14, 1784, by the historic ceremony of "laying on of hands." In this way the "apostolic succession," or line of consecrated bishops from the days of the apostles, remained unbroken. When the Anglican churches in America became independent of the mother church in England they took the name Protestant Episcopal.

Both Like and Unlike the Roman Catholic Church

Anglicans and Episcopalians are closer to the Roman Catholic Church than any of the other Protestant denominations. In England, the Anglican Church is an established church, that is, it is the only church formally recognized by the national government. Its support comes from endowments and government funds, to which are added voluntary contributions. These last are very important when it comes to the upkeep of many of the ancient and magnificent cathedrals and abbey churches. The king (or queen, when there is no royal male heir to succeed to the throne), is titular head. The actual administration, however, is largely in the hands of the two chief ecclesiastical dignitaries, the archbishops of Canterbury and York. Parliament must give its consent before any radical changes are made in ecclesiastical faith or practice. For example, any alterations in the Book of Common Prayer must receive the consent of Parliament. Thus, somewhat paradoxically, such changes might even be blocked by the votes of non-Anglicans in Parliament.

But even though the Anglican Church is the only recognized church in the United Kingdom, there is nevertheless complete freedom of worship and its actual membership is only about 3½ million. However, it is also strong in the British colonies and Commonwealth. There are, for example, about 2 million Anglicans in Canada, and more than a third of those belonging to any church in Australia are Anglican. Yet the Anglican Church in each dominion is entirely independent of the parent church. Each elects its own bishops and may use a slightly different prayer book. The total number of Anglicans and Episcopalians the world over is said to be about 40 million.

The Church of England and many of the Episcopal churches in our own country continue the observance of most of the holy days and religious festivals inherited from the Catholic Church. Indeed, the observance of these is one feature that makes life in the Episcopal Church interesting and religion itself meaningful for many people. Almost every date in the calendar has some special significance.

Although the monastic life occupies a much less important place in the Anglican and Episcopal churches than in the Roman Catholic, there are nevertheless a number of monastic orders. As in the Roman Catholic Church, monks and nuns vow chastity and poverty, and engage in teaching, preaching and frequent prayer. Some also do other kinds of useful work.

Episcopal Church Government

A self-supporting district supervised by a bishop is called a diocese. (There are also missionary districts.) He serves as chairman and administrator of the diocesan convention. This convention is composed of the ministers of all the parishes and of elected lay members, one or more from each parish. The diocesan bishops are elected by these diocesan conventions, but these elections must be ratified by the House of Bishops (that is, by all the bishops of the church), and by standing committees representing all the dioceses. There are three classes of bishops: in addition to what might be called the regular bishops, there are coadjutor bishops and suffragan bishops.

Both the latter assist the former, but a suffragan may not succeed to his superior's post should it become vacant. A General Convention representing all the dioceses meets every three years.

The affairs of the individual church are in the hands of a vestry, the members of which are elected by the congregation. The vestry in each church chooses its own minister (or "rector"), submitting its decision to the bishop, and, even though the bishop objects, the vestry may still have the man of its choice if it insists.

Episcopal Beliefs and Customs

Anglicans and Episcopalians differ among themselves. The group known as "high church" gives great emphasis to ritual and to the sacraments. The "low church," on the other hand, has simplified ritual and puts less emphasis on inherited forms. Although these differences persist, there is less tendency among Episcopalians today to label them and the terms "high church" and "low church" are not heard as commonly as formerly. The "high church" service in many ways resembles that of the Roman Catholics, and such "high churches" are frequently called "Anglo-Catholic." With them the service of Holy Communion is spoken of as the Mass. Their ministers are called "priests," and sometimes "Father." They may hold confession, just as the Roman Catholic priests do. In England the Anglican Church is also bound to accept the Thirty-nine Articles of Faith, but in America Episcopalians are free to accept or reject them, although for all they have historic value.

The "low church" Episcopalians reject the idea of the confessional and the Mass, they recognize only two sacraments —baptism and Communion. Purgatory they also deny, as do Episcopalians generally, nor do they pray to the Virgin Mary and the saints.

There are other important differences which separate Roman Catholic practices from those of Anglicans or Episcopalians. Since the days of Cranmer, marriage of the clergy has been permitted. If the union of two persons who love each other is to be blessed by the sacrament of marriage, as even the Roman Catholics believe, why should it be forbidden to priests? So Cranmer thought, and so it seems to most Protestants. Anglicans and Episcopalians in general do not believe in monastic orders, although a few exist.

Thus Anglicans and Episcopalians are more Protestant than Catholic, and they may well become more so in the future, for the urge to unite with other branches of Christendom has not passed them by. Bishop Pike of California has suggested that Episcopalians, Presbyterians and Methodists, among others, should seriously consider organic union. A similar proposal that Presbyterians and Episcopalians merge was seriously considered some years ago by both churches but finally dropped; there is a fair prospect that more will come of it this time.

Episcopal Forms of Worship

Episcopal church services are usually distinguished by their artistic beauty. There is much ceremony and ritual, especially in the high churches, with a processional and recessional, both headed by a crucifer bearing a cross. Music is given an important place. Much of it consists of choral responses to words spoken by the minister. These prayers and responses are often old and expressive of deep religious feeling. The magnificent works of such great composers as Gounod and Palestrina are often sung. The prayers used are those found in the Book of Common Prayer, much of which is still as Archbishop Cranmer left it after working for years to put the services into the spoken language.

The dignity of the service is increased in most Episcopal churches by the beauty of the church interior. Many American churches have been copied from the old English churches of Norman or Gothic architecture. Almost all of them—whatever the architectural style—are expressive of the close relationship of beauty and religion.

Protestant Episcopal Cathedrals

The Episcopalians, like the Roman Catholics, have cathedrals. A cathedral is sometimes called the bishop's church, for in it is the official seat of the bishop of that diocese. Two such cathedrals, that of St. John the Divine in New York City, and the Cathedral of Sts. Peter and Paul in Washington, are national monuments. Like the ancient cathedrals of Europe, these have been years in building. In the crypt of the cathedral in Washington the bodies of some of the nation's great have already been placed, including those of Admiral Dewey and Woodrow Wilson.

Although built by the Episcopal Church, these cathedrals belong in a sense to the nation, and to the world. The millions of dollars required to build them have been given by people of all denominations and from all over the world. Some of the priceless decorations and furnishings have been contributed by foreign governments.

Episcopal Schools and Institutions

The Episcopalians have founded a number of notable preparatory schools. These are sometimes connected with cathedrals, such as the schools alongside that of St. John the Divine and of Sts. Peter and Paul. There are also Episcopal colleges, including Hobart in Geneva, New York, Kenyon in Gambier, Ohio, and the University of the South, in Sewanee, Tennessee. Columbia University was once an Episcopal institution. There are also many Episcopal hospitals.

Perhaps more richly than any other Protestant Church, the Episcopal Church has preserved the values in the old Roman Catholic art, music and liturgy as aids in worship. Those who from childhood become accustomed to the beauty of these forms often feel that the services in other Protestant churches are crude and lacking in emotional appeal.

7. *Robert Browne*
1550-1631

Therefore woe unto you ye blinde guides, which cast away all by tarying for the Magistrate.... Ye will not have the kingdome of God, to go forward by his spirit, but by an armie and strength forsooth; ye will not have it as Leaven hidde in three peckes of meale, till it leaven all: ... You are offended at the basenesse and small beginnings, and because of the troubles in beginning reformation, you will doe nothing.

—ROBERT BROWNE, *A Treatise of Reformation without tarying for anie, and of the wickednesse of those Preachers which will not reforme till the Magistrate commaunde or compell them.*

Pilgrim and Puritan Reformers

The Plymouth Pilgrims were open dissenters from the Church of England. Although the Rev. Robert Browne had once been a respected leader among them, he was so no longer, and they resented being dubbed "Brownists," as many people mistakenly called them.

As a student at Corpus Christi College, Cambridge University, young Robert Browne had found himself in the midst of a heated religious conflict. Dr. Thomas Cartwright, one of his professors, was a leader of the Puritan group that was seeking to reform the Church of England from within. They said that the reformation under Henry VIII and Thomas Cranmer had gone only half way; that a second reformation was needed. There were still many things in the Book of Common Prayer that seemed unauthorized by the teachings of the Bible. Like Calvin and the Presbyterians, they believed the Bible to be the only infallible rule of faith and practice. The Bible, they asserted, had nothing to say about archdeacons and archbishops. The early churches were governed by deacons and elders. Therefore, all the glamor of the vestments of the prelates and the pageantry of the processions and the rule of bishops seemed contrary to the will of God.

But Queen Elizabeth selected the bishops, and the would-be reformers acknowledged the Queen as the rightful head of the church. They were resolved to be loyal. So these Puritan reformers were in a dilemma. Their reforms had to wait.

In the meantime, the Queen was determined to hold the Church of England together in a powerful organization, of which she was the supreme ruler on earth. To this end, she and her Parliament commanded that all parish priests should read in church the exact words of the English prayer book, without omitting anything, under penalty of trial and possible dismissal. She decreed also that priests must continue to wear surplices, such as were worn by Roman Catholic priests. They must continue the outward pageantry of worship in order to impress the people. The great aim was to secure uniformity. All the clergy who did not fully obey were accused of being nonconformists. To make conformity more certain, Parliament passed a law making it a criminal offense to write or publish any criticism of the church. Such repressive measures forced this second reformation underground; pamphlets denouncing any practices of the church had to be privately printed and secretly circulated.

At Cambridge University, the young Mr. Browne felt keenly the tension caused by these governmental restraints. He believed that true religion could not be forced. He saw Professor Cartwright deprived of his professorship. This stirred Mr. Browne's passion to act. If the reforms were truly required by God's will, was it right to wait "till the Magistrate commaunde or compell them"?

After completing his studies, Robert Browne was for

three years an instructor in Cambridge. During this time he began preaching here and there to informal gatherings. He did not wait to be ordained. In fact, he refused ordination by a bishop saying that "the laying on of hands" by a bishop had no meaning for him. Wherever Browne went, he stirred people up to act "without tarying for anie." He called upon believers to obey God immediately without waiting for the Queen and her bishops to see the light. He insisted that his followers reform their services at once without waiting for the state-controlled church to abolish its "popish ceremonies."

So Independent Churches Began

Such bold preaching soon aroused strong opposition. Before long the young man lost his teaching post. Things became so uncomfortable for him in Cambridge that he retired for a while to his brother's home in the large city of Norwich. But the irrepressible Mr. Browne soon gathered a company of like-minded persons in Norwich who agreed to meet regularly for prayer, thanksgiving, reading of Scriptures and preaching. They met in his brother's home. They worshiped without the help of stained-glass windows, or richly gowned prelates, or processions, or organ music. Mr. Browne read to them directly from the Bible. He usually led in prayer in his own words rather than by what he called a "blind reading" of the prayer book. He preached not once a month, as did many of the Anglican ministers, but every Sunday. After the sermon, the members of the congregation would stay to discuss freely what he had said, for in making their covenant together, they had "agreed to allow any member of the church to protest, appeal, complain, exhort, dispute, reprove, etc., as he had occasion, and yet in due order." Browne was a pioneer in methods resembling those of a modern discussion group.

This worshiping, discussing group is sometimes called the first Congregational Church in England. It was called "Congregational" because the congregation governed its own affairs in the light of the teachings of the Bible, and not according to the dictates of the Queen, the Parliament, or the bishops.

Mr. Browne went out into neighboring towns. By describing "the woful and lamentable state of the church" he stirred up other groups to separate from the Church of England. Thus a number of self-governing societies were gathered which took the Bible to be the only rule of faith and practice. It was the duty of the leaders to "gather" a church of true and tested believers. If any one lapsed morally to a serious degree, the others were first to warn him and then, if this was of no avail, the sinner was to be excommunicated.

Other local self-governing congregations were formed. William Brewster gathered one of them in Scrooby. During the next sixty years, it is said, eighty such Congregational churches were organized in England, and many more would doubtless have come into existence and Mr. Browne's hope of remedying the "woful and lamentable state of the church" might have become a reality, had it not been for the persistent royal and ecclesiastical policy to force conformity.

The Congregational church in Norwich was broken up. The Rev. Robert Browne was jailed, later released, and jailed again and yet again. By his own account he was confined in thirty-two different dungeons, some of them "so dark you could not see your hand before your face at mid-day." Finally, on being given his freedom for a space, he fled with some of his followers to an island off the coast of Holland where his old friend, Thomas Cartwright, had gone before him. Religious rebels of many varieties sought refuge in that small land for it granted a freedom in religion afforded then by no other country of Europe.

While in exile, Mr. Browne wrote a pamphlet to which he gave the awesome title _A Treatise of Reformation without tarying for anie, and of the wickednesse of those Preachers, which will not reforme till the Magistrate commaunde or compell them._ This pamphlet was widely, though secretly, circulated in England, and had considerable influence in encouraging the dissenting movement.

The Sequel to Mr. Browne's Story

The irony in this story came a few years later when this once bold reformer returned to England, made peace with a bishop and accepted a post in an Anglican Church where he served as a rector for forty years. He actually became one of those ministers whom he had himself formerly condemned as "wicked" because they waited to make reforms until commanded to do so by those in authority. Thus his early followers now felt he had deserted the cause of freedom.

The Story of the Plymouth Pilgrims

The story of the Plymouth pilgrims has often been told. Their twelve years of exile in Amsterdam and Leyden; the final blasting of their hope of returning to England; their realization that even in Holland they were not wholly free; their dread of the prospect of their descendants being completely absorbed in the Dutch culture and nationality; their vague hope to better their lot by venturing to the New World; and the tragic story of their long voyage—all these facts are known to the boys and girls of America.

Their great minister, John Robinson, onetime fellow of Corpus Christi College, Cambridge, was unable to sail with them to the New World, but his farewell sermon is among the great religious utterances. A large painting of this scene hangs in the main entrance of the Capitol in Washington. As recorded by Winslow, later governor of Plymouth Colony, we have this eyewitness account:

He took occasion also miserably to bewail the state and condition of the Reformed Churches, who were come to a period in religion, and would go no further than the instruments of their Reformation. As for example, the Lutherans, they could not be drawn to go beyond what Luther saw; for whatever part of God's will he had further imparted and revealed to Calvin, they will rather die than embrace it. And so also, saith he, you see the Calvinists, they stick where he left them; a misery much to be

After a stormy crossing of the Atlantic Ocean in the tiny May-flower, the courageous band of Pilgrims came ashore near Plymouth, Massachusetts. With Elder William Brewster as their spiritual leader, they observed their first Sunday in America. (H. Armstrong Roberts)

lamented: for though they were precious shining lights in their times, yet God had not revealed his whole will to them; and were they now living saith he, they would be as ready and willing to embrace further light as that they had received. Here also he put us in mind of our church covenant, at least that part of it whereby we promise and covenant with God, and one with another, to receive whatever light or truth shall be made known to us from his written word; ...[1]

The Puritans of Massachusetts Bay

Again we find another name that is a key to a long history. Although the Pilgrims of Plymouth have often been referred to as "Puritans," the name does not really apply to them. The Pilgrims of Plymouth were "Separatists." The majority of the "Puritans," on the other hand, although critical of the Church of England in which they had been reared, did not wish to break with it. They wanted to help purify the church of its "corruptions" by working within it rather than by separating from it. Because the Massachusetts Bay Colony had been promoted very largely by a group of rather wealthy merchants in England, the settlers in that colony had more at stake than did the Pilgrims of Plymouth in preserving friendly relations with the king of England and its Church.

Their Earlier Experiences in England

Before coming to America, the Puritans of the Massachusetts Bay Colony had for the most part belonged to the moderate party of reformers. When the Scottish son of Mary, Queen of Scots, came to the throne of England in 1603 as James I, these Puritans had high hopes of seeing some real reforms brought about. They said: "James I comes to us from the land of John Knox. He himself has been reared in the Presbyterian Church. Surely he will side with the reformers."

[1] John Cuckson, *A Brief History of the First Church in Plymouth, from 1606 to 1901* (Boston, 1902), pp. 22-23.

A group of Anglican ministers, therefore, decided to make use of their opportunity, and prepared a long and carefully worded petition. They chose a skillful representative to present it to James I at a specially arranged conference at Hampton Court, a royal palace on the Thames. This petition is remembered as "the Millenary Petition" because the plan was to secure for it the signatures of one thousand Anglican clergymen.

First of all, these reformers made it clear that they wished "the doctrine of the church preserved pure and simple according to God's Word." These Puritans were by no means theological heretics: in fact, they favored longer and stricter creeds. In the petition, they were bent on purifying the Church of corrupt and medieval practices.

They did, however, propose some important changes in the prayer book, and they asked for a new translation of the Bible into English. They protested against "the dumb ministers," that is, ministers who on Sunday morning merely read sermons that had been written for them, or perhaps did not preach at all. These reformers urged the authorities to educate ministers so that they could preach sermons of their own.

The petitioners objected also to the practice of the clergy of wearing at the services the white embroidered surplices over their plain black gowns. Other "popish" practices were condemned, such as kneeling when partaking of the Lord's Supper. This they said was idolatry, making the bread and wine appear as objects of worship. They rejected also the idolatrous use of the sign of the cross in baptism, because the Scriptures do not require it.

The petitioners asked also that the celebration of the many Saints' Days be abandoned and that the Sabbath be made the one most important day. They asserted that after services in the church, the people should not treat the Sabbath as a holiday, with archery contests, dancing and mirth, but should spend it as Moses commanded. They contended that the Old Testament law concerning the Sabbath had not been abolished after the death of Christ, but that God had the Sabbath transferred to Sunday.

"I Will Harry Them Out of the Land!"

All these reforms King James might have granted had not some of the Puritans irritated him by asking in addition for a revision in the plan of governing the churches. These Puritans wanted to have the right to govern vested in small groups of elected elders within each congregation—a plan which did away with most of the powers already exercised by English bishops and archbishops. In short, these petitioners were seeking to introduce into the Anglican Church the Presbyterian form of government.

King James I, however, had already had enough of presbyteries in Scotland. He had come to the English throne determined that, like the Tudor kings before him, he, James Stuart, would continue to hold the supreme power as the earthly head of the church. He would no longer be dictated to by groups of presbyteries.

He, therefore, finally ended the discussion by thundering his scornful reply. " A Scottish Presbytery as well agreeth with a monarchy as God and the Devil." . . . "No bishops, no king." . . . "No! I will make these Puritans reform or I will harry them out of the land, or worse. . . ."

King James meant what he said. The only important reform that came out of this Hampton Court conference was a decision to have a new translation of the Bible prepared. This translation has been ever since the authorized English version of the Bible for all Protestant groups the world over. In this King James' Version, his Majesty's memory has been honorably perpetuated.

The "Millenary Petition," however, had merely stiffened the King's antagonism toward the Puritans. Almost at once he caused to be published a short book of laws governing Church matters. They declared that the Book of Common Prayer must be used word for word in all the churches. All private religious meetings must be suppressed. All ministers must declare their belief in a creed which had been adopted in 1571, called the Thirty-Nine Articles. Every person in the realm must attend Communion in some Anglican church at least three times a year.

The strength of the reforming group within the Church is shown by the fact that within one year fifteen hundred Anglican ministers were deprived of their posts because of their refusal to accept such restrictions.

In 1625, Charles I came to the throne and William Laud became his chief counselor. In 1633, Laud was made Archbishop of Canterbury. An even more determined campaign than had been waged under James I, was then begun in an effort to drive out all varieties of non-conformity. During the reign of Charles I, when persecution of Puritans and open dissenters reached its height, thousands fled to America.

Beginning about 1630, ten years after the Pilgrims first landed, the Puritans began making settlements in and around what is now Boston Harbor. Once in America, they had their chance to build the kind of churches for which they had been hoping, for as yet the English government had not sent any bishops to govern the churches in America. It is not surprising then that the Pilgrims' First Church in Plymouth received brotherly recognition from the Puritans. In the Massachusetts Bay Colony a system of church government was worked out, called at first "The New England Way." Before long these New England churches were given the name Congregational.

All the stone walls, behind which Browne and many others who believed in "reformation without tarying for anie" had been imprisoned, could not stifle the growing democracy within the newly gathered Congregational churches; nor did the broad Atlantic prevent our New England forefathers from bringing with them their strict Calvinism and their stern Scriptural codes of morals.

The Congregationalists

"The Church of the Puritans"

To one who knows America, the mention of New England brings a vision of beautiful wooded hills, rambling old houses painted a spotless white set back on broad streets lined with elms, all radiating from a common grassy green and somewhere, not far from the center of the village, a venerable white pillared wooden church with its spire of white piercing the blue sky overhead. Even from colonial days such vistas have been as characteristic of New England as the Gothic stone churches have been symbols of old England.

Nor is the central position of the little white church in the New England town the result of accident. To our Pilgrim and Puritan forefathers, religion lived at the heart of life. It was the most logical thing in the world to put the house of worship in the heart of the village. The "meetinghouse" under the colonial laws was erected at town expense, maintained by taxation, and used not alone for worship but on weekdays also for town meetings and other public events.

The sturdy initiative which our colonial forebears demanded in political affairs they insisted on even more staunchly in religion. Not only the Pilgrims, but the Puritans as well, organized churches in which each congregation, in accordance with the colonial laws, was free to govern its own affairs, and to call as its minister any qualified man whom the congregation might elect as their pastor or teacher.

Church Life in Colonial Days

In a New England village of colonial days going to church was a major activity, for there were church services twice on Sunday, and usually in the large towns there was a religious lecture in the middle of the week besides. In winter whatever warmth there was in the meetinghouse came from the fiery eloquence of the minister, for there were no furnaces nor even stoves. Little footstoves heated by burning charcoal were carried to church by or for the ladies.

Men, women and children sat by groups in separate sections of the meetinghouse. In the earliest days the children sat in the gallery under the care of a tithing man, who was an official with a long stick. On one end of the stick was a knob;

Church services in the early days in New England lasted many hours. In winter the church was not heated, so many in the congregation—like this mother and daughter—used foot stoves to keep warm. By W. L. Taylor. (The Bettmann Archive)

on the other end a feather. The tithing man used it at his discretion to keep the children awake and quiet.

Sermons were usually long. One wonders what the children thought of as the minister passed from his "firstly" through his "secondly," "thirdly"—and on and on sometimes for two or three hours, or until the last bit of wisdom had been extracted from his text. To Calvinists and to Separatists of all kinds the sermon was far more important than it was to many Anglicans and to nearly all Roman Catholics, for religion to the Separatists was based on a detailed and adequate understanding of the Word of God. By contrast, the Anglicans worshiped in accordance with their Book of Common Prayer.

Children were expected to understand and accept the traditional beliefs at an early age, and to repent of their sins. The Rev. Cotton Mather, one of the eminent Congregational preachers in New England, said in a sermon for children in 1721:

> If you dye in your sins what will become of you? An Aking Tooth for One Month, how tedious it would be unto me here. But if I lie down among the damned I must undergo much worse griefs than that, and after as many millions of years, as there are leaves on the Trees, or Drops in the Sea, or Sands in the Shore, I have no prospect of any peace.[2]

The Discipline of the Children

Some children seem to have caused the authorities trouble, for we find a certain Connecticut judge commenting in court on one child's behavior in these words:

> A rude and Idel Behaver in the meting hows such as Smiling and Larfing and Intiseing others to the Same Evil.
> Such as whispering and Larfing in the meting hows between metings.

[2] Sandford Fleming, *Children and Puritanism* (New Haven: Yale University Press 1933) , p. 96.

Such as Larfing or Smiling and puling the heir of nayber benoni Simkins in the time of publick Worship.

Such as playing with her Hand and fingers at her heir.

Such as throwing Sister penticost perkins on the ice it being Saboth Day or Lords Day between the meting hows and his plaes of abode.[3]

Music in the Church Services

There were no organs in these chilly New England meetinghouses, for our Puritan ancestors did not find in the New Testament authority for having them. Opponents of organs called them "boxes of whistles."

As late as early in the eighteenth century, the Brattle Street Congregational Church in Boston refused the gift of an organ. Even fiddles in some places were objected to because of words attributed to God in the book of Amos, "I will not hear the melody of thy viols." (Amos 5:23) In early days choirs did not exist. When these were finally introduced, they were put into the gallery at the back of the church. In some churches the congregation turned around to face the choir so that the singing of the congregation would not drag.

In place of hymns, the Psalms were put into verse and sung. Since books were scarce, the Psalm was "lined out," that is, one or two lines were first read by the deacon, and then sung by the congregation. The first important book printed in New England was the *Bay Psalm Book*.

The Church Today

Because the local churches have always jealously guarded their independence they came to be known as Congregational, and this name is still given them in many places. Despite this concern for local autonomy they have been pioneers in the movement for church union. Three such fusions have been accomplished, largely through Congregational initiative, and

[3] *Ibid.*, p. 63.

a fourth is being consummated. The first was in 1892, when the Congregational Methodists and Congregationalists united. Then in 1923 the Evangelical Protestants joined the larger Congregational fellowship. A third and greater union occurred (1930) when the Christian Church[4] joined the Congregationalists. This united organization became known as the Congregational Christian Church, and in 1957 had a membership of about 1⅓ million, spread among some 5,500 congregations. In that year, after prolonged negotiations, a fourth union was voted, this time with the Evangelical and Reformed Church, which numbered 2,750 local churches and about 775,000 members.

Unlike the Congregationalists, these Evangelical and Reformed churches had a presbyterian type of organization but both denominations were similar in the emphasis they put on a well-educated ministry. As the name suggests, the Evangelical and Reformed Church was itself the product of a merger. One of the two parent organizations, the Reformed Church, grew out of the immigration about two centuries ago into Pennsylvania of Calvinists from Germany and Switzerland. The other had Lutheran roots and was known as the Evangelical Synod, its churches being largely centered in the midwest. The two merged in 1934 to form the Evangelical and Reformed Church. It was notable for its efforts to better the lot of the aged and orphans. Now, since union with the Congregationalists, the merged denominations are known as the United Church of Christ. They became one of the large Protestant groups in the United States. Their combined membership exceeds 2 million, and they have over 1 million pupils and teachers in their church schools. There are churches in every state.

Organization

Members of these churches still maintain the traditional vigorous initiative of their immigrant ancestors. Local

[4] Not to be confused with the Disciples of Christ, often called the "Christian Church" (Chapter 12).

churches are self-governing, but in case of serious division on some question (such as whether a minister should stay or go), other churches of the neighborhood may be called in to join with the local church in discussing the thorny problem. Congregational churches called this a *council of the vicinage* (neighborhood). Each church invited sends its pastor and a delegate. The council hears both sides and gives advice. Although the local church may vote not to follow the advice, it usually accepts it.

Each church of the merged denomination, as has always been the case among Congregational churches, has the right to decide upon its own creed or statement of faith (if it elects to use one), and the minister who is called is supposed to be in general agreement with this creed, although he is not required to sign any document to that effect.

The National Organization

As the need for cooperative planning developed, Congregational churches gradually developed a truly effective and democratic form of national organization without sacrificing the independence of the local church. It was called the General Council, and was made up of delegates from the local churches, elected by the state conferences. It has now been superseded by a similar body known as The General Synod. Meetings are held at regular intervals to deliberate on matters of general interest. By means of committees with efficient secretaries many kinds of cooperative work are carried out.

Educational and Missionary Work

When there was still an American frontier, Congregationalists were active in founding schools and colleges to keep pace with the westward march of civilization. Among them were Oberlin in Ohio, Beloit in Wisconsin, Carleton in Minnesota, Doane in Nebraska (also Episcopalian-sponsored), and

Colorado College in Colorado. Amherst College in Massachusetts also owed its founding to the Congregational Church. Franklin and Marshall College in Pennsylvania, and Heidelberg College in Ohio, were likewise started by the Reformed Church. Albright, also in Pennsylvania, and North Central College in Illinois, owe their existence to Evangelical efforts.

To the Congregationalists belongs the honor of being the first Protestant Church to send missionaries to the Indians of New England. John Eliot of Roxbury began such work in 1646. The Congregationalists also organized the first American Protestant foreign missionary society. In the summer of 1806 a group of five college students at Williams College were in the habit of taking walks together in the country to talk over their obligation to the heathen in Asia. One afternoon, because of a heavy rainstorm, they were compelled to find shelter under a haystack. There that afternoon they secretly pledged themselves to go to some foreign land and preach the Christian gospel to those who had never heard it. Four years later these same students sent a petition to the Congregational General Association in Massachusetts, telling of their resolve and asking for "advice, direction and prayers." As a result, the American Board of Commissioners for Foreign Missions was organized in 1810, and these five men became the first American Protestant foreign missionaries. Other Protestant groups began to organize missionary societies, and thus the great Protestant movement in America to spread Christianity into all the world was initiated. This work is being continued under the United Church Board for World Ministries, which has an active missionary program in eighteen countries. Williams College is often called "the Mother of American Foreign Missions." The Haystack Monument on the campus of Williams College memorializes that eventful rainy afternoon.

Under the American Missionary Association of the Congregational Church, organized to further Christian work on the home front, active efforts have been made to improve the lot of the Negro, especially in the South. Negro colleges were organized just after the Civil War when there were few other educational opportunities beyond elementary school open to those with colored skins. Among them were Tougaloo Southern Christian College (now sponsored jointly with the Disciples of Christ) in Mississippi, and Talladega College in Alabama. Work such as this, and other humanitarian and missionary activities in the United States, are continued for the United Church under the United Church Board for Homeland Ministries.

Thus this great merged denomination, still as democratic and independent as were its English, Swiss and German founders, though more liberal theologically, less rigid in its moral code, and more sensitive to the larger economic, social and international needs of mankind, continues to be a vigorous element in American religious life.

8. John Bunyan
1628-1688

My sword I give to him that shall succeed me in my pilgrimage, and my courage and skill to him that can get it.
> —JOHN BUNYAN, last words of Valiant-for-Truth before he passed over the River of Death and into the Celestial City

When thou prayest, rather let thy heart be without words, than thy words without a heart.
> —JOHN BUNYAN

The Tinker Who Couldn't Be Tinkered With

To a visitor three centuries ago the town of Bedford, near London, probably seemed a sleepy community where nothing of consequence ever happened. If he indulged any such feeling he might indeed have been pardoned, for the town was already more than a thousand years old, and nothing memorable had ever happened there—that is, nothing memorable to those outside Bedfordshire. Weddings, births and deaths came as unfailingly as the days followed the nights.

For centuries there had been public fields and woods within the township, and any man who plowed a part of these public lands could reap the harvest; or any herdsman who needed pasture for his sheep or cattle could let them graze there. But now the wealthy had been buying up these public lands and enclosing them behind fences, and the poor were left helpless and resentful. Many self-respecting and independent farmers had been forced to beg or to toil as serfs on the large estates. The commerce in coal carried down the Ouse River was still brisk but not what it had been. Like an old man, the town of Bedford was slowing its pace.

A Woman's Bold Pleading

Thus things were one summer day in August 1661. Whether it was the hard times that were bothering old Judge Twisden that morning as his carriage rumbled down the rutted street, or just a recurrence of the gout, one cannot say. Perhaps he was feeling a new burden of responsibility now that Charles II was on the throne, and the Puritan Commonwealth under Oliver Cromwell was a thing of the past. Possibly orders had reached him from London to be more strict with all dissenters, and the judge dreaded facing the prisoners awaiting trial. In any case, his mood boded no good for those whose cases he was to pass upon at that day's session of the Midsummer Assizes.

Nor did it promise encouragement to the peasant woman who ran into the street and threw a petition into his coach. Annoyed he probably was, yet there was a desperation in the woman's actions that compelled his attention. Still the roadside was no place in which to hold court.

"I tell thee, woman, it is of no use. Thy husband must remain in gaol until he promises not to preach."

"But, my Lord, he hath not yet even been permitted to answer the indictment, though he hath languished in gaol from April till now. And what of our four children, my Lord? They are too young to work. They must have food."

"What if it be so! Thy husband might have brought that to mind before. He is a pestilent fellow. Speak to me of him no more."

With that the Judge drove off, and the young woman, with her hopes once more crushed, stood still in the roadway, unable to decide in which direction to turn.

Presently a kindly bystander approached, whom she recognized as the high sheriff. This was scarcely a quarter from which to look for encouragement, but one could never tell.

"Woman, thou mayest yet have a chance to present thy husband's case. Why dost thou not try once more, when the Assize is over, but before the judges depart?"

The woman's face brightened. Perhaps, after all, there was still some hope.

Several days later, therefore, she made her way into the crowded court room, and faced the judges. She told them she had already gone to London to plead her husband's cause before Lord Barkwood. He in turn had presented it to members of the House of Lords, but they had all agreed that there was nothing they could do. She should bring the matter up again before the next assizes in Bedfordshire. In coming before their Honors now she was simply following the advice of the Lords. Her husband had been held in prison over four months without trial. In the meantime she and her four children, one of whom was blind, "had nothing to live on but the charity of good people."

Again the woman's pleadings were of no use. The only justice who showed any sign of mercy was speedily silenced by his angry colleagues.

"Thy husband preacheth not the word of God. He ought rather to have kept to his pots and pans. Instead he runneth up and down the countryside doing only harm. Thy poverty thou usest only as a cloak."

Many other words were said, heartless as these. The courageous mother could do nothing but depart.

The Indictment and the Man

Who then was this man? Why was he regarded as more dangerous to the country's welfare than other dissenters? What had he done to deserve such treatment?

A tinker and the son of a tinker whose ancestors had lived in a cottage in the little village of Elstow near Bedford for three hundred years. This was John Bunyan—red-haired, tall, big-boned, with an infectious personality in spite of his meager schooling. Of his own boyhood he wrote: "Notwithstanding the meanness and inconsiderableness of my parents, it pleased God to put it into their hearts to put me to school, to learn me both to read and write; the which I also attained, according to the rate of other poor men's children."

And what had he done beside mending pots and pans to merit imprisonment? What was the indictment that had been brought against him? The paper read before the court had stated that this John Bunyan "was arrested for devilishly and perniciously abstaining from coming to church to hear divine service, and for being a common upholder of several unlawful meetings and conventicles to the great disturbance and distraction of the good subjects of this kingdom, contrary to the laws of our sovereign Lord and King." Here then was another of these self-made unordained preachers stirring up the people against the established church. But what kind of a nonconformist was this John Bunyan? Again we must take up the story at an earlier date.

A Ringleader in the Village

If we take John Bunyan's own word for the truth, he was a bad boy, "one that had but few equals both for cursing, swearing, and blaspheming the holy name of God." . . . "Until I came to the state of marriage, I was the very ringleader of all the youth that kept me company, in all manner of vice and ungodliness." "I infected all the youth of the town where I was born." Apparently the blackest sin of which he was guilty, at least from our point of view, was a blood-curdling profanity. But John Bunyan included as sins other matters, such as his fondness for pealing the church bells and his love of folk-dancing and games on the village green, especially on Sundays. Under the influence of the Puritan teachings to which he had been subjected as a boy, John Bunyan saw himself as a great sinner. From his early years he was tormented at night with dreams of devils and the sufferings of hell.

When nearly sixteen years old, family tragedies began to tumble in quick succession over his head. In June his mother died. In July his sister passed away. Then in August his father remarried. John Bunyan's home life was completely changed and the depths of bitterness must have been stirred in his heart.

John Bunyan as a Soldier

Fortunately perhaps for John, he left home soon after this series of tragedies, and for about three years he was a soldier in Cromwell's army.

In this army, he was "tossed into a society where·every revolutionary idea was being thrown into the cauldron of debate; ideas not only religious, but political, social, and economic."[1] The depressed classes were roused. Everywhere was heard the democratic cry "All men are equal in the sight of God." "A fair share of the riches of the earth is the people's birthright." It was for these common rights that the soldiers in Cromwell's army thought they were fighting. The rich were being openly denounced as murderers of the poor. They were stealing the public lands for their own special benefit. A communistic dream had come to the people of Bunyan's day.

Religious Debates Over Baptism

In those days, debates over religious questions were as exciting as ball games are to young men today. In one of the barracks a debate over whether or not babies should be baptized had brought on a riot. A new kind of dissenter was scattering the seeds of division in England. No one outstanding person was their leader. The contagion had taken hold of many people. Nor was the idea new. Had the people known their history, they would have realized that as far back as the third century there had been men and women who had pro-

[1] M. P. Willcocks, *Bunyan Calling* (London: Allen & Unwin), p. 37.

tested against the baptism of babies. Hundreds had even suffered martyrdom—banishment, drowning, burning at the stake—rather than be compelled to baptize their babies.

These English protestors were of the spirit and conviction of the Anabaptists in Germany and Switzerland, although they did not go to the extremes of nonresistance to royal authority. These new protestors were now usually called simply Baptists, and many of them were fighting in Cromwell's army. But why should such a fuss be made over the baptizing of babies? What harm in so simple a ceremony as the sprinkling of water over the head of a child and saying a prayer for his soul?

To the Baptists, the whole matter had become a serious issue. In the first place, they said that no reference to the baptism of babies could be found in the New Testament. Baptism in the primitive church was a symbolic act that stood for a change of heart. It marked the entering upon a Christian life, the committing of one's destiny to Christ as Savior. The Baptists held to the Bible, rather than to the traditions of the church, as their authority.

In the second place, the Baptists said that no parent could take such a step for his child. No person could make such an important decision for another. No man could believe for another. Parents could teach their children, but they had no right to commit them to any special line of conduct before they were old enough to know what they were doing. The Baptists said that each individual is responsible for his own life before God, and that baptism should be withheld until a person was able to make his own decision for himself.

Why Riots over not Baptizing Babies?

It seems strange to us today that so reasonable a position should have been fought with such furious resistance. Again the seriousness of the issue is realized only when one understands the generally accepted philosophy of life, as contained in the Old Story of Salvation. If, for instance, one believes that even innocent babies are sinners and liable to eternal damnation unless saved by the power of Jesus Christ, it is important that something be done promptly.

Early in the history of the Roman Catholic Church, the baptism of infants had been made a sacrament by means of which a child was given safety in the protecting arms of the Church. It was a kind of eternal life insurance against hell. Even according to the prayer book used in all the established Protestant churches in England, the baptism of babies was regarded in the same manner. Before sprinkling the child's head, the minister always prayed this prayer. "Sanctify this water to the mystical washing away of sin." In short, the baptism of babies was not a symbol of something that had already taken place in the heart of the child. It was rather a sacrament, an act having divine "grace" in it. It did not matter whether the child understood or not what was being done to him. By the act of baptism his guilt was washed away and God could receive the child into heaven if he died.

These Baptists, like the Quakers, were against all such sacramental acts, against forms without the spirit. They insisted that baptism stood for an important commitment that had already taken place in the heart of the believer. What would happen if babies died unbaptized could be left with God. Some asserted that God would not send innocent babies to eternal punishment. Others even ridiculed infant baptism by saying: "It is as lawful to baptize a cat, or a dog, or a chicken as to baptize an infant."

The Years of Indecision

How much of all this feverish debating John Bunyan heard during his three years in the army, we do not know. He had not yet made his own great decision.

While in the army the turmoil in the life of John Bunyan had to do with the society to which he belonged. During the next several years after his return to the village of Elstow, the turmoil was within John Bunyan's own heart. The story of these years of struggle, Bunyan has told in a book which he called *Grace Abounding to the Greatest of Sinners.* As an honest and vivid revelation of the inner secrets of a man's soul, the book ranks among the greatest autobiographies ever written.

The turning point in his religious interest came with his marriage. "This woman and I," wrote Bunyan, "came together as poor as might be, not having so much household stuff as a dish or spoon betwixt us both." The bride, however, did bring with her a reverent memory of a pious father, and a library of two books. And what were the titles? *The Practice of Piety* and *The Plain Man's Pathway to Heaven*—two of the best sellers of that time. When the day's work was done, John used to sit with his young wife before the open fire in their thatched cottage, and by the light of a tallow candle he would read from one or other of these books. Before long a crib stood between their chairs and a little blind daughter slept peacefully under the spell of the rhythm of Bunyan's reading.

Slowly John Bunyan's interests began to change. He became a faithful attendant at the little village church, going sometimes even twice a day to worship. But for some reason what he heard "did not reach the heart." Something else was beginning to touch it. Perhaps it was his little blind daughter who became so very dear to him that he could scarcely bear "to let the wind blow upon her."

"Sometimes Up and Sometimes Down"

He wrote: "One day as I was in the midst of a game of Cat, and having struck it one blow from the hole, just as I was about to strike it the second time, a voice did suddenly dart from heaven into my soul, which said, 'Wilt thou leave thy sins and go to heaven, or have thy sins and go to hell?' " The issue was just as clear-cut as that, yet, those things which he called his "sins" seemed strangely fascinating. In spite of this definite warning, he made as much haste as he could to have his fill of sin, "that he might taste the sweetness thereof," lest he should die before he had had his desires.

His uneasiness, however, grew. He began searching in the Bible for some word that would give him assurance of peace. But Bunyan had a hearty humor and a vigorous body. He loved his fiddle and the dancing of the Morris dances on the village green. He yearned to drink the full cup of life with all its delicious pleasures.

His swearing had become a symbol of his fearless defiance of restraint. One day a woman of loose living habits heard him swear and curse loudly in a rage and called him the "ungodliest fellow for swearing she had ever heard in all her life." This experience shocked the man into a complete reform on that score. For a whole year he struggled over the question of dancing before he finally gave this up also. As the months passed his conscience became

> sore and would smart at every touch. . . . I durst not take a pin or stick, though so big as a straw. . . . I could not now tell how to speak my words, for fear I should misplace them. . . . I found myself in a miry bog, that shook if I did but stir.
>
> The tempter would also much assault me with this, "How can you tell but that the Turks had as good Scriptures to prove their Mahomet the Savior as we have to prove our Jesus?" And, could I think, that so many ten thousands in so many countries and kingdoms, should be without the knowledge of the right way to heaven (if there were indeed a heaven) that we only, who live in a corner of the earth, should alone be blessed therewith? Everyone doth think his own religion rightest, both Jews and Moors, and Pagans; and how if all our faith, and Christ, and Scriptures, should be but a think so too?

John Bunyan found it hard to escape from Doubting Castle. Sometimes "down I fell, as a bird shot from the top of a tree, into great guilt and fearful despair . . . and would get out of bed and go moping into the field."

The Women Sitting in the Sun

One day while on his rounds mending pots and pans in Bedford, he came upon "three or four poor women sitting at a door, in the sun, talking about the things of God; and being now willing to hear their discourse, I drew near to hear what they said.—But I may say, 'I heard, but understood not; for they were far above, out of my reach.' Their talk was about a new birth, the work of God in their hearts.... They spoke with such pleasantness of Scripture language, and with such appearance of grace in all they said, that they were to me, as if they had found a new world."

These women Bunyan never forgot. Sometime afterward he had a dream or vision. He wrote:

> I saw as if they were on the sunny side on some high mountain, there refreshing themselves with the pleasant beams of the sun, while I was shivering and shrinking in the cold, afflicted with frost, snow, and dark clouds; methought also, betwixt me and them, I saw a wall that did compass about this mountain. Now through this wall, my soul did greatly desire to pass; ... About this wall I bethought myself to go again and again, still praying as I went, to see if I could find some way or passage, by which I might enter therein: but none could I find for some time; at the last I saw, as it were, a narrow gap, like a little doorway in the wall, through which I attempted to pass; now the passage was very straight and narrow, I made many offers to get in, but all in vain. ... At last, with great striving, methought I at first did get in my head, and after that, by a sideling striving, my shoulders, and my whole body: then I was exceeding glad, and went and sat down in the midst of them, and so was comforted with the light and heat of their sun.

To John Bunyan this dream became a parable of his life. The wall was the world. The gap in the wall was Jesus Christ. The life in the sunshine was the life eternal. None but those who were in downright earnest could enter through the gap for "here was only room for body and soul, but not for body and soul and sin."

Bunyan's dream of entering into the sunshine beyond the wall was but a prelude to the commitment of his life to the righteousness of Christ and to the peace of mind that came with his belief that by Christ's great sacrifice he was at last "within the arms of God's grace and mercy." When this decision was once made, John Bunyan sought to symbolize his "downright earnestness" by being immersed in the Ouse River. In so doing he became a member of an independent congregation that was then meeting in St. John's Church in Bedford, a church which later was definitely called Baptist.

A Quiet Period—Then Imprisonment

For five years John Bunyan lived quietly among the country folk with whom he had long been acquainted. Through the day he mended their pots and pans and in the evenings he spoke at informal gatherings—out in the fields, in country barns or on the village green. While Oliver Cromwell ruled the land, all went well. When Charles II ascended the throne, however, the nonconformists found themselves being spied upon and their liberty checked.

So it came about that on a November day in 1660, men and women in twos and threes were going to a farmhouse near the little village of Samsell to hear John Bunyan talk. Bunyan had been forewarned of the rumors that he would be arrested, but he refused to hide. "If we give in so easily," he said, "what will our enemies think of our religion?"

To make a long story short, he was arrested on the charge previously explained. With but one brief interlude of freedom six years later, John Bunyan was kept in the Bedford prison without trial from 1660 to 1672—that is, for nearly twelve long years. Then came about three years of freedom followed by another six months in jail.

The Light Behind the Cloud

Distressing as this long imprisonment must have been both for Bunyan himself and for his faithful wife and children, nevertheless the spirit was never conquered. Nor did he leave his wife and children completely without some help from him.

As a dissenter, John Bunyan spent almost thirteen years in prison at Bedford. Here he wrote the first part of his most famous book whose full title is The Pilgrim's Progress from This World to That Which Is to Come. (*Keystone View Co.*)

During many a long hour of captivity, he knit "many hundred gross of tagg'd laces," from which his wife could earn at least a pittance toward the family's support.

Far more important in the history of the world than Bunyan's fidelity to his family is the fact that during these long years of confinement, he wrote in all about sixty books—some of which proved to be among the most popular books of his generation. Among the last of his writings, and a climax to them all, was the immortal *Pilgrim's Progress,* which after nearly three hundred years is still in print and widely read. During Bunyan's lifetime 100,000 copies were sold. Since that time it has been translated into over 120 different languages. *Pilgrim's Progress* has been perhaps the most widely read book in the world with the exception of the Christian and Jewish Bible.

The Pilgrim's Progress

Bunyan tells the story of *Pilgrim's Progress* as a dream, which he says came to him as he lay asleep in his prison cell. Who has not heard of Christian and of the places through which he passed as he made his pilgrimages from the City of Destruction to the Celestial City of God? Vanity Fair, the Slough of Despond, Doubting Castle, the Delectable Mountains and the Valley of the Shadow of Death. And some of his characters were once household words in many homes around the world, such as Obstinate and Pliable, Mr. Worldly-Wiseman, Mr. Facing-both-Ways, Giant Despair, Great-Heart, Madam Bubble and Mr. Valiant-for-Truth.

The Last Years

Finally in 1672, even before his release from prison, the Bedford church elected John Bunyan as its minister. Fortunately, he did not have to wait long for freedom, for the king

This chart, engraved especially for "Virtue's Elegant Edition of The Pilgrim's Progress," shows the path taken by Christian in that famous allegory. (Keystone View Co.)

had just made a solemn declaration again granting the right
to believe and worship as conscience dictated. This toleration,
however, did not last long. Dissenters were again being persecuted. Ruinous fines were imposed upon them and many lost
everything they owned. The authorities seized the cows,
horses, poultry—even bedding and kitchen utensils—of those
who could not pay the fines.

In 1675, Bunyan was again thrown into prison, but his
friends intervened. He was released after only six months in
jail. From that time on until his death, twelve years later, he
was a free man. Because of the popularity of his books, he was
by then a well-known man. On horseback he roamed the
country as a recognized leader of the Baptists of England.

There was a charm and tenderness and power ·in his
preaching that held his hearers spellbound. One of his con-
temporaries wrote:

When Mr. Bunyan preached in London, if there were but
one day's notice given, there would be more people come together
to hear him preach than the meeting-house could hold. I have
seen to hear him preach, by my computation, about twelve hundred at a morning lecture by seven o'clock on a working day, in
the dark winter-time. I also computed about three thousand that
came to hear him one Lord's Day at London . . . so that half were
fain to go back again for want of room.[2]

John Bunyan was a Baptist, and the Baptist denomination has good reason to be proud of him; but he founded no
Church. There was nothing narrow in his loyalty. Neither the
mode of baptism, nor the time of baptism seemed to him to be
matters important enough to divide the righteous from the
righteous. When once his tolerance was denounced as weakness he protested. "Because I will not let Water Baptism be
the rule, the door, the bolt, the bar, the wall of division between the righteous and the righteous, must I therefore be

---

[2] Charles Doe, *The Struggler* (1692) , quoted by John Brown in his *John
Bunyan: His Life, Times and Work* (London, 1918) , II, 127-128.

judged to be a man without a conscience? The Lord deliver me from Superstition."

John Bunyan's conscience was nothing to tinker with. He refused to evade an issue by two-faced words in order to escape imprisonment. No one has ever stood more foursquare for religious freedom. We can easily hear John Bunyan himself speaking through the words he put into the mouth of Valiant-for-Truth as he talked with By-Ends.

"If you will go with us, you must go against wind and tide. . . . You must own Religion in his rags, as well as when in his silver slippers; and stand by him, too, when bound in irons, as well as when he walketh the streets with applause."

The Baptists in America

When John Bunyan was but a three-year-old toddler, Roger Williams, a radical young Anglican minister, had already separated himself from the established Church, and had fled with his young bride to America. Here he imagined he would find freedom from laws against nonconformity in religion, but the Massachusetts Puritans cared for freedom in religion only for themselves and for those who were like them. They had not yet separated Church from State. No one in the colony could vote or hold office unless he belonged to a "gathered" Congregational Church, even though but one fourth of the colonists met the qualifications required for membership.

In addition, the Puritan churches had not separated definitely from the Church of England. The merchants, who sailed on business trips to England, took communion with their brethren in the Anglican Church. Roger Williams believed that such communion with the Anglicans was sinful because, as he said, the Church of England was founded on anti-Christian principles.

A Man of "Dangerous Opinions"

When, therefore, Williams was invited by the church in
Boston to become its minister, he refused because he felt it
would be wrong to serve a church that had not completely
separated. "Friends," he said, "ye should repent in sackcloth
and ashes for this sinful connection." This the Puritans of
Boston were unwilling to do. Their relations with the English
Crown were already too precarious to permit such an open
insult.

Williams said also that the civil authorities of the colony
should have no power to enforce or punish the breaking of
the first four of the Ten Commandments that deal with one's
duties to God. For example, he declared that the government
has no right to punish men for not observing the Sabbath. In
addition to these two bold criticisms of conditions in Boston,
Williams said that the royal charter granting to the colonists
the right to settle in Massachusetts was worthless. He insisted
that the land did not belong to the king but to the Indians
who had been living on it from time immemorial. It was from
the Indians that the colonists should purchase the land.

All these charges put together were more than Puritan
Boston could take. Many of the colonists were loyal to the
Church of England; and, since they believed that the continued prosperity of their colony was dependent upon the
good will of the king, they dared not risk a drastic separation.

On leaving Boston, Roger Williams was invited to Salem
where he was asked to assist the Reverend Mr. Skelton as
minister of the church. Since Mr. Skelton was a separatist by
conviction, Williams assumed that the church also had separated from the Church of England. Later he discovered that
the contrary was true. So again trouble started.

Roger Williams refused to receive any new member into
the church who would not first renounce all his former connections with the Church of England. He protested against
allowing the rulers of the Church to be also the sole rulers of
the colony. Finally, as opposition to William's "offensive
spirit" grew, he refused even to have communion with the

Salem church. Instead he held meetings in his own home where he continued to "infect" others with what his opponents called "his extravagances." Many of the townspeople were drawn to him, but most of the leaders of the Massachusetts colony were hostile. Cotton Mather wrote that the whole country was "like to be set on fire by the rapid motion of a windmill in the head of one particular man." The sequel to the continuing conflict was that Roger Williams was finally brought to trial before a court in Newton, and a decree of banishment was given, with a six weeks' delay in its execution because of Williams' poor health.

The "Lone Journey"

During this period of respite, Roger Williams secretly laid plans for starting an independent colony on the shores of Narragansett Bay, and arranged a treaty for the purchase of land from two Indian chiefs. Again and again leading men of the Massachusetts Bay Colony urged him to change his mind, but Williams "stood stiffly in his own course." Nor was he willing to keep quiet or to refuse to let his friends gather in his home. Soon the authorities in Boston became so fearful of the contagion of his ideas that they decided it was dangerous to wait to be rid of this burning "firebrand." They, therefore, secretly plotted to arrest him and to put him forcibly on board a ship sailing for England.

Being warned by his old friend, John Winthrop, Williams anticipated his arrest by fleeing. In one short afternoon, he arranged for the carrying on of his business in Salem, and for the temporary support of his wife and two small children. In the bitter cold of a midwinter night, in a driving snowstorm, he set out alone in the direction of Narragansett Bay.

In his extremity, Williams' reputation as a friend of the Indians served him in good stead. Many a cold night he found shelter in their simple though filthy wigwams. During the winter months, he helped three quarreling sachems to resolve their grievances and to smoke together the pipe of peace.

In May of the following year, Roger Williams and five like-minded companions paddled in canoes up an arm of Narragansett Bay and began to build a new settlement. In gratitude for the peaceful ending of his hazardous adventure, Williams named the place Providence.

So began the first real democracy on American soil where the function of the civil authorities and the function of the Church were clearly separated and no man was to be compelled to worship in a way contrary to the dictates of his own conscience. To the persecuted the colony became a happy haven. To its enemies it seemed more like a dirty sink into which Massachusetts and Connecticut let flow their discarded refuse of "fanatics."

Roger Williams Changes His Own Convictions

In the new situation as time went on, Roger Williams' own beliefs changed. He began, for example, to question the validity of infant baptism. As he and his friends in Providence had all of them been baptized as infants in the Church of England, he concluded that none of them had been truly baptized. Therefore, together they must all make a new start.

Following a precedent acted upon in Zurich, Switzerland, in 1525, twelve of the colonists gathered for a true baptism. At Roger Williams' request, one of the company, Ezekiel Holliman, repeated the New Testament formula, "I baptize thee in the name of the Father and of the Son and of the Holy Ghost," and at the same time poured water from a pail over Roger Williams. Then Williams, having been baptized, spoke the sacred words and poured water over Holliman, and in turn over each of the other ten candidates for baptism. Thus was "gathered" a Baptist church, the first of its kind in America.

Some three or four months after participating in this ceremony, Williams came to believe it had all been a mistake. He had been baptized by an unbaptized person and consequently his baptism had been of no value. The line of succession, from the apostles, of truly baptized persons had been

In 1635, Roger Williams was banished from the Massachusetts colony for his radical ideas and sought shelter with the Narragansett Indians in the neighboring colony of Rhode Island. The following spring he founded the settlement of Providence on land purchased from the Indians. (The Bettmann Archive)

broken. What could he and his friends do? Nothing. They must wait for some new revelation authorizing the starting of a new succession. Since while waiting for light he could not call himself a Baptist, he separated from the church which he had just helped to organize. Instead he called himself a "Seeker," a name used by a small number of people in England. By this they meant that they did not see the way clearly and were seeking new light from heaven.

A Great Experiment in Tolerance

This experience made Roger Williams more tolerant of those who differed from him. He was ready now to pray with all Christians regardless of how or when baptized. His slogan was "soul freedom." This did not mean, however, that he approved of all beliefs. What he did was to tolerate differing beliefs. No one was driven from the colony because his religion differed from that of the original settlers. Roger Williams denounced what he thought to be error, but he granted to those whom he opposed complete religious liberty in his colony. To most of the Christians of that day, such an experiment in colonization seemed positively dangerous. They believed that the God of Truth would be offended by a government that permitted the teaching of error within its territory. They expected the colony to be torn by civil war or to be punished by some God-sent plague. But when the Rhode Island Colony continued to prosper and grow, opposition to its fundamental principles slowly began to weaken.

Although this significant experiment cannot justly be called a Baptist experiment, the Baptists of America like to remember that Roger Williams was a charter member of the first American Baptist church.

Who Were the First Baptists?

The Baptists can point to no one pioneer in Europe, England or America, and say, "This man was our spiritual

father." Sometime during the first four centuries the practice
of infant baptism began, and soon those who protested against
it were persecuted. As early as A.D. 414, a council of bishops
meeting in Carthage decreed, "We will that whosoever denies
that little children, by baptism, are freed from perdition, and
eternally saved, be accursed." As late as 1636 in Massachusetts,
a law was passed saying "If any Christian shall openly condemn
the baptizing of infants, or shall purposely depart the
congregation at the administration of that ordinance, and
continuing obstinate therein, he shall be sentenced to be
banished."

Differences Among Baptists

In England there developed two kinds of Baptists, the
"Particular" and the "General." The "Particular" Baptists
preached that God was "Particular" in choosing only a minority of people for salvation. The "General" Baptists, on the
other hand, revised their Calvinist beliefs regarding the predestination of some infants to perdition. They believed that
Christ came to save all men and that only those who refused
his grace when they reached the age of responsibility would
be lost.

In both England and America, many of the "General"
Baptists later became Unitarians. Today there is little trace
of these two divisions among Baptists. But the traditional zeal
of Baptists for independence has led to divisions of many other
kinds; indeed there are in America today at least twenty-seven
varieties. Among them are Free-will Baptists, Primitive Baptists, Seventh-Day Baptists (Saturday is their Sabbath), General
Six Principle Baptists, Duck River Baptists, and even a few
Two-Seed-in-the-Spirit Predestinarian Baptists.

Like other Church families, the Baptists have some close
relatives. Among these are the Mennonites and the Dunkards,
both of whom originated in what is now Germany, and are
descended from the Anabaptists. Both groups were persecuted.
Those who fled later to the Netherlands were called Men-

nonites because they rallied under the leadership of a Dutchman named Menno Simons. Later they fled to America, and in response to a direct invitation from William Penn in 1683, they settled in Pennsylvania.

The majority of Baptists throughout the world now make immersion a condition of membership in the Church. Some of these churches practice what is called "close Communion." None but the immersed may join with them in the Lord's Supper. The number of Baptist churches that practice "open Communion" is increasing. These invite all those present, who have accepted Jesus Christ as Savior, to join with them when the sacrament of the Lord's Supper is performed.

Baptism is usually performed by immersing the candidates one by one in a baptismal tank near the pulpit. Many churches, especially in the South, prefer to immerse their candidates in nearby rivers or lakes. The emotional excitement which often accompanies these outdoor religious rites frequently draws many spectators.

At the large Riverside Church in New York City, of which Dr. Harry Emerson Fosdick has been the noted senior minister, one may be admitted to membership merely on confession of faith, and the exact wording of this confession is not definitely prescribed. The symbolic ceremony of immersion will be performed if asked for, but it is not required for membership. Every year there is held the ceremony of the dedication of children. For this parents bring their babies to the chancel where the minister in an act of prayer dedicates each child in turn to the Christian life.

How the Baptists Govern Themselves

As is the case with the Congregationalists, each Baptist church governs its own affairs. No higher officials or boards can demand obedience from the churches, but they can and do formulate programs for achieving common goals. Some regional Baptist associations are interested in the strict maintenance of Baptist traditions and others are concerned with carrying on educational and missionary enterprises. Northern, Southern and Negro Baptists in the United States are each organized in national bodies called "Conventions."

Their Numerical Strength

Today the Baptists have become the largest Protestant group in the United States. If we include all kinds of Baptists, there are some 21 million in the United States alone, and at least half a million more in Canada. There are also some millions more in other countries, including, it is said, about 3 million in the Communist part of Europe. The largest Baptist groups in the United States are the Southern Baptist Convention (about 9 million), the National Baptist Convention, U.S.A. (about 5½ million), the National Baptist Convention of America (about 2½ million), and the American Baptist Convention with about 1½ million. The latter was formerly known as the Northern Baptist Convention.

The Fundamentalist Controversy

No American denominational family in the twentieth century has been more involved in theological controversy than have the Baptists, unless it is the Presbyterians. Although the Baptists have traditionally stood for freedom in faith and government, they have also usually stood for a freedom that is bounded by loyalty to the Scriptures as the Word of God.

Many conservative Baptists have been alarmed by the progress of critical views concerning the Bible. They have allied themselves with those of somewhat similar views among the Presbyterians and in some other denominations in emphasizing certain doctrines or statements in the Bible which had been set aside or "explained away," as they said, by some of the Biblical critics. These conservatives declare that belief in the truth of all statements of Scripture is absolutely *fundamental,* not only to the well-being but even to the very existence of true Christianity. For this reason such Christians have been called "Fundamentalists." They regard the following five points as the minimum essentials of the true faith: the virgin birth of Jesus, his physical resurrection, the inerrancy of the Bible, the substitutionary atonement, and the truth of the miracles recorded in the Bible.

Many of the Baptist Fundamentalists, as well as others, are putting great stress on the second coming of Christ which they believe will soon take place, but not before a series of more and more dreadful catastrophes occur. They prophesy that the human race will become worse and worse, in spite of all human efforts to reform society. They assert that salvation even for this world can come only through the supernatural intervention of the divine Son of God from heaven. In brief, these Fundamentalists are preaching the Old Story of Salvation very much in the form which it had in the days of Augustine. Since in this terrifying drama the Jewish people are presented as the chief of sinners in having killed the Christ, the Son of God, anti-Semitic hatreds are being kept alive, often unconsciously, by such preaching.

Perhaps the best-known leader of the Fundamentalists was William Jennings Bryan, a Presbyterian, and three times an unsuccessful candidate for the presidency of the United States. He and his colleagues secured the trial and conviction in 1925 of Mr. John T. Scopes, who taught science in a high school in Dayton, Tennessee, a state which by law forbade the teaching of evolution in its public schools.

Dr. Harry Emerson Fosdick, a Baptist liberal, led the fight against the Fundamentalists. His famous sermon, "Shall the Fundamentalists Win?", had a wide and significant influence.

The Missionary Fervor of the Baptists

Most Baptists, like the Methodists, are evangelistic in their emphasis, and have gained a great many members by having revivals of religion. The modern Crusade for Christ has been ardently supported by the Fundamentalists among them. They have also been active in organizing a special Crusade for Children.

In the past few years the Southern Baptists have been engaged in an energetic and successful campaign to gain new members and found new churches in the Northern and Western states. The result is that they are now a national rather than a Southern denomination.

The Baptists have also been among the more zealous missionary denominations. They have been fortunate in having some great leaders to urge them forward. William Carey, a minister in England, in 1786 challenged a meeting of ministers with this question—"whether the command given the Apostles to teach all nations was not obligatory on all succeeding generations to the end of the world, seeing that the accompanying promise was of equal extent." He was told, however, by one of his Calvinistic colleagues to sit down. "You're an enthusiast. When God pleases to convert the heathen, He'll do it without consulting you or me." Notwithstanding this wet-blanketing of William Carey's proposal, the Baptist churches of England did organize a Missionary Society and sent William Carey and his medical friend, Dr. John Thomas, to Bengal, India.

In America it was the great Adoniram Judson who first started for Burma as a Congregational missionary. While on the ocean on his way to India, Judson was converted to the Baptist position. He appealed to the Baptist churches in America to take him on as their missionary. As a result, a missionary society was organized which is now called the American Baptist Foreign Mission Society.

The ringing words from William Carey's farewell sermon before sailing for Calcutta have been a noble motto for the entire Protestant missionary enterprise. "Expect great things from God; attempt great things for God."

Baptist Philanthropy

Baptists have not been merely zealous missionaries, they have also been intensely interested in work for the common good, both here and abroad. Like the Presbyterians, Methodists and some other churches, they have founded hospitals, especially in the larger cities; one of the better-known Baptist hospitals is in Boston. Many a youth has received his education in a Baptist-related college or university. These are to be found throughout the nation. Among them are Brown University in Rhode Island, Baylor University in Texas, Colby College in Maine and the University of Richmond in Virginia. Indeed, we are all the richer for the spiritual legacy of John Bunyan and Roger Williams.

9. George Fox
1624-1691

The Scriptures, what are they but the words of prophets, of Christ and his apostles, uttered by men who enjoyed and possessed this Light which they received from the Lord? What have you to do with the words of the Scriptures, unless you come to the same Spirit which gave them forth? You open the Bible, and say, "Christ saith this," and the "apostles say that," but what do you say yourselves? Art thou a child of the Light? Hast thou walked in the Light? What thou sayest concerning God, does it come to thee inwardly from Him?

—GEORGE FOX

"As Stiff as an Oak, as Clear as a Bell"

In the quiet English village of Fenny Drayton lived another worker's son, George Fox (just four years older than John Bunyan), a man whose ideas were destined to be carried to the four corners of the earth. His father, whom his neighbors called Righteous Christer, was a weaver and a God-fearing Puritan. His mother, though poor and uneducated, had the blood of martyrs in her veins.

Like Bunyan, George early learned a trade in a neighbor's shoe shop. He also served as a hired shepherd and sold wool for his master in the neighboring villages. As a young man, he made for himself not only his own leather boots but leather breeches and jacket as well. In his later wanderings he wore this suit so continuously that he was dubbed "the man in leather breeches."

In writing of his early youth, George Fox said: "In my

very young years I had a gravity and a stayedness in mind and spirit not usual in children. . . . The Lord taught me to be faithful in all things, and to act faithfully two ways, viz: inwardly to God, and outwardly to man: . . . It was a common saying among the people who knew me, 'If George says Verily, there is no altering him.' "

Unlike Bunyan, George was not distressed about his own sinful nature or distraught over the prospect of eternal punishment. Instead, he was troubled about many things that seemed to him wrong in the life of the community. In church he heard people profess to be followers of Christ. On Sundays they prayed long prayers, listened reverently to long sermons; but on Mondays these same people in their shops would cheat their customers. He saw Puritans strict in morals, who at the same time went often to the village inn to drink beer and rum until they were drunk and silly. He saw the minister and others tip their hats and bow when the lord and lady of the castle passed by, but when a butcher or baker came along, they would keep their hats on with never the slightest bow. Beggars "some in rags and some in tags," came almost daily into the town hoping for a mouthful of food or a place to lay their heads, but only the barking dogs seemed to notice them. Did Christ come to save only the rich? For whom was the Bible intended? Such were the things that disturbed George Fox.

A Small Episode Becomes a Crisis

One day when George was a young man of nineteen, he was walking about at a county fair, selling his master's wool, when his cousin and a friend met him. "Come, George, let's have a jug of beer together." Glad for a little fun, George went into the inn with them and each drank his glass. Then the other two boys began asking for more, and each drank a second glass and then a third. "Let's run a race," said the cousin, "and see which of us can drink the most. Then the one who drinks the least will have to pay for us all."

For years George had known the two boys. They had usually been models of behavior, especially at church. But now he saw that they were trying to shame him into overdrinking. Putting his hand in his pocket, he pulled out a groat—enough to pay for his own glass—and laid it on the table. "If it be so, I will leave you."

That night George did not go to bed at all. Anxiously he walked the floor. All his discontents seemed to pile themselves one on another. He longed to talk with some one. He tried to pray. Why did people say one thing in church and act so differently on the street? Wasn't God real? Did the ministers speak the truth? What was the truth? How was it to be discovered?

Finally, it seemed to George that he heard God command him to leave his home and his parents and all his companions in the village and go forth as a pilgrim alone to other towns to find the truth. The next morning, just as truly as any explorer ever set out to find the North Pole, George Fox set out to find God. He walked from one town to another, staying a few weeks in one place and then moving on to another village. Wherever he went he watched people, and talked with them. He talked with Puritans and dissenters and people who had little thought of religion. Some he found were "tender" and treated him kindly. But none seemed able to understand or "speak to his condition."

After some months, conscience-stricken for leaving his parents, he returned to his own Fenny Drayton. His neighbors said his troubles would go if only he would settle down and marry, but he was uninterested. Finally he found courage to talk things over with Mr. Stephens, the minister in his own church; but once more this honest seeker was disappointed. Off he went again to other towns. He talked with ministers wherever he could find them, but they all seemed as "empty casks."

The hours George spent in the woods alone proved more profitable to him. With a tree stump for a chair back, he would sit and read his Bible. Now and then a new thought was "opened" to him.

"I saw that being bred in Oxford and Cambridge did not qualify or fit a man to be a minister of Christ."

"It was opened to me that God, who made the world, did not dwell in temples made with hands... but in people's hearts." The so-called holy churches seemed but places of idol worship with steeples pointing to a faraway God.

The Experience That Freed Him

Finally, after nearly three years spent in this solitary search, "when all my hopes in them and in all men were gone, so that I had nothing outwardly to help me, nor could I tell what to do, then, oh then, I heard a voice which said, 'There is one, even Christ Jesus, that can speak to thy condition,' and when I heard it, my heart did leap for joy."

From this experience George Fox returned home "wrapt in the love of God." For him life had begun. He was a new man. And the thought came to him, "If God can speak to me, so clearly and directly, He can speak to any man, woman, or child. In every one there is a 'seed' of life waiting to grow. In every one is 'an inner light' which may at any time become a greater light." From that time on George Fox believed he had a mission to live for. His purpose was clear as a bell. He would do all in his power to bring people off from "all the world's fellowships, and prayings and singing, which stood in forms without power... that their fellowship might be... in the Eternal Spirit of God... that they might know the pure religion, might visit the fatherless, the widows, and the strangers, and keep themselves from the spots of the world."

With the ending of his terrific inner struggles, George Fox's outward struggles began. In all sorts of places people would gather to hear him talk. His denunciations of wrongdoing often made people tremble. For this reason his followers were first called Quakers. His ways of speaking were never softened by tact or because of fear of offense. Whatever else George Fox was or was not, he was determined to be honest and outspoken.

The Taking of an Oath

During the seventeenth century whenever any one was suspected of plotting against the king, he was brought before a court and compelled to take an oath of allegiance, by kissing the Bible and swearing his loyalty. This George Fox refused to do, not because he had the slightest intention of plotting against the king, but because it had been "opened" to him that all swearing was wrong. He had found Jesus' own words: "Swear not at all, but let your speech be 'yea, yea; nay, nay'; for whatsoever is more than these cometh of evil."

Yet there was the law. "If any person, not noble, and above eighteen, shall refuse the oath of allegiance" he may be sent into another country away from the king's protection; his lands, houses and all his property may be confiscated; or he may be imprisoned for as long a time as the king shall determine.[1]

One morning George Fox had been standing a long time at the bar before the judge. Much had been said but nothing had been proved against him. The learned man with the gray wig and scarlet gown had the power to send his prisoner to jail for life or even to the gallows. George Fox was ready for anything; he felt that God's power was over all weakness and over death. Finally, the judge said, "Give him the Book and let him take the oath of allegiance."

So George Fox took the Bible; and turning the pages he found Jesus' words about swearing. With the open Bible in his hand, the prisoner lifted his sharp gray eyes and watched the judge.

"Read the oath to the prisoner," said the judge, eager to be through with his grim business.

When the clerk had read the solemn oath, the judge turned to the prisoner and said: "Wilt thou or wilt thou not take this oath?"

"Ye have given me a book here to kiss, and to swear on, and this book which ye have given me says, 'Swear not at all . . . but let your speech be, yea, yea; nay, nay; for whatsoever is

---

[1] This was called the penalty of *Praemunire*.

more than these cometh of evil.' I do as the Book says, yet ye would imprison me. How chance ye do not imprison the Book for saying 'Swear not at all'? How comes it that the Book is at liberty amongst you, which bids me not to swear, and yet ye imprison me for doing as the Book bids me?"

Such answering back was impudence. The clerk snatched the Bible from the prisoner's hand, and the judge cried, "Nay, but we will imprison thee," and to prison George Fox was sent.

Honesty Every Day

In his everyday conversation George Fox went to the minutest care to speak the truth. He began watching even his casual remarks. He caught himself saying "Good morning" to a stranger one day passing on the street. "Do I really wish him a good morning?" he asked himself. "I must not say 'good morning' unless I mean I want him to have a good morning. It is better to be rude than to be dishonest."

He even began asking the meaning of words others never thought of questioning. He found out, for example, that Sunday really meant the sun god's day; Monday meant the moon god's day; Tuesday, the day of Tyr, the war god; Wednesday, the day of Woden, or Odin, the father of gods and men; Thursday, the day of Thor, the god of thunder.

"I can not call the days of the week by the names of gods I do not believe in," he said. For this reason George Fox called Sunday the First-day, and Monday the Second-day, and so on. Even yet, three hundred years after George Fox's time, the Quakers do not speak of Sunday Schools, but of First-day Schools.

This determination of George Fox to be honest was contagious. Hundreds and thousands of those who gathered about him in the towns and cities of England also began trying always to be honest. Some of these Quakers were tradesmen. They had dry goods shops and grocery stores. They were tailors, shoemakers and carpenters. Like George Fox, when speaking to their customers, they would not put off their hats or bow. They refused to say, "Your humble servant." The customers, feeling slighted, grew shy of these queer people and refused to go to their shops until many of the Quakers were able to earn scarcely enough to buy bread for their children.

As months passed, however, the people came to see that these Quakers never cheated them. If a Quaker promised to do a thing, he did it. Slowly the reputation of the Quaker merchants changed. A stranger coming into a town would ask, "Where is there a Quaker grocer or tailor or shoemaker? I like to trade with the Quakers because they are honest." Ever since George Fox's day, the Quakers, or Friends as they prefer to be called, have had the reputation of being honest.

Should a Man Fight for a Good Cause?

Another matter about which George Fox was "stiff as an oak" was his conviction about fighting. In the days of Charles I and of Oliver Cromwell, it was customary for every man in England to wear a sword in his belt. It was assumed that he should be prepared at any moment to fight. Fighting for a good cause was regarded as a Christian duty. The great Protector was a notable soldier of the Lord. Had he not taken up arms against the king for the good of the people? Had his armies not gone into battle singing hymns and before fighting had they not always prayed?

It was "opened" to George Fox, however, that he should never carry a sword and never fight. Again Jesus' words were final for him. "Resist not evil . . . but whosoever shall smite thee on thy right cheek, turn to him the other also. . . . Love your enemies. . . . Do good to them that hate you."

His Practice of Nonresistance

One Sunday morning as the church bells were ringing and "struck at his heart," as he said, God seemed to be calling him to go to the church and speak. George Fox sat quietly until the sermon was ended, then stepping to the platform, he motioned to show that he had something to say. This in itself was not such an unusual thing to do. Men often spoke in this way after the church service.

What he said, however, was different from what the minister had just been saying. For a while the people listened eagerly, but not for long. Soon a judge in the audience interrupted. "He is not speaking according to the Bible. He is an enemy of the country. He is plotting against the king and the Church. Put him out."

The judge's words were like a match setting fire to a haystack. In a moment the church was in a turmoil. Some tumbled over the seats in their excitement. They struck George Fox with their fists. They threw him on the floor. Some pulled him by the collar; others by the hands. They dragged him away to an open meadow a quarter of a mile from the town. A crowd shouting and jeering ran after him. On their way they broke off boughs from the trees and picked up sticks from the ground and pulled branches from the prickly holly bushes. They struck him on the arms and shoulders; they hit him on the head until he was so weak that he fell in a heap on the wet grass. As he lay there unable to move, George Fox asked himself, "What shall I do?" Then the words of Jesus came to his mind, "Love your enemies. Pray for them that abuse you."

The crowds were watching. They saw his body move slightly on the ground; they pushed closer and raised their sticks ready to strike. They watched him struggle to his feet. But what did they see? How dared he stand so straight and look so fearlessly at them? Was he bewitching them, too? The crowds stepped back, as if stunned when they saw his two bloody arms stretched out and heard his voice clear as a bell. "Strike again. Here are my arms. Here is my head. Here are my cheeks. Strike them again. I will not strike you back."

Only one man in the crowd had any daring left. With a hard laugh, he pushed his way forward and with his stick struck George Fox such a blow on his wrist that the arm fell as if dead at his side. The crowd groaned. "His hand is crushed. He will never be able to use it again!" One by one the people walked away, for they had lost their courage.

As for George Fox, he felt "the Lord's power spring through him." Instead of leaving the town as he had been ordered to do, he walked back into the market place and made his way about calmly among the very people who had been flogging him so short a while before.

Soon he was holding as many meetings as ever, now in this city and now in that. Everywhere he went he made a disturbance. He even had the daring to walk up to the drawbridge of a castle and preach to those on guard. Some soldiers were throwing away their swords and refusing to fight. One ship's commander had written to Cromwell saying that his very best gunman had turned Quaker and now refused to fire a gun. It is not strange that George Fox was imprisoned as a traitor.

Cromwell's Offer of Freedom

Later, messengers were sent to the prison. They ordered the jailer to bring the prisoner forth into the market place where a band of soldiers was gathered.

Without lifting his hat to salute the officer, the prisoner in the leather breeches faced him. Paying no attention to the insult, the officer spoke, "Oliver Cromwell, the Lord Protector of all England, offers you your freedom if you will become captain of his army." On hearing this the soldiers cheered.

"Stiff as an oak" the prisoner stood and in a voice "clear as a bell" he answered: "All wars and all fighting come about because men are selfish and jealous of each other and hateful. Every soul is important in the eyes of God. I could never use my sword to kill any man, not even my bitterest enemy. I am a follower of Jesus Christ, the Prince of Peace. He would have us live such lives as will take away all occasions for war. I will accept orders only from Him."

With his hands tied behind him and with the taunts of the soldiers ringing in his ears, George Fox was led away once more behind the prison walls, this time to share a room with thirty criminals of the worst sort, with not a bed for any of them.

Twice during the long winter, Cromwell sent messengers with the same offer of freedom. Finally, the prisoner was ordered to appear before one of the very highest officers of Cromwell's army, who commanded Fox to become a soldier.

"You are commanding a dead man."

"You seem very much alive."

"I am dead to all war. Where there is envy and hate, all is confusion. I will have none of it."

So once again this man of peace was sent to the small bare prison to join the thirty thieves and murderers.

In the filthiest, most sickening prison dungeon, he would sing and talk with his fellow sufferers about God's love and power. On the hard stone bench or on the cold damp floor of his prison cell, he would write letters to the judges pleading for mercy, not merely for himself but for some thief beside him. With swollen fingers he would pen words of cheer to other Friends who like himself were sitting lonely behind barred doors.

Free again, he would go at once to some market place or to a fair or perhaps to a Quaker meetinghouse and there he would preach.

Three Great Principles

These then were three of the great convictions which George Fox proclaimed: first, the endowment of every human heart with an "inner light" or a "seed of divine life" which makes possible direct relations with God; second, the primary importance of honesty in all relations and the despising of all shams; and third, the complete allegiance to the principle of nonresistance, or to the belief that all wars and fighting are evil.

Out of the first of these three principles grew George Fox's democratic philosophy of life. It was because of his belief in the "inner light" in every person that he also believed that men everywhere were equal in the sight of God. In a day when even some ministers said that women had no souls, George Fox

To spread the word of his great convictions, George Fox visited America in 1671, journeying to various colonies scattered between New England and North Carolina. Here he is shown preaching to a group of settlers and Indians in Maryland. (The Bettmann Archive)

encouraged women to be leaders of his societies. He included the "heathen" also among those who had "the light of the Spirit of God."

This fundamental respect of George Fox for every man deeply influenced his great disciple, William Penn. Penn's colony in America and the one established in Rhode Island by Roger Williams were the only colonies that consistently treated the Indians in the spirit of friendliness and justice. William Penn's famous treaty with the Indians is one of the few political events in the white man's relation to the Indians of which the nation can be proud.

The Harvest Reaped Before His Death

In spite of years of imprisonment and persecution, George Fox lived to see fifty thousand persons in Great Britain and Ireland, who, to use his quaint expression, had "suffered convincement." These people of like convictions were formed into a working, growing body with equally well-organized meetings in Holland, New England, New York, Pennsylvania, Maryland, Virginia and the Carolinas.[2] Before his death, Fox knew also that more than twelve thousand of his followers in England had been imprisoned because of their beliefs, and that over three hundred of these imprisonments had ended fatally.[3]

Unlettered and uncouth himself, Fox was honored as a prophet not only by peasants but also by judges and scholars. William Penn, the most famous of the disciples of Fox, was the son of a famous admiral, a man of wealth, social standing and education. Late in life the "man in the leather breeches" even married the beautiful widowed lady of Swarthmore Hall, Margaret Fell. For years this large and charming country estate was the meetinghouse for Friends and a refuge for the perse-

[2] Rufus M. Jones, ed., *George Fox: An Autobiography* (Philadelphia, 1903-1906) , I, 43.

[3] Ernest E. Taylor, *Cameos from the Life of George Fox* (Headley Brothers) .

cuted. Because of her activities, Margaret Fell herself was held as a prisoner for four long years while her husband languished for almost as long in another castle dungeon.

William Penn wrote this frank estimate of his master in Christ:

> And though the side of his understanding which lay next to the world, and especially the expression of it, might sound uncouth and unfashionable to nice ears, his matter was nevertheless very profound, and would not only bear to be often considered, but the more it was so, the more weighty and instructive it appeared. And as abruptly and brokenly as sometimes his sentences would fall from him about divine things, it is well known they were often as texts to many fairer declarations. And indeed it showed beyond all contradiction that God sent him . . . he was an original, being no man's copy."[4]

The Society of Friends

Persecution of Quakers in Massachusetts

If the way of the Quaker was hard in England, it was no less so in America. Puritans desired freedom of conscience, but only for those whose consciences were like their own. To the New World followers of Calvin, the Bible was the infallible guide. The Quaker belief in an "inner light" as a guide seemed to the Puritan to be an outright denial of the all-sufficiency of Holy Scripture.

Quakers whose "concern" for spreading the gospel brought them to the New World found New Englanders concerned about keeping them out. Sea captains who brought Quakers to America in their ships were required to return them under penalty of heavy fines. The few Quakers who

---

[4] Quoted in Thomas Hodgkin, *George Fox* (London: Methuen and Co., 1896) , pp. 274-275.

landed were promptly thrown into prison. Anyone caught importing Quaker books was liable to a $25 fine. In the eyes of the law the Quakers were "that cursed sect of heretics," and were liable to "be whipt with rods so it exceed not fifteen stripes" and banished.

A law passed by the Massachusetts House of Deputies in 1658 decreed the death penalty for these "fitt Instruments to propogate the Kingdom of Sathan," and the sentence was actually executed on some of these intrepid pioneers, including the saintly Mary Dyer. After the death of Governor Endicott in 1665, persecution relaxed, but even as late as 1775 there was a law still on the statute books forbidding Quakers to hold meetings.

Whether because of the unrelenting persecution these Quaker missionaries had to endure, or for other reasons, the Quaker movement never prospered in New England. It was quite the reverse in Pennsylvania. William Penn's charter for his colony granted freedom for all religious sects. To this haven in the New World large numbers of English Quakers emigrated. It is still a stronghold of the American Society of Friends. There are also many Friends in Indiana, and other parts of the Midwest.

Beliefs by Which Friends Are Known

All Friends still cherish belief in the "inner light," as the ultimate authority, rather than the creedal statements or traditions of a church. This central conviction has made Friends staunch advocates of the democratic faith. No denomination has been more consistent in its respect for personality than they. Women have stood side by side with men in the leadership of this society. No Christian group has been more persevering in its defense of outcast racial or social groups. With a remarkable degree of unanimity, and in spite of persecution, Friends have opposed all wars. They are renowned for their thrift and honesty. Although substantial wealth has come to no small number of Friends, yet for the most part they have maintained simplicity both in dress and in manner of living. Many of them still retain a preference for "thee" in conversation, as a symbol of friendship and mutual respect. Among themselves they refrain from all use of academic titles. Still true to the spirit of George Fox and other early Quakers, they are against all forms without the spirit to give them meaning. They do not baptize or celebrate the Lord's Supper, and their marriage ceremonies are beautifully simple.

Their First-day Meetings

Most Friends still speak of Sunday as the First-day of the week, and their Sunday services are called First-day meetings. These are usually without singing or instrumental music or sermon. When some member, man or woman, of the Meeting feels the prompting of the Spirit he speaks; otherwise nothing is said. The group worships in silence. The helpfulness of silence in group worship and fellowship is one of the greatest lessons the Society of Friends has demonstrated. If there is business to transact no formal vote is taken. The clerk simply records as a "minute" what seems to be the consensus of the group. When the meeting is over each person shakes hands with the one sitting next to him and greets him before leaving for home.

Their Places of Worship

Quaker places of worship are called meetinghouses rather than churches. These, like the meeting held in them, are usually plain and unadorned. There is no pulpit. Sometimes a raised platform takes its place at one end of the room, where a group of the leaders of the meeting sit. Plain wooden benches for the other worshipers fill the rest of the room. Originally the women sat on one side and the men on the other. In some of the larger cities, present-day meetinghouses are beautiful colonial structures, but without stained-glass windows or ornate decoration.

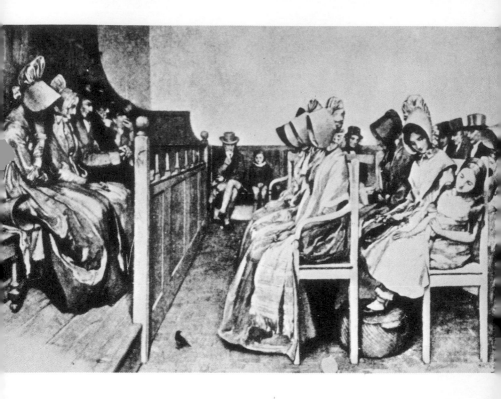

Quakers worshiping in spirit at the Friends meetinghouse in Jordans, Pennsylvania, where William Penn worshiped. From a painting by J. Walter West. (Ewing Galloway)

We can appreciate the feelings that younger Quakers sometimes have had because of the lack of art in Friends' meetinghouses, and because so little seems to happen in the meeting. Richenda Gurney, sister of the famous Elizabeth Fry, who did so much to reform English prisons in the nineteenth century, wrote in her journal, "I had a truly uncomfortable sort of meeting. It was really bliss to hear the clock strike twelve . . . Oh, how I long to get a broom and bang all the old Quakers who do look so triumphant and disagreeable." There is, however, a spirit of quiet reverence and worship in such meetings which the sensitive and more mature person cannot forget.

The Simplicity of Organization

The Society of Friends for a long time had no paid ministers. Their organization has been as simple as possible, and thus as different as could be from that of most other denominations. In some areas the meetings have salaried pastors and their use is increasing, although these leaders are still independent of any higher ecclesiastical control. They are not ordained, but they are often called "Reverend."

The local society is known as a "Monthly Meeting." A group of these Monthly Meetings is known as a "Quarterly Meeting." There are now five "Yearly Meetings," with a total membership of about 22,000; and three other groups. There are also a "Five Years Meeting," a group known as the Religious Society of Friends (Conservative), and one called the Religious Society of Friends (General Conference). All told, Friends in the United States and Canada number rather more than 125,000. The Five Years Meeting is much the largest of the three groups.

Liberalism vs. Conservatism

With such a belief as that of an inner divine light in every one, the members of the Society of Friends have always re-

spected nonconformity. From the beginning they have struggled valiantly against requiring assent to any doctrine as a test
of the reality of religious experience. Unfortunately, however,
even the Friends have been split into several separate groups
because of beliefs that once seemed irreconcilable.

In the early part of the nineteenth century, in the Society
in Jericho, Long Island, there appeared Elias Hicks, a dynamic
and original leader who preached ideas which, to those who
could not accept them, seemed destructive of the very gospel
itself and of true religion.

This Elias Hicks, without benefit of Biblical scholarship,
came to the conclusion that a clear distinction must be made
between "Jesus of Nazareth" and "Christ." To Hicks, "Jesus
was a model man who lived in Palestine at a definite date."
Hicks said, "This outward historical Jesus is not our Saviour."
His physical death on the cross cannot save anyone. There can
be "no other Saviour, but such as one who takes His residence
in the very center of the soul." It is "the portion of God"
within a man that saves him. This may be called the "Divine"
in man. Some call it "the indwelling Christ." This "Spirit of
Life, Light and Grace" was in the Jesus who lived in Palestine,
and it may also be in any man. It is an eternal principle. It is
only through the soul's obedience to this light or principle
that salvation can come. No other person's righteousness can
be substituted for one's own righteousness and the power to
achieve that righteousness is within and cannot come from
outside. The story of the Jesus who died on the cross and rose
again should be thought of as "entirely figurative," a symbol
of the death of sin and the growth of righteousness within the
spirit of man.[5]

Here was a Quaker of Quakers who carried the doctrine
of the "inner light" to its logical and full conclusion. His
thinking resulted in a division among Quakers into two
groups: the Orthodox and the Hicksite, or Liberal, groups.
Today, however, there are many liberal Quakers who prefer

---

[5] Rufus Jones, *Later Periods of Quakerism* (New York: Macmillan, 1921).
I, 444, 452, 455.

not to be labeled as Hicksites, since they regard the nineteenth-century form of liberalism of Elias Hicks as unsatisfactory to a liberal of the twentieth century.

Furthermore, they believe that true liberalism should mean the breaking down of the dividing walls in the fellowship. They are, therefore, working for unity and are accenting anew respect for originality and individual freedom to follow "the inner light."

Significant Activities

Although the membership of the Society of Friends, both in America and in England, is comparatively small, their influence far exceeds their proportionate numbers. Through the work of the Friends Service Committee, Quakers have become known far and wide. After both world wars this committee performed an immense and exceedingly difficult work, feeding and caring for prisoners, war orphans, refugees from annihilation, and stricken populations in friendly and enemy countries alike. In the postwar years their humanitarian work has been continued throughout the world: relief and rehabilitation of war refugees in west and central Europe; food, clothing and medical care in Korea; aid to victims of the Hungarian uprising; help to homeless Arabs in the Gaza strip and Suez Canal Zone; and famine relief in India and Pakistan.

Nor has the work of the Friends been confined to disaster relief; they are even more interested in educating for peace. They have organized seminars for international affairs, conferences of diplomats, race relations committees and work camps in which young people aid in constructive activities, such as repairing the school in an Indian fishing village in Alaska, and building a tuberculosis recovery home in Kenya. In all this they have no thought of making more people Quakers, but only in making a hard world a better place in which to live. They well deserve the name of "Friends."

Many Quaker young men who, because of religious convictions believed it wrong to fight, served without pay during World War II in work camps under the civilian control of a board of Friends, Brethren and Mennonites. Other young men of similar views, who had no religious connections, humanists who reject all beliefs in a supernatural God, served with them. Some of these conscientious objectors were sent to jail for their refusal to register for the draft. Most of these pacifists, however, were allowed to do certain kinds of useful work, and in some cases dangerous work that involved suffering and even death. Some served as nurses in hospitals for the insane, while others volunteered as guinea pigs for experiments in preventive medicine and starvation diets.

A number of preparatory schools under the leadership of Friends have been noted for the quality of democracy they teach. Friends have also established in the United States a few colleges of the highest scholastic rank. Among these are Swarthmore, Haverford and Bryn Mawr.

Of all the humanitarian work that the Quakers have carried on, perhaps none was more desperately needed in the early days than prison reform. Elizabeth Fry, an Englishwoman of the early nineteenth century, was a pioneer in this work.

Friends have lived up to their name in many other ways. Throughout their history as American colonists, they were able to maintain consistently peaceful relations with the Indians. William Penn's treaty with the Indians and his subsequent dealing with them belong with the few nobly great events which Americans should never cease to celebrate.

Friends the Quakers also were to the Negro slaves. Although a few Quakers fell into the social pattern of the times and employed slaves for a while on their estates, when once convinced of their error, they freed their slaves even before Lincoln's Proclamation of Emancipation. Before the Civil War by establishing the so-called "underground railroad," many Friends risked their own lives to help slaves reach the north and freedom.

The "inner light" that illuminated the hearts of such

men and women as George Fox, William Penn, Margaret Fell and Elizabeth Fry has helped to light a very dark world, and it continues to do so. Perhaps the Friends' solution to the conflicts which create so many of the world's problems, and from which so many conflicts spring, may be the only practical one after all.

10. John Wesley
1703-1791

Give all you can. Hoard nothing. I defy all the men on the earth, yes all the angels in heaven, to find any other way of extracting the poison from riches.

—JOHN WESLEY

A Revivalist Prevents a Revolution

Early one Sunday morning about the year 1730, a student wit of Christ Church College, Oxford, looked out his window and saw some half dozen other students walking into the cathedral for Communion.

"There goes the Holy Club!" said he laughingly to his visiting friend. "A new set of Methodists is sprung up here at Oxford."

"Why call them such names?" asked his companion.

"Because they think they must be singularly holy or be damned, and because they regulate their holy deeds by clock and bell. They imagine they can not be saved if they do not spend every hour, nay every minute of their lives in the service of God. They sleep but little. Rise early in the mornings. Meet every evening from six to nine. Like moths they patiently crawl through the Holy Book eating the words. Each Saturday night they rehearse their sins one by one and weep for five minutes, then thank God for granting them repentance, and laugh immoderately as if they were mad."

"Methinks that to strain so hard after holiness is folly."

"I've not told you half. They are the jest of the whole university. They fast two days a week like the Pharisees. Give every penny they save to feed the poor or to buy books for them to read. They try to reform notorious harlots and preach to criminals in prison, and hire teachers for the children of house drudges."

"Let them have their 'Holy Club.' It's nothing to me," said the visitor in disgust. "If I have to work that hard to gain heaven, let me have the flames of hell!"

Extreme and foolish as the activities of this small group of students seemed to their fellow students, the world has never forgotten this "Holy Club," and, strange as it seems, the title "Methodists," first given in derision to these college men, is now the official name of the second largest Protestant denominational family in America.

The Two Brothers

In this small group of serious young men were two brothers, John and Charles Wesley, sons of an Anglican minister in the small English village of Epworth. Charles, the younger, was the organizer: a sociable, excitable and impractical young man "with more genius than grace," who loved to write poetry and to sing. Disorderly in mind and habits, he had been drifting gaily through life, with little thought of his ultimate destiny.

John, Charles's older brother by four years, was of an opposite temperament, more like his competent and serious-minded mother, Susanna Wesley. Even as a child John began to guide his life by reason. Said his father one day, "Susanna, I think our boy Jack would not attend to the most pressing necessities of nature unless he could give a reason for it."

The strict discipline of an Anglican home had taken effect on John. But Charles, like his poetical father, was always bursting the bonds of routine. He had once petulantly protested to his brother, "Would you have me become a saint all at once?" John, the leader of the "Holy Club," was methodical to the core.

The Epworth Home

Susanna Wesley was the mother of a family of nineteen children. John was the fifteenth child and Charles the eighteenth. Although her husband's stipend was considered reasonable, it required a Spartan manager to make ends meet. But the cause of the Wesley's poverty lay deeper than the size of the family, for the father, unfortunately, seemed to love books more than his children, and was constantly getting himself into debt in order to finance his literary productions. In fact, for a period of several months he was actually jailed for his indebtedness, which put the whole burden of the family's finance upon his wife. Later, when Susanna was asked if they ever actually lacked for bread, she replied: "I had so much care to get it before it was eat, and to pay for it after, as has often made it very unpleasant to me. And I think to have bread on such terms is the next degree of wretchedness to having none at all."

"A Brand Plucked from the Burning"

Nor was the Rev. Samuel Wesley really popular with his parishioners—particularly with the dissenters, those uncouth doubters of official religion. Perhaps this unpopularity was the cause of the crisis that came on the night of February 9, 1709, when John was but six and Charles was a baby in arms. The old thatched parsonage caught fire (or was set on fire, as some rumors had it). John was asleep in a room on the second floor. All the rest of the family had escaped. The father tried to run up the stairs to rescue his son, but flames blocked his way. John was awakened by the crackling of the fire. He opened a door to run down stairs but was met by a hot blast. He slammed the door shut, ran to the open window, saw the shouting crowds below, cried for help, and by means of a human ladder he climbed down to safety and to his mother's arms. "A brand plucked from the burning!" she cried in her joy. From that day John had a special place in his mother's heart. She determined, as she said, to be "more particularly careful of the soul of this child." Often in later years she reminded John that he must have been "plucked from the burning" for some great purpose.

Susanna's Discipline

Susanna Wesley, however, was a careful mother of all her many children. When but a year old, each was taught to fear the rod and to cry softly. If any child visited the kitchen for something to eat between meals, he was "most certainly beat." "I insist," said Susanna, "in conquering the will of children betimes, because this is the only strong and rational foundation of a religious education, without which both precept and example will be ineffectual, but when this is done then is a child capable of being governed by the reason and piety of its parents, till its own understanding come to maturity, and the principles of religion have taken root in the mind."

On each child's fifth birthday, she planned what she called an "Alphabet Party." This meant that the child spent the day learning the letters of the alphabet. The next day he began to spell words, with the use of the Book of Genesis as his first reader and speller. The hours for instruction were from nine to twelve, and from two to five. A tough schedule for a five-year-old, judged by modern standards.

In spite of poverty, two sons went to Oxford University and were enabled to enter the ministry of the Church of England. While John served with a good salary as don at Lincoln College at Oxford, his brother Charles was a student. It was during this period that the two were members of the "Holy Club," and John, the elder, became the leader.

But the methodical religion of the "Holy Club" was not the power that brought to England the great religious awakening. The actual beginning of the Methodist Church was still a long way off. To learn how these two loyal Anglican ministers later started another dissenting church, we must trace the story further.

The American Venture

On his father's death John was given the assignment of taking his father's latest volume to Queen Caroline in the hope that she might become interested in its promotion. Something more important, however, than the promotion of his father's treatise on Job happened as a result of this journey. While in London, John met an old friend of the family, James Oglethorpe, a man of wealth, interested in organizing a royal colony in America. Called Georgia in honor of the king, the colony was to be a refuge for debtors and Protestants of all kinds. Oglethorpe also had the ambition to spread the Christian faith among the Indians. The Wesley sons hesitated to venture so far away from their widowed mother and wrote to ask her advice. Her brave answer settled their minds. "Had I twenty sons, I should rejoice that they were all so employed, though I should never see them more."

The Moravians and the Storm

It was what John Wesley learned from his fellow travelers during the eight weeks' voyage across the Atlantic that played the most important part in changing the course of his life. Unused to the ocean and from childhood afraid of dying, John found it difficult to be calm during storms. Among the passengers were some Moravians from the Continent. One evening, just as they were in the midst of singing Psalms, a heavy storm broke. It split the mainsail in shreds, water flooded the deck and began pouring down into the ship. Wesley wrote in his diary, "I was vaulted over with the water in a moment, and so stunned I scarce expected to lift my head till the sea should give up her dead." Most of the passengers ran below deck screaming in terror. But the Moravians calmly continued to sing.

Afterwards Wesley asked one of them "Were you not afraid?"

"I thank God, no."

"But were not your women and children afraid?"

Again the answer was "no." Why should they be afraid to die?

From that day on there lay buried in John Wesley's heart a wistful longing for a surer faith, unsatisfied until he found for himself the kind of peace of spirit that his Moravian brethren had in the presence of death.

Failure of the Venture in Georgia

Such a change in John Wesley, however, did not come for a long time. During his stay in Georgia, he remained the faithful and formal minister of the church in Savannah. Neither the Indians nor the colonists felt the need of this religion of ritual and ceremony. Indeed, a certain Indian chief said to Mr. Wesley one day, "Those are Christians in Frederica; those are Christians in Savannah, Christians lie, Christians steal, Christians beat men. Me no Christian."

In addition to this failure John Wesley became involved in a love affair. He had been disciplined to fear the fires of passion lest he might be led to love a woman more than God. His holding back was misunderstood. Finally, because of his lack of tact, a scandal was falsely publicized, and both Charles and John Wesley took ship for England with the weight of failure resting heavily upon them.

John poured out his unhappy soul in his journal: "I went to America to convert the Indians, but O! who shall convert me? who, what is he that will deliver me from this evil heart of unbelief? I have a fair summer religion; I can talk well, nay, and believe myself, while no danger is near; but let death look me in the face and my spirit is troubled. . . . O who will deliver me from this fear of death?"

No one could have been more in earnest than John Wesley. But he felt himself working as a servant in fear of his master, rather than as a happy child of God.

A Moravian Teaches His Don

Back in England, John Wesley resumed his duties as a don at Oxford. Peter Böhler, a Moravian, came to be taught

English, and John Wesley in turn was taught the faith of the Moravians. Luther's gospel of "justification by faith" was Böhler's meat and drink. On the soul's acceptance of the love of God in Christ, all fear of eternal damnation was destroyed. "This philosophy of yours must be purged away, Mr. Wesley," Böhler would say. "Accept the truth in simplicity."

But Wesley had to be clear about the reasonableness of his faith. He began preaching again from a sense of duty, but his gospel continued to be one of alarm rather than a call to peace. He antagonized his hearers. One by one the pulpits of London were closed to him. He began to question whether he should not cease preaching entirely. "By no means," said Peter Böhler.

"But what can I preach?"

"Preach faith till you have it, and then because you have it you will preach faith."

The Great Day of Awakening

Wesley saw the promise, as he wrote in his diary, but it seemed afar off. At last, when thirty-five years old, his great day of release came. It was May 24, 1738, his spiritual birthday. His brother Charles had found the great joy of conversion only a few days before.

Here is the memorable extract from John Wesley's journal.

"In the evening I went very unwillingly to a society in Aldersgate Street where one was reading Luther's preface to the Epistle to the Romans. About a quarter before nine, while he was describing the change which God works in the heart through faith in Christ, I felt my heart strangely warmed. I felt I could trust in Christ, Christ alone for my salvation; and an assurance was given me that he had taken away my sins, even mine, and saved me from the law of sin and death."

After the meeting, John walked over to his brother's room to tell of the experience. Standing in the open door, he hailed his brother with the rapturous words, "I believe!" In their great joy they began to sing.

John Wesley facing the mob at Wednesbury in England's "Black Country" near the Midlands city of Birmingham. (The Bettmann Archive)

For John Wesley, a transformation had taken place, like that which came to St. Paul on the way to Damascus. What days of fasting and prayer had never achieved, the love of God fulfilled in a single moment. With a new life within himself, he had a new enthusiasm that was contagious. The "brand plucked from the burning" now began itself to burn with an intense, but friendly and warming flame.

The Great Revival

For the next fifty-three years, John Wesley traveled the length and breadth of Great Britain, preaching usually several times a day, frequently out of doors, and to audiences that often numbered thousands. He traveled on foot over unfrequented paths, making at times thirty miles a day. He went more often on horseback, covering during his lifetime a quarter of a million miles. He met angry mobs with confidence, he endured exposure to wind and storm without complaint, and he even faced tuberculosis and conquered.

By his side went his fascinating brother Charles, who taught the people how to sing and love it. Up to that time England had known no religious songs except the Psalms put to stately and measured meters. John Wesley translated for them the stirring songs that the Germans sang in Luther's time. And Charles composed literally thousands of new songs of his own—songs that were vibrant with a passionate love of God. Charles put the songs to lilting and rhythmic tunes, some of which were borrowed from the folk ballads of the day and sung to other words in dance halls and on the street.

Over and over again the hills echoed with the full tones of the hearty singing of the crowds. Some of these new songs are still loved and sung in our churches even after two hundred years have passed. "Hark! the herald angels sing," "Love divine, all love excelling," "Jesus, lover of my soul."

The hymns of Charles Wesley were sung all over England. ...A thousand hearts were hungering for love, and here they found what they longed for in full measure, pressed down and running over. . . . The world looked on and wondered. It saw tears washing the faces of the begrimed miners in the King's Wood, Bristol . . . and marvelled. Before, such men had been the terror of all sedate citizens and had marched into Bristol murdering and rioting and looting shops for food. Now like so many lambs they followed the sweet singer, Charles Wesley, to Holy Communion in Temple Church.[1]

John Wesley's Tutelage

John Wesley, however, did not come to this outdoor preaching easily. In the famous "Holy Club" of Oxford had been one George Whitefield, who as a boy had tapped the beer in his widowed mother's barroom. Even earlier than John Wesley, Whitefield found freedom in the love of God, and had turned to preaching out of doors as easily as a duck turns to water. Endowed with qualities money could not buy, being tall and strong of frame, having a marvelous voice and a native ability to make dramatic every thought, it is said, George Whitefield could electrify a crowd of fifty thousand people. Garrick, the most famous dramatic artist of his day, remarked that Whitefield could say the word "Mesopotamia" in such a way as to move an audience to tears.

George Whitefield, therefore, loved to preach in the open fields. "There is no pulpit like a mound," he said. "And no sounding board like Heaven." But John Wesley had been long accustomed to the decorum of a service in a church. He said, "I found it hard to reconcile myself to this strange way of preaching in the fields . . . having been all my life (till very lately) so tenacious of every point relating to decency and order that I should have thought the saving of souls a sin if it had not been done in Church."

But hearing his old friend Whitefield convinced Wesley that he must change his habits. When he yielded and preached

[1] G. Elsie Harrison, *Son to Susanna* (Nashville: Abingdon, 1938), pp. 182-183.

out of doors, Wesley soon learned by experience that he could preach to twice the number of people that he had reached before in the churches. "What marvel the devil does not love field preaching! Neither do I; I love the commodious room, the soft cushion, a handsome pulpit. . . . Field preaching is a cross to me. But I know no other way of preaching the Gospel to every creature."

So John Wesley began preaching on village greens, in churchyards, under trees, during the rain, standing on a chair, a table, or even on his father's tombstone when locked out of the church. As the years went by he trained others to preach also—men without an Oxford education, men on whom the hands of bishops had never been laid to sanctify them for their ministry. Although Wesley was against preaching at the hour of the Sunday morning service, yet after the church service was over, sometimes more people would gather outside to hear these Methodists than came into the church.

The enthusiasm and the extreme emotionalism of these meetings were sharply criticized by the clergy of the day. Bishops wrote books denouncing the "Methodists." Plays were given in the theatres in which the "Methodists" were held up to ridicule. Professional clowns climbed trees and performed their antics before the eyes of the listeners. Drummers marched through the crowds, cow horns were blown in the ears of the preachers. A miller opened the sluiceway of his dam to drown out Mr. Wesley's voice as he preached. In the midst of a meeting, the Wesleys and their assistants were carried in wagons to the house of the justice of the peace. But even in the face of all such opposition, the revival spread.

The Methodist Organization

Along with the tenderness and fire of his enthusiasm, John Wesley was still an efficient minister. He knew that merely preaching to crowds and stirring them up would prove of little lasting worth. He made it a policy not to enter a city or section of the country unless he and his preachers could stay

*John Wesley preaching at his father's grave in the churchyard at
Epworth, on Sunday, June 4, 1735. Lithograph by Currier & Ives.
(The Bettmann Archive)*

long enough to organize small classes or societies, with leaders who would instruct the people and watch over their conduct. Together the class members were to examine their everyday activities to see if they were living in ways worthy of their Savior. Wesley, the revivalist, was still a practical man who believed in discipline. He tells of finding a society whose members were doing an "accursed thing"—well-nigh all bought and sold "uncustomed goods." Considering the low state of morals at that time, such dealing in smuggled goods was probably deemed quite proper by most people, but not so by Wesley. He tells that after he had talked with them they "severally promised to [live in this way] no more." It was not always easy to be a Methodist.

A Preacher of Social Justice

Like Amos of old, Wesley was also a strong preacher of justice and mercy. A few quotations from his sermons will show the social temper of the man's mind. "The more you lay out on your own apparel, the less you will have to clothe the naked, to feed the hungry, to lodge the strangers, to relieve those that are sick and in prison, and to lessen the numberless afflictions to which we are exposed in this vale of tears . . . therefore, every shilling that you needlessly spend on your apparel is, in effect, stolen from God and the poor."

John Wesley was a prolific writer, having published during his long lifetime several hundred books and pamphlets. These achieved a wide circulation, and there is a project planned to collect and republish all of them, a task which is expected to take ten years and result in the production of thirty-five volumes. Through his writing, Wesley earned thousands of pounds, and it is said that he gave away in all at least the equivalent of $125,000. He wrote in his journal that he never spent more than twelve shillings (about four dollars in those days) a week upon himself, although, of course, the purchasing power of money in those days was greater than it is now.

During Wesley's lifetime England was engaging openly in the most insidious forms of the slave trade. Wesley published a treatise giving his *Thoughts Upon Slavery*. There was no mincing of words. "I absolutely deny all slave-holding to be consistent with any degree of even *natural justice*... Captains, slave owners, kidnappers, murderers. . . . Thy hands, thy bed, thy furniture, thy house, thy lands are at present stained with blood. . . . Whether you are a Christian or not, show yourself a man."

Only a week before his death Wesley wrote a letter, his last, to William Wilberforce, the great pioneer in the British anti-slavery movement, saying, "Go on in the name of the Lord and in the power of His might till even American slavery, the vilest that ever saw the sun, shall vanish away before it."

Wesley writes in his journal of visiting the sick. "I found some in their cells underground; others in their garrets, half starved both with cold and hunger, added to weakness and pain. But I found not one unemployed, who was able to crawl about the room. So wickedly devilish is that common objection. 'They are poor only because they are idle.' "

Wesley was also militant against the liquor traffic. In his day it is said that every sixth shop in London sold gin. Passersby might get drunk for a penny—or dead drunk for a twopence.

His Practical Benevolent Projects

Wesley not only preached righteousness, but he also organized societies to carry on many kinds of benevolent enterprises. In the days before hospitals, Wesley organized clinics for the sick. The rise of the modern hospital may rightly be attributed in part to the efforts of the Methodists to give nursing care. John Wesley even wrote a book on medicine. He started schools for the education of poor children. He organized lending societies. He insisted that all members of the Methodist societies, even though themselves poor, should justify their acceptance of God's grace by doing deeds of helpfulness.

The religious revival led by the Wesleys did not achieve the thoroughgoing economic and social reformation the eighteenth century really needed, yet its results should not be discounted as being of no value merely on the grounds that "the pie-in-the-sky" assurance given the downtrodden masses deadened their ambitions to struggle for their rights. In fact, the evangelistic revival did the very opposite. It awakened the ambition of all the neglected poor. It freed, at least in spirit, the captives in the Castle of Giant Despair. It saved them from madness and hate against their oppressors.

As a result England was spared the horrors of a revolution such as devastated France, and the slower but more effective process of change without the use of armed forces was made possible. "An ounce of love is worth more than a pound of compassion," said John Wesley.

The Methodists

The spirit of the first Methodists was contagious. In Wesley's time one of the Anglican vicars, when preaching against these Methodists, said: "There is sprung up amongst us a new religion called Methodism; it is like the plague. They that have it infect whole families." If but two or three Methodists were in a town it was always possible to form a Society, and some lay preacher was soon found who could come to them and help to spread the gospel. John Wesley's societies were like an army of lay missionaries, always recruiting others. When Wesley died at the ripe age of eighty-eight, the Methodists in Great Britain numbered one hundred thousand strong. Now after a century and a half, Methodists are found in most countries of the world and their numbers have reached a grand total of well over 12 million in the United States alone.

Separation from the Church of England

"John Wesley was great enough to be outrageously inconsistent. He was devoted to the Church of England, and also at the same time broke some of her most honored and sacred rites."[2]

Even to the day of his death, he remained a loyal minister of the Church of England. The members of his societies might belong to any sect they wished—Presbyterian, Baptist, Quaker, Moravian, or even to no church at all. Wesley meant that they should partake of the Lord's Supper and worship on Sundays in the churches of their own choosing. But when Anglican clergy began to refuse the right of Communion to Methodists, and when the doors of more and more churches began to be closed to him and to his lay preachers, then a break finally became inevitable. The formation of a separate Church, however, did not come until after Wesley's death.

The Pioneer Genius of the Methodists

Both the message and the organization of the Methodists made them peculiarly fitted to follow the westward migration in America that advanced so rapidly during the first few decades of the nineteenth century. It required a religious body that knew how to move quickly if churches were to be established in these new settlements before the pioneers forgot all about religion.

The gospel the Methodist circuit riders preached was a simple one of God's free love and man's free will to accept or reject that love. The message fitted well the growing belief in equality and democracy. It granted the pioneers the right to believe that they could be masters of their own destinies.

The type of organization begun in England also lent itself to these same pioneering conditions. Lay preachers, without formal education or special training, but filled with zeal

[2] W. Bardsley Brash, *Methodism* (New York: Doubleday, Doran, 1928), p. 167.

and prepared to meet hardships, were quickly recruited. They rode on horseback from settlement to settlement even to points farthest out.

In America these circuit-riding preachers were ready to preach every day of the week in any sort of place, indoors or out. They shared without complaint in the labor and deprivations of the log-cabin settlements. If but two or three converts were made, these were gathered into a class and a leader appointed. They were enjoined to meet once a week "to confess their faults one to another and to pray for one another." In the meantime the "circuit rider" rode off to another settlement to gather another class of converts. Some of these preachers were in charge of circuits so large that it took them a month or more to go the rounds even though they preached in a different place every day of the week except Monday.

Sometimes an especially gifted person was discovered in the leader of a class. He was encouraged to develop his leadership. Later on some qualified ordained minister would visit the settlement and if this young leader proved worthy of the task, he would be given a license first to exhort and later to preach. Thus, although he continued to earn his own living as before he would preach to his society on Sundays. Soon a log meetinghouse would go up, and a church organization would be started. In this way the Methodists enlisted hundreds of local and lay preachers, who were given a little instruction from time to time by their supervisors, yet whose main qualifications were their personal character and their zeal for the cause.

The Methodist Organization in the United States

"John Wesley must be ranked with Ignatius Loyola and William Booth as the greatest organizers in Christian history."[3] Each Methodist class was looked after by a leader responsible for seeing that members attended the weekly meeting and that

[3] Paul Hutchinson, *Men Who Made the Churches* (Nashville: Cokesbury Press, 1930), p. 175.

in their daily lives they lived according to the rules prescribed by Wesley. The classes in a given town united and formed a society. Some of the societies had their own lay or ordained preachers, but most of them were ministered to by itinerant preachers who traveled and preached to a whole circuit of societies.

In the United States the class meetings have now been rather generally discarded. A district superintendent travels about to all the churches in his district regularly and guides the ministers and officers in making their policies. A group of such districts is called an Annual Conference. Once a year ministerial and lay delegates from all the churches within the conference meet under the presidency of a bishop. At these Annual Conferences, the ministers receive their appointments from the bishop and his "cabinet" of district superintendents.

Above the district superintendents are the members of the Council of Bishops. The bishops are elected for life by the Jurisdictional Conferences which are set up to administer the geographical areas of the church, though, except for such elections, these conferences have no other important duties. One of the conferences (the so-called Central Jurisdictional Conference) consists of Negro churches not otherwise assigned. Once in four years representatives, ministerial and lay, from all the Conferences in the world-wide connections of the Methodist Church meet for a month in what is called the General Conference. This body has full authority to revise the Discipline of the church or to rule on all matters of concern to the whole church. In the four years interim between the meetings of the General Conference, the Council of Bishops has large powers. Individually each bishop has the final word regarding the placing of every minister in the area under his jurisdiction.

The Methodist Discipline

During his lifetime John Wesley worked out in detail many rules for the guidance of the conduct of ministers and all members of the societies. These rules form the Methodist

Discipline. Although Wesley's rules have been revised from time to time, they are still a powerful factor in the control of the life of Methodist churches. They resembled in certain regards the rules for a monastic order. He was against all forms of luxurious living. He decreed against theatergoing, dancing and card playing. He disapproved of smoking and all "dram-drinking." Although in some Methodist conferences, a minister may now be ordained without making a promise not to smoke, the question will be put to him since a rule about smoking by ministers is contained in the Discipline.

Until 1900, Methodist ministers were allowed to serve a given parish for only a few years. Originally the term was one year or even less, but now a bishop may appoint a pastor without any time limit if his congregation ask for him and he wishes to remain.

This closely knit organization has certain advantages. No Methodist minister once ordained and admitted to conference need be without a "charge" unless for illness or after he is retired for age or other cause. District superintendents know all their ministers. Every pastor submits regular reports of his work. If the standards set by the Discipline are not met, or if the churches do not carry their allotted shares of the general church expenses and benevolences, the pastor is held responsible. Although the organization may lack much of being completely democratic, it has been highly effective in building up a strong church.

> The arbitrary Methodist system . . . was greatly tempered by the fact that the early bishops moved about the country, from north to south, from east to west; stayed in the rude cabins on the frontier, preached at camp-meetings and received the same salary as the humblest circuit rider.[4]

Divisions in the Methodist Societies

Neither Methodists nor their leaders in America have always been able to agree, and as a result there are now

[4] Sweet, *The Story of Religions in America* (New York, 1930), pp. 319-320.

Methodists of a variety of kinds. The most important split occurred over the matter of slavery. Wesley had been unrelenting
in his condemnation of slavery, and in the United States the
Northern churches, for the most part, were loyal to his attitude. But in the South the problem became very complicated.
The climax came when one of the bishops in the South married into a slaveholding family. The law of his state prohibited
emancipation. The Northern churches refused to accept him
as a bishop, so the Southern churches withdrew from the
parent church.

Earlier another group began to fight for more democracy
in church government. They opposed the rule of bishops.
They also insisted on lay representation in the Annual and
General Conferences. These withdrew in 1830 and formed
the Methodist Protestant Church.

About a century later, in 1939, these three divisions
reunited in one church now called simply Methodist, a great
organization with a membership within the United States of
almost 10 million people. Despite this merger there are still a
number of independent Methodist bodies, some with names
that stir the imagination, such as the Lumber River Annual
Conference of the Holiness Methodist Church. This is a very
small sect, with only seven churches and 360 members, but
others are of some size: the Wesleyan Methodist Church of
America and the Free Methodist Church of North America
have a membership of about 44,000 and 56,000, respectively;
they tend to be rural and rather strict.

Although many Negro churches and several Negro Annual Conferences belong in this united or Methodist church
proper, and their Negro bishops to the Council of Bishops, yet
a majority of Negro Methodist churches in America still maintain a separate denominational existence and have their own
organizations. The largest of these is the African Methodist
Episcopal Church, with almost 6,000 congregations and a
membership of well over a million, but the African Methodist
Episcopal Zion church is not very far behind with its almost
800,000 members. The Christian Methodist Episcopal Church
also claims some 400,000; thus the total of Negro Methodists
exceeds 2½ million.

Benevolent and Missionary Enterprises

In Wesley's day the Methodists were not only interested in saving people for a happy life throughout eternity, they were also concerned with better living conditions in this present vale of tears. Like their founder, Methodists still tend to be practical in their good works. They have been leaders in many benevolent enterprises. The starting of the Goodwill Industries in the Morgan Memorial Methodist Church in Boston in 1907 is a good example. A local project begun to help the aged and handicapped and unemployable to find work has grown into a national enterprise having headquarters in many cities. Training is given in many trades and more than 30,000 handicapped and disabled people are thus helped annually. The total daily labor force now numbers more than 13,000 and the annual payroll almost $20 million.

Hospitals and homes for the aged and orphans have also been established in many communities, at home and abroad. There are more than 200 such institutions in the United States alone, with some 35,000 full-time workers. Some Methodist hospitals have a world-wide reputation, such as the New England Deaconess Hospital in Boston.

The Methodists have also continued the tradition, started by John Wesley, of book publishing. Their Methodist Publishing House is the largest of the Protestant book concerns.

In the fight against the evils of the liquor traffic, the Methodists were in the vanguard. The passing of the Eighteenth Amendment was due in no small measure to the propaganda and sacrifice of Methodist enthusiasts.

Since the Methodists have done so much of their work in pioneer regions and among people of relatively small or ordinary financial means, they early realized that if their young men and women were to have an education, the church must establish colleges where an education might be gained at small expense. Consequently, the Methodist have planted their denominational schools in almost every state of the Union. Some of these pioneer colleges have since become large universities of the highest rank, and are no longer wholly controlled by the Methodists. Northwestern, Vanderbilt, University of Southern California, Ohio Wesleyan, Wesleyan in Connecticut, Duke University, Syracuse University, De Pauw in Indiana and Boston University speak for themselves.

The foreign missionary work of the Methodists has been outstanding in scope and in outlay of money. Methodist churches, affiliated with American Methodism, are scattered widely over the world in many mission lands. Membership in such churches outside the United States is probably over a half a million.

Although there have been wealthy people in Methodist churches as well as elsewhere, the example of John Wesley is always with them. Having earned thousands of pounds through his writings, he might well have died a wealthy man. Instead he died poor, not leaving after debts were paid, even as much as ten pounds. Thus he extracted "the poison from riches" and turned them into a powerful means for building the Kingdom of God on earth.

11. Hosea Ballou
1771-1852

If the servants of Christ here on earth desire the increase of holiness, and the decrease of sin, which would be most agreeable to
such a desire: the belief that the greatest part of mankind will grow
more and more sinful to all eternity, or, to believe that sin will
continually decrease and righteousness increase, until the former
is wholly destroyed, and the latter becomes universal?

—HOSEA BALLOU, *Treatise*
on the Atonement

God Does Not Punish Eternally

A Mother's Distress

On a September day in 1770, in a small village on the
New Jersey coast a little south of Sandy Hook, Mr. John Murray and his fisherman host knocked at the door of a farmer's
home. On being welcomed, they saw a woman sitting in a
rocking chair, weeping over a babe asleep in her arms. "Sup-
posing that her tears flowed from some domestic distress or
pecuniary embarrassment," Mr. Murray endeavored to con-
sole her by observing that "the world was very wide, and that
God was an all-sufficient Father."

"Alas! sir," she replied, "I never, in the whole course of
my life, experienced a moment's anxiety from the dread of my
children or myself suffering the want of either food or rai-
ment. No, sir, my fears are that they will be sufferers, through
the wasteless ages of eternity, in that state of torment from

A rare portrait of Hosea Ballou at the age of thirty-six. (Univer-salist Historical Library)

whence there is no reprieve: and that they will continually execrate their parents as the wretched instruments of bringing them into being. I have eight children, sir; and can I be so arrogant as to believe that all these children are elected to everlasting life?"

"But, my dear lady, you have reason to believe that they will all be saved, whether they be elected or not, because Christ Jesus is the Savior of all men."

This, however, did not satisfy the mother. Had not God elected some to eternal happiness and others to eternal damnation? Mr. Murray picked up the Bible on her table and expounded to her from the Scripture that God's love included all, that by the death of Jesus all the world had been saved. There was no one who would be eternally damned in hell. All who are born are God's children and he would not desert them.

Again and again the mother took the Bible up into her own hands and read with her own eyes the words that Mr. Murray quoted. Slowly the strained lines on her face relaxed. At last she burst into tears of joy, and hugged her babe to her breast. "Blessed, blessed God, they are not mine; they are thine, O Almighty Father; and thou wilt not be regardless of thine own!"[1]

Unthinkable as such an episode seems to most of us today, it is a startling reminder of how seriously Calvin's doctrine of election had taken hold of the consciousness of Christian people in the eighteenth century.

John Murray in England

Only a short while before this episode John Murray had come ashore from a sloop caught on a sandbar—another refugee from religious prejudice and ostracism. Naturally a vivacious and temperamental child, he had been reared in a godly English home by a strict and pious disciplinarian of the Calvinistic faith. John Murray had struggled with serious persistence to keep his religion alive; yet he shifted from time to time

[1] *The Life of Rev. John Murray . . . Written by Himself* (Boston, 1870), p. 220.

between a life of "mirth and frolic" to a life of exacting devotions and churchgoing. Although his father never allowed him the opportunity for an education, John had access to an unusual library. He became a popular leader in the Methodist classes promoted by John Wesley.

It was not until John Murray was a grown man and married, however, that he discovered a religious faith that relaxed his spirit from morbid fears. It was a Rev. Mr. Relly who freed him by convincing him that the doctrine of eternal damnation for an elected number of sinners was not based on the teachings of Christ. This free-lance minister had been ostracized by the clergy in the other churches and his character had been falsely maligned. Yet when Mr. and Mrs. Murray finally screwed up their courage to go to hear the man for themselves, they went away feeling that they had listened to "the first consistent sermon they had ever heard."

But to deny the doctrine of eternal damnation for all unbelievers was to destroy the whole plan of salvation, so their Presbyterian friends all said. Without the fear of hell, there would be no motive for living a good life. The prejudice and slander to which Mr. Murray was subjected is difficult today to understand. Almost every friend he had disowned him. To add to his loneliness his first child died, and his wife became ill with a lingering but fatal disease.

Discouraged and isolated from his friends, he finally decided to flee to America, hoping to find here a quiet place where he might live a simple life and might never again teach or preach or become a public figure who would be hurt by slander.

The Unexpected Summons to Preach

A strange reversal of his expectations came about without his wishing, for John Murray could not hide his light under a bushel. Shipwrecked in a sloop off the coast of New Jersey, with a small crew of men and without provisions, he went ashore in search of fish. Instead he found a friend and a church waiting for his ministry.

Mr. Potter, his host, was an illiterate though successful fisherman who lived alone. "Come," said he, "I've been expecting you for a long time."

Mr. Murray was puzzled. How could he have been expecting him?

Mr. Potter had built a small church near his house. Whenever he could find a minister to preach, the church was opened and all the people living in the neighborhood around were summoned. But Mr. Potter had not been satisfied with the preachers who had come. "The preachers we have heard are perpetually contradicting themselves . . .," he explained. "When the house was finished I received applications from the Baptists and I told them, if they could make it appear that God Almighty was a Baptist, the building should be theirs at once. The Quakers and the Presbyterians also tried. No, said I. As I firmly believe that all mankind are equally dear to Almighty God, they shall all be equally welcome to preach in this house which I have built. My neighbors assured me that I never should see a preacher whose sentiments corresponded with my own. My constant reply has been, 'He will by and by make his appearance. The moment I beheld your vessel on shore, it seemed as if a voice sounded in my ears, 'There, Potter, in that vessel is the preacher you have been so long expecting.' "

Mr. Murray was terrified. Like Jonah he had tried to run away, but God had followed him. John Murray had to obey the voice. Two days afterwards he preached a Universalist gospel to nearly seven hundred curious people, who crowded into the little church. So once again John Murray became a public servant who had to stand out in front of the rank and file and take the slanderous darts from those who opposed him.[2]

The Growth of a New Movement

News spread of the young and vivacious minister from England. Invitations came for him to preach in New York

[2] *Ibid.*, pp. 196-212.

City, in Philadelphia, in New Jersey and later on in New England. A church in Gloucester asked him to be its pastor and by a very simple ceremony he was ordained as a minister of the gospel. Later on he was called to be minister of a church in Boston.

Wherever he went, John Murray made both friends and enemies. His followers, too, found themselves the butt of ridicule and the objects of scurrilous accusations. In Boston the crowds became most vociferous in their hostility. One evening the audience found themselves deluged with buckets of water thrown in upon them, as well as with rotten eggs. On another occasion, Mr. Murray ascended the pulpit only to find it had been sprinkled with foul smelling asafoetida, and later stones were thrown at him through the windows. One large stone which came near to hitting Mr. Murray, he picked up and waved in view of all his audience saying: "This argument is *solid,* and *weighty,* but it is neither *rational,* nor *convincing.*"[3]

Although John Murray was the most famous pioneer of Universalism in America, other preachers before him in America had been boldly denouncing the Calvinist doctrine of eternal misery in hell. There were others also who secretly sympathized with the more hopeful belief in universal salvation, yet because of the scornful popular prejudice against the idea they held their peace.

Like other independent thinkers before him, John Murray had no desire to organize a separate denomination, but those who followed his leadership were obliged by their opponents to establish themselves in separate churches. Fifteen years after he landed on the New Jersey shore a national convention of Universalists was held in Oxford, Massachusetts.

A Greater Than Murray Appeared

Attending the national Universalist Convention in 1791 was a twenty-year-old young man who had just been excommunicated from the Baptist Church, of which his father had

[3] *Ibid.,* p. 306.

long been the pastor. Ten years before in a small village in New Hampshire, Hosea Ballou had first heard this new doctrine of universal salvation from a preacher in a neighboring town. Having been thoroughly trained in Calvinistic teaching, the boy was as antagonistic toward this denial of the faith as were all the rest of the villagers. It seemed a horrifying and dangerous heresy. It was said that those who accepted the teaching would no longer have any motive for being good. They would lie, cheat, indulge in dissipation, wallow in sin of every kind, not hesitating even to take the lives of their neighbors or to commit suicide. These were the very words Hosea Ballou heard over and over. He began to feel uneasy. To be condemned to eternal suffering through no fault of one's own seemed unjust. He found himself wishing that all people might attain happiness. Could it be a sin for him to wish for this? Did not God also really care for all his creatures?

Hosea Ballou was not one to rush after a new idea, nor was he one who would close his mind and refuse to think his way through a question when once it was raised in his mind. There were, however, few with whom the boy could talk. He found no book on the subject. Ballou's one guide was the Bible. He began studying this with great diligence, having this one question continually on his mind. It was not until he was twenty that he openly made his decision, and the result was that his Church excommunicated him.

As this young man sat among the ministers in convention in Oxford, Massachusetts, he was dreaming wistfully of the day when he, too, might become a minister. John Murray and the other older men encouraged Hosea Ballou; but little did they dream that by the time he was their age, this young New Hampshire farmer would be carrying the Universalist banner to thousands of people all over New England, New York and as far west as Ohio.

Hosea Ballou—the Architect of Universalism

John Murray was like an enthusiastic scout who discovers a thrilling site for a new building. Hosea Ballou was the

Portrait of John Murray. (Universalist Historical Library)

architect whose genius created plans for a noble structure on sound foundations. With scarcely more than a year's regular schooling in his life, Hosea Ballou learned for himself how to use his brilliant logical mind. He could look squarely at an old idea and think originally on it until he had created a better one to take its place. He had the ability also to state his reasons in clear, striking terms so that people could understand and were challenged. No Unitarian of his day denounced the doctrine of the Trinity with more effectiveness than did Ballou; and he did it twenty years before Channing preached his famous Baltimore sermon. It was a sore disappointment to Ballou that so few Unitarians of that time could break loose also from the old belief in everlasting punishment for part of mankind.

While John Murray had preached a cheerful but naive gospel of universal salvation, Hosea Ballou thought through the meaning of punishment and salvation. His psychological insight into the therapeutic value of love in contrast to condemnation was far in advance of his generation. "God saves men to purify them," he said one day to a woman about to mop her floor. "That's what salvation is designed for. God does not require men to be pure in order that he may save them."

Hosea Ballou was not dogmatic in denying all punishment in the life after death, but he asserted that whatever there was, it would be similar in kind and degree to the punishment that results from sin in this present life. He said:

Men are now as happy as they are righteous, and they are as miserable as they are sinful; therefore, to my understanding, if all men are to be rewarded in the future world according to their works in this, they will be just as happy and just as miserable as they are in this world.[4]

He decried also a superficial thought of salvation, saying: "No man understandingly wants salvation any further than he wants holiness." Ballou's own sympathies were too wide for

[4] Thomas Whittemore, *Life of Rev. Hosea Ballou* (Boston, 1854) , II, 213.

him to accept with satisfaction the thought of the ultimate division of humanity into two separate groups, one in bliss and the other in agony. "I do not conceive," he said, "that part of humanity can be made perfectly happy while the rest is in misery."

Hosea Ballou was a strong preacher. He traveled widely over the eastern United States organizing Universalist churches. Many of his sermons were printed and given a wide circulation. His most noted book was a *Treatise on the Atonement.*

The Universalist Magazine

For a number of years, Hosea Ballou was editor of the first *Universalist Magazine.* In the initial issue he wrote that the object of the paper was to promote "the growth of truth, religion and morality." "Whatever correspondents might contribute to aid in these objects would be gratefully received; nor would the editor exclude articles advocating doctrines opposite to his own, if written in a proper spirit, provided he should retain the liberty of pointing out any errors that seemed to be of a dangerous tendency." He answered the objections that some might raise to having the paper open to writers of all sects by pointing out that this very feature would make the magazine universalist. Consequently, the paper became for many years a kind of forum in which the lively theological issues of the day were discussed.

The glory of both John Murray and Hosea Ballou is that they helped to tear down a high and long-standing wall that had confined men to a partial view of humanity and of humanity's God. In so doing they made possible a broadening of the horizons of religious thought. These men were reaching after a universal instead of a partial God. Theirs was a God for all rather than a God who chose to show his love only to the elect, one whose love shines both "on the evil and the good," both in this world and on in the world to come. Such a broadening insight prepared the way for the possible development of a "religion for greatness."[5] With this ennobling heritage, modern Universalists may lead the way toward even richer insights, toward the achieving of a religion universal in more aspects than the founders of the church could imagine. Our "one world" sorely needs such leaders.

The Universalists

Their Bond of Union and the Liberty Clause

At the meeting of the Universalist General Convention (since called the Universalist Church of America) held in Washington in 1935, the following Bond of Fellowship and Statement of Faith was voted into the constitution of the Church.

The bond of fellowship in this Convention shall be a common purpose to do the will of God as Jesus revealed it and to cooperate in establishing the Kingdom for which he lived and died.

To that end we avow our faith in God as Eternal and All-Conquering Love, in the spiritual leadership of Jesus, in the supreme worth of every human personality, in the authority of truth known or to be known, and in the power of men of good will and sacrificial spirit to overcome evil and progressively establish the kingdom of God. Neither this nor any other statement shall be imposed as a creedal test, provided that the faith thus indicated be professed.[6]

The final sentence in this avowal is called "the Liberty Clause" and the Universalists lay great emphasis upon it. They explain that it is merely an agreement in "the essential spirit" of the statement that concerns them. All ministers and all

[5] Clarence R. Skinner, *A Religion for Greatness* (Murray Press, 1945).
[6] Frederic W. Perkins, *Beliefs Commonly Held Among Us* (Boston, 1945).

members of the church should feel free "to state the faith in the manner that shall seem to them right."

John Murray and Hosea Ballou would have stated their faith in different terms, yet they would, if they knew, feel the bond of union in the universality of their outlooks and in their common spirit of confidence in humanity.

"Not a Creed but a Hymn of Fellowship"

Most creeds have been formulated to serve as tests by means of which heretics would be kept outside the Church. This Universalist avowal of a common faith was put into words in order "to rally believers rather than to repel heretics." "It is not a password but a hymn of fellowship, and its rallying power is not so much in the words of the song as in the spirit it sings."[7] The door is as wide open as faith in "the authority of truth, known or to be known"; and the call is to a united effort to establish the kingdom of God in this present world.

The Numbers of Universalists

Like the Unitarians, the Universalists (prior to merger of the two denominations) comprised a relatively small group. They had about 387 churches and 70,000 members in 1960. The influence of a Church, however, should not be measured in numbers, but rather by the quality and significance of the contribution it makes. Great philanthropists have been within the Universalist fellowship. Among these have been Thomas Mott Osborne, pioneer in prison reform, and Clara Barton, founder of the American Red Cross. Owen D. Young, a lawyer and industrial executive, was widely known for his services to education and government, and for his gifts to colleges and to his denomination. The Universalist women have long maintained a summer camp for diabetic children at Clara Barton's

[7] *Ibid.*

birthplace in North Oxford, Massachusetts. From the beginning, the Universalists were vigorous in their opposition to
slavery.

Universalist influence has also been exerted through
their colleges, of which they now have two, St. Lawrence University in Canton, New York, and Tufts University at Med-
ford, Massachusetts.

American Unitarians and Universalists Become One Church

Despite traditional differences in emphasis, the Unitarians tending to stress the intellectual approach and appeal
to reason in support of religious truths, while the Universalists
have insisted on the importance of "love" as the heart of religion, the two groups have long realized that they had much
in common. There has been agitation in each of the denominations for merger with the other for many years. Indeed, the
first overtures for union date to the early nineteenth century.
But for a long time nothing came of such movements, and
it was not until 1959, when both groups held simultaneous
meetings in Syracuse, New York, that each voted approval of
union with the other.

This was confirmed by a large majority of the individual
churches the following year, and the merger finally became a
fact in May 1960, when both denominations held their last
meetings in Boston as separate denominations, and in May
1961, when the organizational meeting of the new denomination was held in the same city. The new denomination is
known as the Unitarian Universalist Association and, like its
parent organizations, maintains headquarters in Boston. It
consists of just over 800 churches in the United States and
Canada, together with several hundred Fellowships. The latter
are lay societies destined to become churches when they are
large enough for self-support. The combined membership of
this Association is about 180,000 adults.

Although organic union has only just been realized, cooperation of the two churches has been going on for many years. Both have long openly avowed their desire to be churches of a free spirit. Since the National Council of Churches of Christ in America and the World Council of Churches have both thought it their duty to make the basis of membership in their organizations a creedal statement, Unitarians and Universalists have been excluded from participation as members.

The Council of Liberal Churches (Universalist-Unitarian), Inc., was created in 1954 in the hope that many liberal, non-creedal groups might join in a larger common effort. This did not happen, and the Council of Liberal Churches was dissolved in 1961.

The preparation and use of a hymnbook, *Hymns of the Spirit,* helped develop a common bond between the two denominations. In the judgment of some, this was the most original collection of hymns made in the United States during the last century. Hymns with outworn theology have been replaced by those expressive of modern man's religious feeling.

The two churches have also cooperated in the preparation and use of new books for their church schools. Indeed, under the Council of Liberal Churches, the educational departments of the two denominations had been organically united since 1955. The educational philosophy has been opposed to indoctrination, and has worked toward the development of independent and creative religious living and thinking. The young people of the two denominations have been completely merged in what is now called Liberal Religious Youth since 1953.

There are, of course, many individual churches and individual Christians of other denominations who are also thinking and acting with as much liberty and vitality as members of the new denomination. Yet the tendency seems to be toward greater orthodoxy and religious rigidity. Unitarians and Universalists value religious freedom, and are convinced that only through it can man's greatest potential be achieved.

12. *Thomas Campbell 1763-1854*
Alexander Campbell 1788-1866

Where the Scriptures speak, we speak; where the Scriptures are
silent, we are silent.

—THOMAS CAMPBELL

Nothing is essential to the conversion of the world but the union
and cooperation of Christians.

Nothing is essential to the union of Christians but the Apostles'
teaching or testimony.

—ALEXANDER CAMPBELL

"The Campbells"

A Family Matter

The road was dusty—indeed, it was little more than a
trail. But it did not discourage Thomas Campbell who was
riding along it in a wagon one fall day in 1809. He was on his
way from his parish in western Pennsylvania to meet his
family, who had just arrived from Scotland. Campbell had
traveled many miles on roads far worse than this, and besides,
he had many other things to think about. It had been two
years since he had left his home and the academy where he had
taught in Rich Hill, near Armagh, Ireland, for the great New
World across the sea. Now he was on his way to meet his wife
and children. They had disembarked in New York, had taken
the stage coach to Philadelphia, and then had set out by wagon
on their own. Anywhere now they might meet.

So the horse continued her trot, and Campbell continued his thinking. Mails were slow, and only reached the little town where he had been living after long delays. What would his eldest son Alexander be like? And the younger children? Two years may make a lot of difference when children are growing up.

The Reunion

Suddenly Campbell was all attention. He thought he heard voices in the distance, but there was still a hill ahead and nothing could be seen. No doubt it was just another party of travelers like himself, but to pass anyone at all on that lonely road was an event. So he whipped up his horse, and soon he saw, over the brow of the hill, a wagon rather heavily loaded. There was baggage in it, and several children. Walking beside the vehicle were a young man and an older woman. Now the voices could be distinctly heard, and they had a familiar sound.

Almost at the same time he heard a shout: "It's Father! It's Father!" And the children came running up to greet him, while the young man and his mother jumped into the wagon and made what speed they could in the heavily loaded vehicle. After the first enthusiastic welcome was over, the children distributed themselves in the two wagons and the young man took his seat beside his father.

Shipwreck, an Ocean Voyage and Decision

There was much to talk about. Young Campbell had been still a schoolboy when his father bade the family farewell in 1807. Now he was a young man, almost ready to begin training for a lifework.

But first there was the just completed voyage for the boy to tell his father about. It had been exciting, as all such trips across the Atlantic were in the days of sailing ships. Yet it had been nothing like the first attempt, a year earlier, of the Campbell family to get across that great ocean. For then they were shipwrecked just off the coast of west Scotland, and for a time it looked as if the ship might break up before rescue arrived. God had seemed very near in that trying time, and a life spent doing his work had come to seem the most rewarding a young man could choose. To help bring together the separated and often bitterly competing churches of Christendom had come to be his consuming ambition. His father's reminder that it would mean hard and unremunerative work only met with the answer: "Paul made his living as a tentmaker. I could labor with my hands, too, or perhaps I could teach."

But both teaching and the ministry would require an education. This would cost money, and the elder Campbell had little of it, for he was himself a minister in a little country parish. Still, although college might be out of the question, the father might teach the son that thorough knowledge of the Bible a minister required, and the Hebrew and Greek needed to translate it in its original tongues, without which one could often not get its real meaning. And in return, the son was more than willing to be of all the help he could in his father's parish.

A Scottish Education

So the two continued to talk. The boy told of his struggles to keep the family together since his father's departure, and of the year of study at the University of Glasgow. There he had worked very hard, rising at four o'clock, going to his first class at six, and having no time for breakfast until ten. Besides his regular college work he had been able to find time for a great deal of general reading. The year had ended all too soon.

Too Many Churches

The elder Campbell had much to tell, too. The ocean voyage and the rugged life in the New World had benefited his health, as the doctors told him it might do. The town of

Washington, Pennsylvania, in which he settled was small but the people were good to him. Most of the inhabitants of that part of the state were Quakers or Lutherans, but there were Presbyterians, Reformed Churchmen, Baptists and Methodists, and not infrequently several varieties of each. Indeed there were far too many kinds of churches, and each believed itself the only true one. Worse than that, there was often quarreling and un-Christlike rivalry.

The Goal: Christian Unity

For the Campbells this day of reunion was a day of celebration, but it was also a historic day for America, for these two men were to play a major part in founding one of the great Protestant religious bodies. Oddly enough, this was what both wanted least of all. Even today "Disciples," as their followers are usually called, much prefer to think of themselves as a movement toward human brotherhood and not as a denomination. The Campbells had dedicated their lives to the cause of making the Protestant Church unite. But they did a great deal for Protestantism even though they could not achieve their great ambition, and the emphasis they put on Christian unity is a leaven still at work.

In recent years some very important mergers have occurred among the churches. Though the great majority of denominations remain distinct, the feeling among them is much better than it was a century ago. Few of them any longer think of themselves as God's sole elect.

Alexander Chooses the Ministry

As the Campbells talked, father and son were surprised to find on how many things they felt alike. The elder man had already been urging more Christian unity, and had been censured by his presbytery for inviting all members of his congregation to share in the Communion service, regardless of what sect they might be. The presbytery had taken this stand, despite the fact that there were no other churches in the neighborhood which non-Presbyterians might have attended.

Alexander had made up his mind on the matter when he noticed that only those whose membership in a Presbyterian church was attested by a little metal token were permitted to take Communion in his home church in Glasgow. When he realized that this meant the exclusion of all other Christians, he had thrown the token back into the collection plate.

The years that followed seemed all too short to both father and son. Alexander spent them taking a rigid course of study laid out by his father. The major part of it was devoted to the Bible. He read it with minute care, and learned to translate it from the original Greek and Hebrew versions. Different passages were compared with painstaking diligence. There was also much church history, and some of the classics of literature. He became known in later life for the breadth of his knowledge on many subjects.

Thomas Campbell Expelled From the Presbytery

Thomas Campbell had already been compelled to leave the presbytery, after being found guilty of administering the Lord's Supper with "unbecoming laxity" and expressing sentiments "very different from sentiments held and professed by the (Presbyterian) church." During this time the father continued to preach, usually in farmhouses or even barns, wherever he happened to be, and it was not long before his followers organized a religious society which they called the "Christian Association of Washington" to avoid any suggestion of denominationalism. This was to be, according to the famous "Declaration and Address" formulated at the same time by Thomas Campbell, an association "free from all mixture of human opinions and inventions of men," which "by no means considers itself a church," and which would only "practice that simple original form of christianity, expressly exhibited upon the sacred page." Two years later, however, the Christian Association organized itself as a Church and in 1813 joined the Redstone Baptist Association—thus becoming denominational after all. Thomas Campbell became an "elder" of the church; Alexander, who at twenty-two was now ready to be a minister himself, was licensed to preach in its pulpit, although, like his father, he also often spoke in farmhouses and barns. It was not long before the younger man was also widely known for his able and fearless utterances.

Alexander Campbell Marries

About this time, too, he met a very attractive young girl of eighteen with whom he promptly fell in love, and they were married on March 12, 1811. They had much in common, for both were intelligent and well educated for the time, and sixteen years of happiness followed. For a wedding present (and also to dissuade his somewhat venturesome son-in-law from leading a party to Ohio to form a religious colony) the bride's father gave the couple his large farm, and this solved the problem of a livelihood. The house became the Campbell homestead, and furnished room for a study and later even a post-office, from which his *Christian Baptist* and other publications could be mailed. Nearby was a little stream which Campbell liked to call "the beautiful flowing Buffalo" and which also served to premoisten the paper on which his tracts were printed; a small building on its banks housed the printing press.

Accused of Heresy

But other matters now claimed the attention of the Campbells, father and son. Study of the Bible had convinced them that baptism by immersion was the only proper way, and so they and their congregation were baptized in a neighboring river; previous baptism by sprinkling no longer seemed valid.

It was then that they applied for admission to the local Redstone Baptist Association, and were accepted.

Not long afterward, however, Alexander was asked to preach a sermon at the annual meeting of the Association and soon found himself accused of heresy by certain older ministers because he had suggested that the teachings of Christ had made certain Old Testament laws out of date. Acquittal followed, but his enemies continued to press the charge each year, and so he eventually withdrew.

A New Church Founded:
Disciples of Christ

Now it was that the crucial question came up. The Campbells had won many followers in Pennsylvania, Kentucky, Ohio and Virginia, and yet no existing denomination would receive them. So, very reluctantly, it was decided to found a new religious society. This, they hoped, would be the beginning not of a new denomination, but rather of an organization patterned on the original or apostolic Church founded by Christ himself. It was to be based only on New Testament teachings, and dedicated to the cause of Christian unity. To carry out this idea, the name "Disciples of Christ" was chosen. By some it was and is still known as the "Christian Church," but this name is shared with several smaller sects.

The Christians

One of these sects was largely due to the reforming work of an itinerant Kentucky preacher named Barton W. Stone, to whom the Disciples also owe much. He had previously been a Presbyterian, but he was of an independent turn of mind and even when ordained into the Presbyterian ministry would only agree to accept the Westminster Confession "as far as I see it consistent with the word of God." Later he and a small group

The meetinghouse (restoration) in Cane Ridge, Kentucky. (Disciples of Christ Historical Society)

of other like-minded men led a group of churches known as the "Springfield Presbytery" out of the Presbyterian fold, after writing a somewhat whimsical list of articles of dissolution which they called "The Last Will and Testament of the Springfield Presbytery." A portion of this remarkable document[1] is worth quoting:

> The Presbytery of Springfield, sitting at Cane-ridge, in the County of Bourbon, being, through a gracious Providence, in more than ordinary bodily health, growing in strength and size daily; and in perfect soundness and composure of mind; and knowing that it is appointed for all delegated bodies once to die; and considering that the life of every such body is very uncertain, do make and ordain this our last Will and Testament, in manner and form following, viz.:
>
> *Imprimis.* We *will,* that this body die, be dissolved, and sink into union with the Body of Christ at large, for there is but one Body, and one Spirit. . . .
>
> *Item.* We *will,* that our powers of making laws for the government of the church, and executing them by delegated authority, forever cease; that the people may have free course to the Bible. . . .
>
> *Item.* We *will,* that each particular church, as a body . . . choose her own preacher. . . .
>
> *Item.* We *will,* that the people henceforth take the Bible as the only sure guide to heaven; and as many are offended with other books, which stand in competition with it, may cast them into the fire if they choose; for it is better to enter into life having one book, than having many to be cast into hell.
>
> *Item.* We *will,* that preachers and people, cultivate a spirit of mutual forbearance; pray more and dispute less. . . .
>
> *Item.* We *will,* that the Synod of Kentucky examine every member, who may be *suspected* of having departed from the Confession of Faith, and suspend every such suspected heretic immediately; in order that the oppressed may go free, and taste the sweets of gospel liberty.

. . . .

[1] Quoted from W. E. Garrison and A. T. DeGroot, *The Disciples of Christ: A History,* rev. ed. (St. Louis: Bethany, 1958).

Item. Finally we *will,* that all our *sister bodies* read their Bibles carefully, that they may see their fate there determined, and prepare for death before it is too late.

Springfield Presbytery, } L.S.

June 28th, 1804

To this was appended the names of six men, of whom Stone was one, as "Witnesses."

As these quotations suggest, Stone came to believe that the only creed of Christians should be the Bible, and when the problem of finding a new name for the seceders arose, it seemed best to call them simply "Christians," although by some they were called "Stoneites." Later Stone met Alexander Campbell and the two became close friends, with the result that it was agreed that "Christians,"—of whom there were then about 13,000 spread rather widely through the South and central West—and "Disciples" should "act as one," despite the fact that they did not at the time actually merge.

Stone continued to be an independent thinker as long as he lived, but he tells us: "My opportunity to read was very limited, being compelled to manual labor daily on my farm, but so intently engaged was my mind . . . that I always took with me in my cornfield my pen and ink, and as thoughts worthy of note occurred, I would cease from my labor and commit them to paper." During a long life (he died in 1844, at the age of seventy-two) he wrote a great deal. Some of his opinions stirred up considerable controversy, for he even questioned the orthodox view of the Atonement, and doubted the Trinity, with the result that he was sometimes (though inaccurately) accused of being a Unitarian.

A New Plan for Preaching

Another pioneer preacher to whom the Disciples owe much was Walter Scott, a distant relative of the great English novelist of the same name. Scott had gained a good educatior at the University of Edinburgh and journeyed to America in the spring of 1819. He became a teacher in a school in Pittsburgh, made up of "humble, pious people, mostly Scotch and Irish." These people were attempting to live as did the early Christians, practicing foot-washing and the "Holy Kiss," and baptizing by immersion. Locally they were known as the "kissing Baptists." A few years later Scott became minister of their little church, but was never happy about the religious atmosphere in it or in others like it. Religion seemed to lack a popular appeal.[2] Eventually he devised a plan of preaching that seemed to solve the problem—present the *evidence* that Jesus is the Messiah, the Son of God (based on the Gospel story, which no one then doubted). Then his hearers need only to repent of their sins and resolve to sin no more, with the implicit obligation thereafter to lead a godly life, and be baptized. God would then forgive their sins, confer on them the gift of the Holy Spirit and grant eternal life.

This was a presentation the common people could understand, especially when made by such a consummate orator as Scott, and converts flowed into the local Baptist churches. But many of the more orthodox were not happy: emphasis on Biblical teaching alone, irrespective of the Philadelphia Confession of Faith, to which Baptist churches were then required to assent, was too radical an innovation. So, after Scott met Campbell in the winter of 1821-1822, it was not long before they became fast friends, and the eventual result was that the dissenting churches were added to the rapidly growing body of Disciples.

Yet their very growth stirred up vigorous opposition and ridicule. They were often derisively dubbed "Campbellites." One Congregational missionary to the Middle West spoke of "the deluded Mormon (s) and Campbellite (s)"; another declared "Campbellism" to be "the great curse of the West." Others lumped together atheism, Campbellism and drunkenness. A Presbyterian revivalist in 1841 said:

---

[2] This was a time when organized religion in America was at a low ebb; only about 10 per cent of the population belonged to any church.

It seemed as if the Devil was allarmed from the first & began his work; letters were dropped in the street, reports of all kinds were circulated & the Campbellites the common enemy of all came with the expectation of setting in ful operation their water-works for converting men—but they failed—some have left them & are now saying they have been deceived & are now rejoicing in hope through the blood of the lamb—Others say they have no religion. O! That God would sweep this dreadful delusion from the land.[3]

"The Prince of Preachers"

Alexander Campbell spent the rest of his life furthering the interests of the new Church. He was a brilliant public speaker, but his kindly, learned and yet simple manner also fascinated people. His utter sincerity carried conviction. He traveled extensively, and great audiences greeted him everywhere. Some called him "the prince of preachers." He was even invited to address Congress. His greatest success was with the common people. Much of his travel was on horseback or on foot, over poor roads or over none, and in this frontier country of the South and West he gained his greatest following. Even today it is in these states that the Disciples are strongest.

Though interested primarily in religious questions, Campbell successfully ran for election as a delegate to the Constitutional Convention of 1829, held to rewrite the constitution of Virginia. He had hoped to have introduced into the new constitution some provision against slavery, but when this proved impossible he stood solidly for a more democratic system of state government—also without much success.

When he was at home, Campbell was accustomed to rise at three in the morning and write until breakfast time. In this way he often accomplished enough to keep his printers busy for the rest of the day. In seven years more than 40,000 copies of his work were sold. Among them was a new translation of the New Testament, but this was not a great success—no doubt because it was difficult for readers to become accustomed to

[3] Quoted from W. E. Garrison and A. T. DeGroot, *op. cit.*

the use of contemporary English, and especially to changes
such as substitution of the word "immersion" for "baptism"
(for Campbell was convinced that no other mode of baptism
was practiced in New Testament times), and reference to
"John the Immersionist" for "John the Baptist" of the Authorized Version. All this was in addition to the circulation of the
paper he edited, at first known as *The Christian Baptist* and
later as *The Millennial Harbinger*. Yet, in spite of these many
activities, he found time to manage his farm so skillfully that
it furnished him a good living. Popular minister that he was,
he never drew a salary from any church.

Bethany College Founded

Somehow he also found time to found and teach in Bethany College. It was to be a school for teaching "vigorous
young men" to carry on the cause to which he had dedicated
his life, and with this aim the college was built on a beautiful
hilltop in what is now Bethany, West Virginia; it was formally
opened in 1841. Though no longer limited to "vigorous young
men" interested in the ministry, Bethany still gives young men
and women a liberal education without which true tolerance
and appreciation of ethical values is difficult; thus it carries on
the ideals of its founder. The college and the old Campbell
homestead together still make the town of Bethany a kind of
shrine for Disciples.

As the years passed, his life was saddened by his father's
failing sight and eventual total blindness and, in 1854, by the
old man's death at the age of ninety. Nevertheless, even at the
age of seventy, when many men are glad to retire, Alexander
Campbell was still young enough to undertake the arduous
task of raising money to rebuild the college after a disastrous
fire. It has today one of the most scenic campuses in West
Virginia. The Disciples also have a number of other schools;
among them are Drake University in Iowa, Butler University
in Indiana, and Texas Christian University.

Portrait of Alexander Campbell. (Disciples of Christ Historical Society)

The Disciples

Campbell died in Bethany in 1866, leaving behind him a movement which had already become great; even then it could claim more than 350,000 members. What is there about it that is distinctive?

In belief, the Disciples are convinced—as are also the Baptists and Mormons—that immersion is the only proper method of baptism. (It is interesting that some of the early Disciples later became Mormons; among them, Sidney Rigdon, at first a Disciples preacher and later an unsuccessful candidate for the leadership assumed by Brigham Young.) Like the Baptists, they are also congregational in church government, each church being entirely independent in the management of its own affairs. They have evangelists, pastors, elders and deacons, but no bishops or higher ecclesiastical officials. The Lord's Supper is celebrated every Sunday. Since Campbell thought all creeds man-made, the Church he founded never had one. Nevertheless, the emphasis he placed on the Bible as the foundation of Christianity has resulted in a very literal interpretation of it by many Disciples. Others believe that new translations, for example, may throw new light on its meanings. They also share Campbell's conviction that Christianity represents a "new dispensation" not dependent on the Old Testament in any way.

Membership

The Disciples of Christ, or the International Convention of Christian Churches as they are officially known, have slightly more than 8,000 churches and nearly 2 million members in the United States. There are also Disciples churches scattered in many other parts of the world, with about 100 in Canada, and they carry on an extensive missionary program. One of the areas where they are especially active is the Congo, in which they have organized more than 1,000 churches, totaling about 125,000 members; here, too, they maintain hospitals and numerous schools.

Schism

The elder Campbell had said, "Where the Scriptures speak, we speak; where the Scriptures are silent, we are silent." But this led eventually to trouble for the Disciples as it has for many other Protestants. For who was to decide just what the Scriptures meant? If nothing was said in Holy Writ about a thing, was it therefore to be regarded as forbidden because it was not expressly permitted, or permitted because it was not expressly forbidden? As a young man, Alexander Campbell himself took the former position, saying, "It is not enough that it is not forbidden [in the Bible]—it is not *commanded*," and he therefore opposed Sunday Schools, missionary societies, organs in churches, and the use of the title "Reverend" for ministers. He modified this viewpoint somewhat in later years.

Thus the young Church became involved in controversy in later years about just these things. Nothing is said in the Gospels about Sunday Schools, Church societies of any kind, stained-glass windows or even organs. The dispute finally became bitter, and the "anti's" founded a religious group of their own, which they called the "Churches of Christ." They now claim over 2 million members, and are thus larger than the parent group; their membership is largely in the far Southwest. In accordance with what they believe has been the custom of the early Church, they even refuse to have any central organization and there are no officers above those of the local churches. But one may ask, perhaps, whether doing without whatever people did not have when Christ walked the earth is really being Christlike.

The story of the Disciples again illustrates the obstacles that beset Christian unity. Can any one system of belief or of worship meet with the needs of all men, or with universal acceptance? Mankind differs, and perhaps religious experience that satisfies one person may not another. Yet only in union is there strength. Christians have not solved the problem, although the widespread movement toward denominational mergers is an attempt to do so. Campbell did not solve it either, when he proposed to substitute for the "iron creed" a rather literal acceptance of the Bible, and emphasized a coming millenium when righteousness would rule the earth. Yet his insistence on the un-Biblical character of denominations has undoubtedly done much to further mutual understanding among them in our time.

13. Joseph Smith
1805-1844

We believe all that God has revealed, all that He does now reveal, and we believe that He will yet reveal many great and important things pertaining to the Kingdom of God.

. . . .

We believe in being honest, true, chaste, benevolent, virtuous, and in doing good to all men. . . . If there is anything virtuous, lovely, or of good report or praiseworthy, we seek after these things.

—JOSEPH SMITH

"Westward Ho!"

In the winter of 1820 the small town of Manchester, New York, had a protracted series of exciting revival meetings, and almost everybody in the town was converted. When the meetings were over, however, the Presbyterian and Methodist and Baptist ministers, who up to that time had been working most heartily together, began competing for the new converts. All their former friendly feelings were "entirely lost in a strife of words and a contest about opinions."

In the Smith household, the mother, two brothers and a sister decided to join the Presbyterian Church. Joseph was partial to the Methodists; yet the Presbyterians talked so violently against the Methodists, and the Baptists tried so hard to prove all others wrong but themselves that Joseph was left confused. Who was right and who was wrong? How could a boy of fourteen know, having so little knowledge of these things?

While laboring under these difficulties, he was one day reading his Bible. The verse he came upon was in the Epistle of James. "If any of you lacketh wisdom, let him ask of God, that giveth to all men liberally, and upbraideth not; and it shall be given him."

Joseph Smith's First Vision

Joseph was startled by the words. Wisdom was exactly what he needed, and he hadn't known how to get it. But now he had found his directions. The words must be true since they were in the Bible. Could he really ask God for the wisdom he needed? Joseph determined to do just that.

So, on the morning of a beautiful clear day in spring, he took a stroll into a nearby woods. Soon finding himself alone, he knelt down and prayed. He asked God to give him the wisdom he needed. For a few moments, all seemed black about him. He felt tongue-tied and his body bound as if by an invisible enemy.

What happened next is best told in Joseph's own words.

I saw a pillar of light exactly over my head, above the brightness of the sun, which descended gradually until it fell upon me.... When the light rested on me I saw two personages, whose brightness and glory defy all description, standing above me in the air. One of them spake unto me, calling me by name, and said, pointing to the other—*This is my Beloved Son, hear Him....* No sooner, therefore, did I get possession of myself, so as to be able to speak, than I asked the personages who stood above me in the light, which of all the sects was right—and which I should join. I was answered that I should join none of them, for they were all wrong. ... All their creeds were an abomination in his sight; ... and many other things did he say to me, which I cannot write at this time. When I came to myself again I found myself lying on my back, looking up into heaven.[1]

Naturally enough Joseph told his experience to his family

[1] Joseph Fielding Smith, *Essentials in Church History* (Utah: Deseret Press, 1924) , p 44.

and to some of his friends in the town. When opportunity came, he related his story to the Methodist minister. But this good man treated Joseph's experience "not only lightly, but with great contempt, saying it was all of the devil, that there were no such things as visions or revelations in these days; that there never would be any more of them."

This was humiliating to Joseph. For three long years he had no more revelations. He was just a farmer's son doing his daily chores. Although his family seems to have been sympathetic with his independent attitude toward the churches, many in the town ridiculed his claims.

Joseph Smith's Second Vision

The young man himself grew deeply troubled. He longed for more wisdom. A second crisis came in September 1823, after he had gotten into bed for the night. Again he saw a wonderful light and a person in shining robes stood above his bed. This heavenly messenger said his name was Moroni, the son of Mormon, the last of the prophets of God in America.

At first Joseph was frightened, but the angel said: "Do not be afraid. I have come to call you to a great work." Then Moroni told the young man many things. He opened to him a new understanding of the history of America and of the world. He said that the time would soon come when Christ would return to the earth to reign as king over the world. These were the "Latter Days" before Christ's second coming. And Joseph Smith was to be a prophet to prepare people for this great day of the Lord.

Three times during the night this same messenger appeared. He told Joseph of a book written on sheets of gold that lay hidden under the ground at a certain spot near the top of Cumorah Hill near Palmyra. Mormon, Moroni's father, had written most of the chapters before his death, and Moroni had completed them and hidden the book. If Joseph would humbly accept the sacred task, he would be given the wisdom needed to translate the book. But until it was translated and printed in the English language, it was not to be seen by any other eyes than his own.

That very afternoon Joseph climbed the hill and found the hidden book of golden sheets. But when he tried to pull it out he was unable to lift it. Again the angel appeared and told him that the time for him to take it had not yet come. "A year from today return to this spot." For four consecutive years Joseph made his annual visit alone to this spot. Finally taking with him a chest from home, he returned with the treasure inside.

For several years Joseph Smith[2] labored in translating the book, which is about one-third the length of the Old Testament. Sitting behind a dark curtain, he dictated his translation to a faithful amanuensis on the other side of the curtain.

When finally an edition of five thousand copies was printed, three names besides that of Joseph Smith were signed to it, under a sworn statement that they had seen the golden plates. Martin Harris, one of these witnesses, was later asked: "Did you really see the plates with your natural eyes just as you see the penholder in my hand?" He answered: "Well, I did not see them just as I see the penholder, but I saw them with the eye of faith."

In this manner, the Book of Mormon was presented to mankind as a second inspired Word of God—not to replace the Old and New Testaments, but to be added to them, giving a later sacred record of God's dealings with men. When the translation was completed the golden plates were said to have been returned to the angel.

What Is the Book of Mormon?

The Book of Mormon continues the great Story of Salvation as it was begun in the Old and New Testaments. It deals

---

[2] Mr. Israel Smith, president of the Reorganized Church of Jesus Christ of Latter Day Saints, and grandson of Joseph Smith, states that "All authentic historic sources show that the plates were received from the angel on September 22, 1827, and translated in less than two years."

The Angel Moroni delivering the plates of the Book of Mormon to Joseph Smith. (The Bettmann Archive)

especially with the spread of the gospel to the new world. Joseph Smith called the letters in which it was written "Reformed Egyptian Hieroglyphics."

The Book of Mormon tells of two major migrations to the new world. The first came from Chaldea after the destruction of the Tower of Babel. In eight barges and under divine guidance, this group of God's "Chosen People" sailed across the Atlantic and settled in South America. For hundreds of years they thrived, increased in numbers and achieved a high civilization in Central America and Mexico. They were disobedient, however, to the law of God and later were exterminated.

A second migration came from Jerusalem after the two great capitals of Samaria and Jerusalem had been destroyed and the tribes of Israel scattered. These emigres were remnants of the lost tribes of Israel. About A.D. 400, guided by divine providence, they too crossed the ocean and settled in the Americas. These came in two groups named after their leaders. One was called the Nephites; the other, the Lamanites. The Lamanites, because of their wickedness, were later cursed with "dark skins" and became wild. These were the ancestors of the American Indians. The other group, the Nephites, were more civilized and for hundreds of years were the dominant race in America. Jesus, after his resurrection, appeared among the Nephites and gave them the gospel. Later, from time to time, prophets were sent to them, but even the Nephites gave themselves over to wickedness, and they, too, were finally exterminated. Mormon, the last of these Nephite prophets, before he died wrote a history of all these events. His son Moroni completed the writing, and hid the book so that the story might be preserved and found in the "Latter Days," when God would send another prophet to prepare mankind for the second coming of Christ after which he would rule the world in peace and righteousness for a thousand years.

The whole story, as told in the Book of Mormon, is depicted annually in a mammoth outdoor pageant acted on the slopes of the "Hill Cumorah" near the site where Mormons believe Joseph Smith found the golden plates. Each year tens of thousands of people flock to this great spectacle from all over central New York.

The Mormons, therefore, believe that they are the modern descendants of God's "Chosen People," and that the coming of their prophet Joseph Smith and the establishment of their church was prophesied in the Old Testament. From this belief they derive the name by which they prefer to be called "The Church of Jesus Christ of Latter-day Saints." They have always had a special interest in the American Indians, since they share with the Indians the honor of being descendants of the Lost Tribes of Israel. The Indian ancestors are called Lamanites. One branch of the Mormon church has its headquarters in Lamoni, Iowa, a town named after them.

The Beginnings of the New Church

The publication of the Book of Mormon created a great stir. Some were contemptuous, yet many others were impressed. In the home of Peter Whitmer in Fayette, New York, six men met—Peter and David Whitmer, three of the Smith family, Hyrum, Samuel and Joseph, and the faithful amanuensis Oliver Cowdry. These six men together partook of the Lord's Supper and made a solemn covenant with one another and God and prayed for one another. In this way the new Church of Jesus Christ of Latter-day Saints was organized. Six men, from three families—in an insignificant town—what could they accomplish?

The story of the years from that memorable date to the time when the Mormons were peacefully established in Utah, is a story of intense enthusiasms and devotion, coupled with almost continuous persecution. They believed themselves to be inheritors of a new Kingdom. They were divinely commissioned to build the New Jerusalem on earth, to prepare a righteous city fit for the throne of the returning Messiah.

Although none of the six men was religiously educated or ordained, they went from town to town gathering small groups in little parlors or in woodland groves, and proclaimed to them the new revelation. As the groups increased and enlarged, they tended to form their own communal societies, separate from the "Gentiles" as they called all who were not of their Church. Their first large settlement was in the lovely little town of Kirtland, Ohio, near the present site of Cleveland. Their beautiful building still stands and is in regular use by the Mormons of the area, who belong to the Reorganized Church.

Joseph Smith was continually pushing his converts farther west, partly because of the persecution they met and partly because he dreamed of their building the New Jerusalem. For this they needed to find a beautiful spot where they could own their own homes and build a new city. From the beginning, it was revealed to him that each person who joined the Church should give one-tenth or a tithe of all he possessed to the Church, and from that time on should continue to give one-tenth of his yearly income. So the treasury of the church grew. Within three years they dedicated their first temple, a truly imposing structure for the town of Kirtland.

Nauvoo—the City Beautiful

Mormon settlements grew rapidly in different towns in New York, Ohio, Illinois and Missouri. The largest and most famous city was called Nauvoo—the City Beautiful. On the east bank of the Mississippi River it rested peacefully, as if in the river's folded arm. In spite of the unfriendliness of their neighbors, the Mormons soon dominated the city of Nauvoo, with its population of nearly 20,000 people. They made it not only the largest city in the state but also one of the most beautiful. In the center of the city they built a temple costing $600,000. They also started a university.

Joseph Smith became mayor. He even organized a Nauvoo Legion and wore the uniform of a commander. Unfortunately, he became tyrannical in his government, and, as some believe, profligate in his own private life. Slanders multiplied. It was here that he first announced a revelation regarding multiple marriage for men. Some of his own people became antagonized.

A few enemies within his own Church began publishing a newspaper, in which they expressed their criticisms of Joseph Smith's rule. As mayor, he saw to it that the newspaper was suppressed after the first issue. Just to be doubly sure, he had the presses thrown into the street and the type pied.

A Mob Lynches the Mormon Leaders

The fat was in the fire. Enemies inside and outside the Church rallied against him. They succeeded in having him arrested on a trumped up charge. Joseph Smith and his brother Hyrum were taken to the neighboring town of Carthage where they were jailed.

The rough-and-ready pioneers of Illinois were not content to let the law take its course. A mob stormed the jail and shot to death both Joseph and his brother Hyrum.

Now the new Church had what it most needed—martyrs.

Who was to take the "Prophet's" place? This was now a pressing problem. Many wished to do so and Joseph Smith himself had designated no one.[3] Fortunately, the man who was chosen to succeed the fallen prophet had extraordinary administrative ability. This was Brigham Young, a former house painter and carpenter from Vermont. His faith in Joseph was tinctured with no hint of skepticism or shred of doubt about the Prophet's revelations. Moreover, this new leader had learned much of human nature as a missionary of the Church in England. Of formal schooling he had little, but life itself had taught him much.

The Exodus from Nauvoo

The popular prejudice against the Mormons grew into hatred. The governor of the state was informed that he would have to find a way to force the Mormons out of the state. The Mormons, sensing the growing enmity, promised to leave in the spring. All they asked was that they be given an opportu-

[3] Mormons of the Reorganized Church believe that Joseph Smith, while he was still in Nauvoo in 1843, selected his son Joseph as his successor.

nity to sell their property at fair prices. Brigham Young, as well as all his followers, saw clearly that if the "Saints" were to survive, they would have to migrate to virgin territory far from the Gentile world. Just where their final New Jerusalem would be established, neither Brigham Young nor any one else knew, yet they had faith to believe that God would lead them.

The town of Nauvoo began to bustle with new kinds of activity. Houses, furnishings, land were quickly sold and the money secured was turned into wagons, horses, oxen and provisions for a long trek. By the middle of May 1846, Brigham Young and about sixteen thousand of the inhabitants of the City Beautiful had crossed the Mississippi River and were on their way through Iowa to their rendezvous on the banks of the Missouri near the present site of Council Bluffs.

The Mormons staying behind hoped to remain till a new settlement could be established. But the irate neighbors in towns nearby grew impatient. In September a battalion of 800 armed men laid siege to the town for three days. The enfeebled Mormons tried to resist, but finally, being so poorly armed, they had to surrender. The invaders promised to give the Mormons time to make their departure in an orderly fashion.

When once in the city, the invaders began to plunder the houses and mistreat the people. They gave some families an hour and others a day in which to gather up their belongings. The old and sick and mothers with small children were ruthlessly forced into wagons or rushed on foot to the river ferry, without adequate supplies of clothing or food. The winter was just beginning. The deserted city was then further plundered. Many homes were burned and the beautiful temple, for which the Mormons had sacrificed their money and devoted labor was turned into a heap of rubble.

The Long Trek

The long line of covered wagons made a trail across the state of Iowa. On the banks of the Missouri and the Mississippi rivers these exiles set up winter quarters. Many died of privation and sickness. With the coming of April, 15,000 of the exiles were able to begin once more their westward pilgrimage. The long line of covered wagons again rolled across the plains toward the setting sun.

Finally on July 24, 1847, Brigham Young and about two hundred of his hardiest pioneers reached the mouth of the canyon through which they "gazed with wonder and admiration upon the vast valley" they were seeking. Before them to the west was spread like a glistening sheet of silver the Great Salt Lake, and below stretched a wide gray desert, encircled by a wall of purplish and rust-colored cliffs, with snow-capped mountains on the far horizon. Brigham Young, sick with mountain fever, was reclining in one of the carriages. Yet like all his company, he was captured by the grandeur of the scene. He ordered his driver to stop till all had feasted their eyes upon it. Finally, he said: "This is the place. Drive on!"

"The Promised Land"

To those pioneers, seeking only freedom of worship and liberty to live as they thought right, the experience must have brought mingled feelings. Freedom they certainly would have, for the world of the Gentiles had been left a thousand miles behind them, but what would the freedom be worth? The land was dry, the climate severe. Natural resources seemed utterly lacking.

Brigham Young, however, saw what his people did not. Here and there were mountain streams trickling into the valley. Within an hour after the caravan halted, his men had their plows out of the wagons and they were breaking up the soil, while other men with spades began damming up one of the mountain streams.

It was not long before Brigham Young's engineering genius and Mormon industry made a garden spot of what had been desert. The Territory of Deseret, as this vast land was called by these pioneers, became indeed a "Promised Land," "flowing with milk and honey."

At the mouth of Emigration Canyon, Utah, Brigham Young announced to his followers, "This is the place," and chose it as the end of their trek across the plains. This mural painting by John McQuarrie is on the walls of the Union Pacific station in Salt Lake City. (Ewing Galloway)

To be sure, primitive and distressing conditions faced the first settlers, but these were slowly overcome. Converts even from foreign lands, especially from England and Scandinavia, flocked to this inter-mountain country. When they had come as far as boats and trains could carry them, these immigrants continued their journey across the Great Plains in covered wagons. Some even came on foot, carrying their baggage or pulling it behind them in handcarts. Little children of seven or eight trudged along beside their parents. There were babies, too, some even born on the way. Many a child, and many a grownup, perished on the road. Those who survived pushed on, leaving small heaps of freshly turned sod behind.

Of such stuff were these Mormon pioneers. Faith and courage are noble partners, yet these two alone would scarcely have sufficed without the genius and able leadership of Brigham Young. Some historians have called him the ablest colonizer of modern times.

The Mormon Church

The Mormon gospel was planted in the West at a time when the country west of the Missouri was largely uncharted and unknown. In spite of contempt, hatred and persecution, the Church has grown and prospered. It now numbers more than a million and a half members, of whom all but about 150,000 belong to the parent Church, which has its headquarters in Salt Lake City. The Reorganized Church, with headquarters in Independence, Missouri, accounts for most of the others. The Mormons are the largest sect in Utah (about 70 per cent) and Idaho, and are also strong in neighboring states; they are growing rapidly even in the East. Many new chapels (the Mormon term for a local church) have been built in this area in the past two decades. Few large cities are without their congregations of Latter-day Saints. Although their membership is largely confined to the United States, yet in normal times about two thousand Mormon missionaries, most of whom are young men, and all of whom serve without pay, are spreading their gospel in other lands and continents. These young men are usually in the field for two years. Salt Lake City in a way is their Holy City, although only about 40 per cent of its present population of 200,000 people belong to the Mormon Church.

Reasons for Their Persecution

By many, Mormonism is identified with polygamy. This has been not only unfortunate, but unfair. In the first place, the Mormon practice of having a plurality of wives and being sexually promiscuous should not be equated. It is to be doubted whether any Church has valued chastity more highly than have the Mormons.

Furthermore, it was not until Brigham Young made public in 1852 a revelation, which he said had been given to Joseph Smith nine years earlier, that polygamy became an accepted Mormon practice. He defended the new rule by the example of Old Testament "men of God," such as Abraham, Jacob and David, and on the basis of the command to Adam to be "fruitful and multiply."

The tardily announced proclamation promptly stirred up bitter dissension, with the resulting secession of a rather large group now known as the Reorganized Church of Jesus Christ of Latter-day Saints. This group also rejects such Mormon doctrines as the "baptism of the dead" and "celestial marriage." All the direct descendants of Joseph Smith have chosen to ally themselves with this Church, and several of them have been leaders of it.

In 1890, now over a half-century ago, the parent Church banned all plural marriages. Whatever we may think about the practice among Mormons in the past, we should realize that plural marriage is now a dead issue.

It would seem, therefore, that the practice called polygamy by outsiders, was in reality an excuse for violence rather than the real cause of the widespread hatred of Mormons. There must have been other reasons. What were they?

Joseph Smith's early claim that he had received an important new revelation was naturally a challenge to all creedal churches that held the Bible contained a full revelation of all saving truth. His further claim that all the other churches were fraudulent made the Mormons no friends. Their tactlessness in calling themselves "saints" while others were "sinners," and their claiming to be the "Chosen People" while others were "Gentiles" also seemed arrogant.

The Mormons set themselves off as different from others, not only in their beliefs but in their everyday practices. Wherever they gathered, they formed a community life of their own apart from others. They were organized for cooperative living. It was communism with a religious motive within the boundaries of their sect. Their people were not merely admonished to be generous to their neighbors, they were told just how much was expected of them and in just what ways their contributions should be made. Religion was a matter of life in this present world as well as a concern for eternity. As a result, wherever the Mormons were allowed to settle for any length of time, they became prosperous and their communism seemed a threat to the American way of private competing enterprise. Because of their numbers and their growing prosperity in Nauvoo, they held the balance of political power in the state of Illinois.

Their Present Prosperity

The Church of the Latter-day Saints is now an immensely wealthy organization. In Utah it owns or has important holdings in numerous factories and industries. In Salt Lake City it owns office buildings, banks, mills, insurance companies, and has a large interest in Zion's Co-operative Mercantile Institution, the biggest department store between the Missouri and the West Coast, doing annually a business of many million dollars. The Church also owns two hotels, two hospitals, and the *Deseret News,* an afternoon newspaper. They have a welfare organization so efficient that few Mormons are unemployed and none are allowed to suffer want. Included in it is a process involving the storage of surplus commodities for future use. To make this possible, a wheat elevator with a capacity of 318,000 bushels stands in Salt Lake City, and was built by volunteer labor. There are also numerous other smaller storehouses.

The tithing rule, early established, has contributed and continues to contribute large funds for the promotion of the Church. Even today one of the old tithing houses still stands near the former home of Brigham Young. To this house the early settlers brought every tenth egg or ear of corn or basket of fruit as their share in the common enterprise.

While Brigham Young lived, he dominated both the Church and the territory of Utah. For a time he was governor. Even today in Salt Lake City names, monuments, buildings continually remind one of this great leader. When he died in 1877, he had been husband to over twenty wives and had fathered fifty-six children; his present-day descendants are estimated to number more than 4,000. He had amassed a fortune of over a million dollars and had built a truly beautiful city. Beyond all these achievements, he had won the wholehearted and lasting respect of his people, and had seen the triumph of the faith to which he had given his abounding energies throughout a long life.

How the Church is Organized

According to Mormon claims, the organization is patterned after that of the early apostolic Church. Over all is the president (who is also called "Prophet" or "Revelator"). He is chosen by the "Twelve Apostles" and elected for life. He has also two other counselors or "High Priests" to assist him.

The churches are organized into regional units known as "Stakes of Zion." There are now 305 such Stakes. The Stakes are divided into wards, each containing about 800 people (al-

though the number varies considerably). Each ward is under
the jurisdiction of a bishop, assisted by two counselors. His
duties are varied: visiting the sick, arranging for relief of the
poor, conducting worship services, performing civil marriage
ceremonies, seeing to it that the ward building is kept in re-
pair. In many respects the bishop's duties are those of a minister of other denominations, but he is elected to office and is
unpaid. Mormons have no paid or full-time ministers. The
organization of the Church is closely knit and autocratic.
Authority is centralized. Yet the welfare of the individual within the organization, regardless of social status, financial resources or race is given primary importance.

Outstanding Beliefs

There are other Mormon beliefs of significance which
have not yet been explained. Some are unique among Christian churches. Such is the belief that the dead may be baptized,
even including the heathen who have had no opportunity to
hear of Christ. This baptism is accomplished by proxy, some
relative or friend taking the dead man's part in the ceremony.
More than 17 million such baptisms have been performed.
So also is the belief in "celestial marriage." A marriage ceremony, sanctified (sealed) by the church, binds the partners not
only for this world but also for the next as well. The marriage
promise is not merely "till death do you part" but "for all
time and eternity." Such marriages, however, may only be
solemnized in Mormon temples, of which there are now eight
in various parts of the world, by a "few men delegated with
authority so to do." Civil marriages are performed by bishops.
The relationships between parents and children are also believed to continue through eternity. Women who remain outside of wedlock in this life, it is believed, do not enter heaven.

Yet there is no hell in Mormon theology. Like the Universalists, Mormons teach that everyone will be saved, but they
add that since some are more deserving they will receive a
higher place in heaven than others. Not only does this life not
end with death, it did not begin with birth, for they think that

every human spirit has existed since the beginning of time; it was "in the beginning with the Father."

Mormons also believe in large families, and do not approve of birth control. They have a highly developed program of recreation and education, which accords with two beliefs on which they place special emphasis: that happiness is one of the supreme ends of life, and that education is essential. "Men are, that they might have joy," declares the Book of Mormon, and, "A man cannot be saved in ignorance."

Other major elements in their faith, however, the Mormons share with other evangelical churches. Like the Baptists they believe that baptism must be by immersion. They observe Communion each Sunday as do the Disciples, although they substitute water for the wine or grape juice used in most churches. Like the Friends, the Mormons believe in the possibility of present and new revelations. Each person may have direct access to God. Joseph Smith declared that all had not been revealed in the sacred words of the Bible and many great and important revelations are still to come. Such a belief makes change and growth possible.

Instead of the trained and professional clergy of most other churches, Mormons recognize two orders of priesthood —the Aaronic and the Melchizedek. The former has to do with the temporal affairs of the Church, and its lowest grade, that of deacon, is open even to boys of twelve. Both orders, and all grades, may be held by any man who conforms to the necessary standards of character set by the Church.

In regard to daily conduct, the Mormons are strict. "The Word of Wisdom," the Mormon health code, prohibits the use of alcoholic drinks, tobacco, and even tea and coffee. Undoubtedly these rules are often honored in the breach, yet to their observance the Mormons ascribe their unusually low death rate. Many of them live active lives well into the nineties.

These Latter Days

The name "Latter-day Saints" refers to a belief that Christ will soon come again to rule mankind. This doctrine is known as "millenarianism," because when Christ comes it is thought he will reign for a thousand years before the end of the world will come. (The Latin word for a thousand is *mille*.) Joseph Smith believed that he was living in the "Latter Days" and that he might witness the second coming of Christ. This belief in Christ's second coming is shared by a number of other denominations, such as the Seventh-day Adventists.

The Mormon Temple in Salt Lake City

In the center of Salt Lake City is a ten-acre park. Here, surrounded by a beautifully kept lawn and brilliant beds of flowers, stand two great Mormon buildings—the Temple and the Tabernacle. The Temple is a tall, spired building constructed of white Utah marble. None but Mormons is allowed to enter this sacred temple. Here baptisms, marriages and other rituals are performed. The Tabernacle is a large oval-domed audience hall open to all and capable of holding 8,000 people. Here the Sunday morning services are held. Like the temple in Jerusalem, it was built without nails or steel of any kind. The music from its great pipe organ, with its nearly 8,000 pipes, is often broadcast on nationwide hookups. Annually a choir of 5,000 singers gathers from all the surrounding "wards," and leads the great assembly in a stirring music festival.

Mormon Education

Three years after Brigham Young and his pioneer band rolled into the valley of Great Salt Lake in 1850, he started a university. It is now the oldest state university west of the Mississippi, with an enrollment of over 4,000 students. The Mormons also have a university of their own in Provo, Utah, with an enrollment of nearly 9,000 students, known as Brigham Young University. In Idaho they maintain a junior college.

Night view of the Mormon Temple in Salt Lake City, Utah. (Ewing Galloway)

Although the church does not believe in religious instruction in the public schools, it does believe in giving children special instruction in religion. Beside almost all public high schools, wherever Mormonism is strong, there stands a smaller Mormon school building, to the number of some two hundred in all. After school hours each day every Mormon son and daughter is expected to attend a class in religion.

Few churches have a saga as full of tragedy and of romantic drama as is the history of the Mormon Church. It is American to the core. It fed on the belief in enterprise and success. It grew from the grass roots of the American pioneer struggle. It was originated by a young man, a farmer's son, who believed in his own worth in the sight of God. It was led to strength and prosperity by a man who had the eyes to see in a dry and barren valley the possibility of a City of God. It was established by an engineering genius, with a will power that refused to acknowledge defeat, and a religious enthusiasm and conviction that inspired and commanded all his people.

The Mormons are still significant in our American life. What their future may be none can predict. That all churches might learn much from them is certain.

14. Mary Baker Eddy
1821-1910

Prayer cannot change the Science of being, but it tends to put us into harmony with it.

. . . .

God is love. Can we ask Him to be more? God is Intelligence. Can we inform the infinite Mind of anything He does not already comprehend? Do we expect to change perfection? Shall we plead for more at the open fount, which is pouring forth more than we accept?

—MARY BAKER EDDY

"As a Man Thinketh..."

Mary Baker—the Child

First it was just Mary Baker, the youngest of six children in the family of a New Hampshire farmer. A pretty child, with big blue eyes and brown curls, but frail and subject to illness.

Whatever may have been the cause, Mary was too frail and too emotionally unstable a child to attend school regularly. The two-mile walk to and from the country school was too much for her. The noise and confusion of school life also upset her. As a result, Mary's education was given her largely at home, either by her grandmother or her mother. Her favorite teacher was her older brother, Albert, who was attending Dartmouth College during the time when Mary was of elementary age. Later she went for a while to a private school near Tilton.

From the outset Mary had personality. She was independent and willful like her father, and sensitive and adorable like her mother. When first her father expounded to her the doctrine of eternal damnation and predestination, Mary's distaste of the idea was so great that it gave her a fever. Only her mother's tender assurance that God was wholly love healed her nerves. When her grandmother told her the story of how Daniel prayed three times a day, Mary determined to do even better. She prayed seven times a day, chalking up her score on the wall of the woodshed.

Mary Baker Glover—the Bride

Next it was Mary Baker Glover. When Mary was nineteen a romantic lover appeared—a handsome, dark-eyed friend of the family who was starting out in the building trade in the South. Two years after their meeting, Mr. Glover carried his delicate and supremely happy bride away with him to Charleston, South Carolina. The two were passionately in love and the next months were perhaps the happiest in all Mary's long lifetime.

Only six months later, while on a business trip in Wilmington, Mr. Glover was suddenly taken with yellow fever and died. There was nothing for the bereft widow to do but to return to her New Hampshire home and there await the arrival of her expected child. When the child finally was given her, however, Mary was unable to take care of him and he grew up in the home of a friend. Financially, Mary had no resources. The difficult birth·had left her with a spinal ailment and she was more of an invalid than before.

Mary Baker Patterson—the Dentist's Wife

Next after nine years of loneliness without an abiding home, the heroine of our story became Mrs. Mary Baker Patterson.· Her Prince Charming was a large and handsome man

who was adept at setting feminine hearts fluttering wherever
he was. With his masterful physical strength and gallantry he
captivated the fragile young widow. She with her delicate com-
plexion and charming manners won his love over all other
competitors.

"At last," thought Mary, "I can have a home again and
my son George can return and live with us." But Dr. Patterson
seems to have had more art with the ladies than with his dental
practice. He seems never to have been able adequately to support his invalid wife. To add to their troubles, Dr. Patterson
enlisted in the Union Army and was taken prisoner. For
several years the two had no way of communicating. Mrs. Patterson was again left dependent on her relatives, and the hope
of having her son with her was once more frustrated. The
family who had taken him soon moved to Minnesota. For years
his mother neither saw him nor heard from him.

Mary Baker Patterson tried living with her sister, Mrs.
Tilton. Hers was a large and comfortable home and finances
were not a consideration. But Mrs. Tilton had settled down
satisfied to live according to the accepted New England ideals
of the past. Mary's face was turned toward the future. Hers was
an ambitious, experimental mind, and she was not afraid to be
different.

Once in her sister's home, when an evening party of
guests were discussing slavery, Mary had expressed a view contrary to that of most of her sister's friends. Mrs. Tilton in
protest interrupted. "Mary, do you dare to say that in my
house?" "I dare to speak what I believe in any house," said
Mary decisively.

Later Mrs. Tilton even offered to build on her estate a
cottage for her sister where she might live in comfort the rest
of her life. But there was one proviso: she must cease to talk
with her friends about her new theories of religion and health,
and she must go to the Tiltons' church. To this, Mary gave a
quick and spirited response. She could not give up her religion
for any one. So the Tilton door was closed upon her.

Mary Baker Patterson might almost as well have been an
outright widow. She was past forty years old, without an ade-

quate income and with but a small circle of friends. Not one
of them could have imagined then that in twenty years she was
to be perhaps the most famous American woman of her time.

Phineas Quimby—the Healer

What was it that had been happening to this spirited invalid that so annoyed her sister and had made it impossible for
her and her husband to be congenial? To understand the
powerful effect that her new ideas had upon her we must live
imaginatively in the atmosphere of the latter half of the nineteenth century in America. At that time the science of medicine was in its babyhood and the science of mental hygiene was
even less developed. It was like an embryo just beginning to
stir in the womb of American thought.

The forerunner of the science of mental hygiene went by
various names: animal magnetism, hypnotism, mesmerism and
spiritualism. Hundreds of books and pamphlets were being
circulated telling of the wonders of the power of mind over
matter. Quack medicines were everywhere advertised for
which exaggerated claims were made. Mesmerists were traveling about the country demonstrating their powers. To some,
mesmerism seemed a return to witchcraft and was frightening.
To other braver (or perhaps more naive souls) it held out the
great hope of relief from sickness and pain.

Mary Baker Patterson, instead of gaining strength
through the years, had been steadily losing ground. She had
tried doctors wherever she had lived. She had gone to spiritual-
ist seances and she had been experimented upon by a mes-
merist. But year by year she had to spend more time in bed,
until she became but a shadow of her former self.

At this juncture came excited rumors of the wonderful
cures performed by "Doctor" Phineas Quimby in Portland,
Maine, who was healing hundreds of sick people without any
kind of medicine. Mary listened and read everything that came
her way. In spite of her sister's violent objections, she finally
found a friend who would take her to Portland. She had to be
assisted up the stairs to the doctor's office in the International
Hotel.

The doctor met her with friendly understanding and sympathy. He talked with her, telling her she was "held in bondage by the opinion of her family and physicians," and that "her animal spirit was reflecting its grief upon her body and calling it spinal disease." To add to his patient's confidence, the doctor included some manipulation of her head and body in his treatments.

Mary Baker Patterson's hope and faith were strong, and she was rewarded. She came for treatments daily for a week, and at the end of that time, she was so much improved that without any one's help she climbed the one hundred and eighty steps to the dome of the City Hall just to prove to herself that she had been healed. The prayers of years seemed to be answered. However, her healing was not permanent and she soon suffered a relapse.

The Fall and "the Revelation"

In the meantime, Dr. Patterson had been released from prison. When his wife returned to her home in Lynn, she said she felt as much like a released prisoner as he did. The new science, however, germinated slowly in her mind. Like an exotic plant it required time before it became naturalized in the soil of her own mind, until it became her conviction.

With the daily problem of adjusting herself to the husband from whom she had been so long separated, she found it difficult to retain her belief in the reality of Mind and Spirit in contrast to the error of bodily pain and sickness. She began relapsing toward her old condition.

Then it was an accident that brought her "the revelation." One evening in February 1866, she was returning with friends from a party when she fell on the ice and struck her head and back such a blow that she was left unconscious. She was carried into the home of a friend. A physician was called. As she gradually recovered partial consciousness, she became the victim of spasms and the doctor feared she might never be able to walk again.

On the third day after the accident when she was alone

on her bed, she had what later seemed to her to have been the most important revelation of her life. The miracles recorded in the Bible, which had before seemed supernatural, grew divinely natural. All her pain seemed to evaporate. Love shone down upon her. She thought she heard a voice say: "Daughter arise!" At once she dressed and walked downstairs and greeted her astonished friends.

That morning February 4, 1866, is held to be the most important date in Christian Science history. For on that day, Mary Baker Patterson discovered "Christian Science."

The Massachusetts Metaphysical College

After she secured a divorce from Dr. Patterson on the grounds of infidelity, Mary assumed again the name of her first husband. It was Mrs. Mary Baker Glover who spent the next three years as a kind of itinerant boarder. During this period, her major ambition was to write a book that would express the revelation she had received. Yet she had to earn her own support in some way. First she began trying out her theories on her sick friends. She gathered small groups about her in the evenings and she instructed them in the new "science," as she called it.

After four years of this healing, writing and informal teaching, she went into a partnership with one of her abler disciples, Richard Kennedy. He nailed a doctor's sign to a tree in front of a house which they rented in the shoemakers' city of Lynn. She had a professional card printed for herself which read:

> *Mary B. Glover*
> *Teacher of*
> *Moral Science*

Before long Dr. Kennedy's waiting room was filled with patients, and Mrs. Glover was having regular classes for the instruction of those interested in the new "science." Later she

Portrait of Mary Baker Eddy. (The Bettmann Archive)

started a school, which was chartered in 1881 as The Massachusetts Metaphysical College.

Soon she was charging $300 for a course of twelve lectures given during a period of three weeks' duration. Those who completed the course were expected to become practitioners.

Unfortunately, the partnership with Dr. Kennedy lasted but two years. Indeed, during the years that followed there was a succession of gifted and magnetic personalities that followed the teacher of moral "science" for a while but who later went their own ways.

Mary Baker Eddy

Finally, in 1876, a new figure appeared in the drama of Christian Science. A bachelor of forty-four years arrived from Boston to become a student in the college. He was broad shouldered, immaculate in his dress, modest, self-effacing. He had a gentle temper and a quiet efficient way of going about his work. Before long Asa Eddy became the favorite student.

Next he became Dr. Eddy, the star practitioner, and before a full year had passed he and the head of the college had become man and wife. Being himself a plodder with little imagination, he had no personal ambitions. It was his joy to devote himself utterly to the forwarding of the cause of Christian Science. Mrs. Eddy needed just such a helper, for during those years misunderstandings, jealousies, lawsuits piled one on another. Asa Eddy was always the peacemaker and the defender of his wife's activities. When he died, but five short years after their marriage, Mrs. Eddy wrote of him: "This was the perfect man."

Science and Health

Science and Health with Key to the Scriptures is the great Christian Science textbook. During the thirty-five years that elapsed between the time when the book first appeared until

Mrs. Eddy's death, it went through many editions. In spite of
the large sales, she was never complacent about what she had
achieved. Each prospect of a new edition was a challenge to her
to see if she could express more clearly or more fully the revelation which she never doubted God had given her.

The importance of the book in Mrs. Eddy's mind is
shown by the instructions given in the Church Manual to each
new member. "The Bible, together with *Science and Health*
and other works by Mrs. Eddy, shall be his only textbooks for
self-instruction in Christian Science, and teaching and practicing of metaphysical healing." Consequently every good
Christian Scientist owns a copy of *Science and Health* and
reads from it daily.

The practice of connecting *Science and Health* always
with the Bible is due to Mrs. Eddy's conviction that the sole
authority for her teachings came from the Bible. In more than
2,800 Christian Science churches throughout the world, twice
each week passages are read from the Bible and from *Science
and Health* alternately in a manner that makes clear that Mrs.
Eddy's teachings are intended to explain certain passages from
the Bible. In her reverence for the Bible, Mrs. Eddy was true
to the Protestant tradition that the Bible is "the sole rule of
faith and practice."

The Christian Science Monitor

One of the most original and successful ventures which
Mrs. Eddy initiated was the publication of a Christian daily
newspaper. The daily newspapers were unavoidable, yet they
contained much news about the sordid affairs of the world, the
reading of which, she felt, was dangerous to moral health. She,
therefore, conceived the idea of a newspaper that would present truthfully only those parts of the news that were fit to
print. That Mrs. Eddy was able to launch a profitable and
useful enterprise of this sort when she was in her eighties is
indeed a monument of which Christian Scientists may be
proud. Today *The Christian Science Monitor* is widely read

and valued far outside Christian Science circles. It is especially famous for the accuracy and richness of its international news and for the broadmindedness and intelligence of its editorial comments.

Up to almost the very end of her long life of eighty-nine years, Mary Baker Eddy kept her hand on the helm of Christian Science. The profits from her teaching and royalties had grown very large, but she personally supervised their investment. Even at the age of eighty-six, when her mental competence was questioned in the famous "Next Friends" suit, she was able to satisfy the court and attorneys on both sides, as well as a group of psychiatrists, that she was still quite able to handle her own affairs.

The Important Things in Christian Science

To most people the name "Christian Science" means faith healing. Such an assumption is to miss a vital point. Mrs. Eddy refused to speak of herself as performing cures. She insisted that the healing that resulted from her ministrations came not because she had performed something miraculous. The healing she regarded as coming through a natural process. What the practitioner does is to help the individual who is sick to accept that which is a true principle of life and to act accordingly. Just as truly as Isaac Newton believed he had discovered a law of the physical universe, Mary Baker Eddy believed she had discovered a spiritual law or principle.

"Who would stand before a blackboard, and pray the principle of mathematics to solve the problem? The rule is already established, and it is our task to work out the solution." These words are to be found in the chapter on prayer in *Science and Health*. Let us not forget that Mary Baker Eddy believed that she had found a "Science" in the spiritual world, and that to understand and act on that "Science" would mean health. We may disagree with the findings of her "Science," but we should acknowledge the significance of her assumption that there is a "Science" of the spiritual life.

And what is the principle which Mary Baker Eddy believed she found? Briefly it is this: Only the spiritual is real while all that is material and mortal is an illusion. The spiritual is God. God is Mind. God is Love. God is all that is real. Evil, sickness, death are illusions. They are the product of our erring mortal minds.

"Become conscious for a single moment that life and intelligence are purely spiritual—neither in nor of matter—and the body will then utter no complaints." (*Science and Health*)

Even the Newtonian law of gravitation the scientists have now revised, yet they still say there is truth in what Newton discovered. May we not take a similar attitude toward the principle which Mary Baker Eddy so fervently set forth? Many of us can not today accept her principle completely, yet we should find a truer way to state the core of truth for which she searched. Instead of looking for either our spiritual or physical salvation by pulling down to earth some supernatural power to help us, let us also search for the true and natural principles that are inherent in the full and noble living of life. Let us study the Science of spiritual health.

The Church of Christ, Scientist

The Church of Christ, Scientist, was organized in Boston in 1879 with twenty-six members. This congregation quickly grew. It met in private homes or in rented property. Mrs. Eddy herself was its preacher. In 1894, the first church building was erected. Although its auditorium held 1,100 people, it soon proved to be too small.

Consequently, in 1906 a beautiful white-domed, 2-million-dollar annex was built in which 5,000 people could gather. This is called the Extension of the Mother Church. At the time of the dedication of this building 30,000 Christian Scientists from almost every large city in the English-speaking world gathered to celebrate Communion in six successive services.

Mrs. Eddy's Strict Control

The First Church of Christ, Scientist, in Boston, Massachusetts—The Mother Church—is administered by a self-perpetuating Board of Directors. All other Christian Science churches are branches of this church. They have their own form of government, but are organized in accordance with the manual of the Mother Church. The by-laws contained in this manual were written by Mrs. Eddy herself. According to the terms of the deed by which she gave the land for the church, it is declared that no services shall ever be held there "which shall not be in strict harmony with the doctrines and practice of Christian Science as taught and explained by Mary Baker Eddy in the seventy-first edition of her book entitled *Science and Health. . . .*"

This manual and this trust deed perpetuate the form of government which Mrs. Eddy established when she was the active head of the Christian Science movement. Consequently, into whatever Christian Science service you may go on a Sunday morning, you will hear readings from the Bible interspersed with readings from *Science and Health*. The subjects for the readings, which are designated Lesson-Sermons, for each Sunday were all worked out by Mrs. Eddy and the Sunday services will be identical in whatever place one attends, as far as the Lesson-Sermon is concerned. Hymns, solos, Scriptural readings and benedictions are not the same. Only the Lesson-Sermon and closing readings are identical.

The Mid-Week Gatherings

In the middle of the week Christian Scientists gather for a testimony meeting, at which time they tell publicly of cures they have experienced or seen accomplished through the practice of Christian Science. In addition to this meeting, every good Christian Scientist spends time each day in private study of the Lesson-Sermon.

Four buildings make up the world headquarters of the Christian Science Church in Boston, Massachusetts. At the left is the administration building; behind it, the Christian Science Publishing House; in the center is the extension of the original edifice, with its 224-foot-high dome; and to the right, with its 124-foot-high tower, is the original First Church of Christ, Scientist. The two churches together are called the Mother Church. (Ewing Galloway)

"Healing"

Although in theory each person is supposed to be able to maintain his health, or recover from illness, by the exercise of his understanding of Christian Science, Christian Scientists may employ more experienced Christian Scientists, called practitioners, to help them. These practitioners, who devote full time to the healing work, of course receive fees for their services. The treatment they give can be administered either to the patient personally, or even by the practitioner at a distance. Christian Science teaches that injuries and disease are equally curable by the application of its rules. Although there is no denying that many sick persons have been made well by the exercise of faith, especially religious faith, yet it is well to remember that Christian Science has no monopoly of such healing. It was practiced in modified form by the ancient Greeks, and is taught today by the "Immanuel Movement" in the Episcopal Church and in the Roman Catholic Church. The shrines of St. Anne de Beaupré and Lourdes, with their piles of discarded braces and crutches, tell their own stories.

Financial Resources

The work of Christian Science churches is supported by individual contributions. The per capita tax of the Mother Church amounts to at least $1.00 per member per year. Church buildings are seldom built, and never dedicated, until the money to pay for them is already in hand. Profits from the publishing house, revenue from endowment, and individual gifts finance denominational expenses.

How Many Christian Scientists Today?

It is difficult to get accurate and up-to-date figures as to the number of Christian Scientists in the country since the Church publishes no figures. It is, however, actively engaged in promotional efforts, using reading rooms open to the public and well stocked with Scientist literature in almost every community where there is a church. Christian Scientists also broadcast regularly over many radio stations. There are no missionaries in the traditional sense, but trained lecturers often speak to the public on Christian Science. So it seems probable that the Church is still growing. There are at least 2,000 churches and 300,000 members in the United States alone.

Much more could be said about this interesting Church, and also about its founder. Few persons who have achieved greatness have done it in a more incredible fashion than Mrs. Eddy. Despite personal weaknesses, of which she undoubtedly had her share, and the flaws which those outside the ranks of Christian Science feel there are in that religion, the doctrine which she taught has emphasized certain vital truths.

Medical Science and Christian Science

The issue that medical science raises with Christian Science may be stated in this way: whether or not our material bodies are in a metaphysical sense real or no, the medical doctor insists that in dealing with organic injuries or damaged tissues he must at least deal with the physical causes and with the physical means of cure. Not to do so, he regards as dangerous to health. The extraordinary progress made by such scientific procedures, even since the time when Mary Baker Eddy lived, has yielded too much release for mankind from pain and sorrow to be disregarded.

On the other hand, medical science, by this very process of scientific investigation, has discovered many and surprising evidences of the influence of the mind or of spiritual attitudes on health. To the medical man it is no longer a choice of an either/or—either dealing with the body or with the spirit, either the use of physical means or the use of psychical means. Up-to-date doctors are seeking a better understanding of both the physical and mental causes and means of cure of disease.

To some who are outside the Christian Science fold, it

would seem that if they are to be true to that word "Science" which Mrs. Eddy had the insight to put into the name of the Church she founded, they also must insist on freedom to retain and to encourage just such a determination to search and such a readiness to change as characterized the spirit of the remarkable leader we have been studying.

15. *The United Church of Canada*

The notion that one's own Church has a monopoly of the truth as it is in Jesus is a relic of intellectual childhood.

If we love and pray and work for the same things, let us love and pray and work together.

REV. S. DWIGHT CHOWN

The United Church of Canada

The Realization of a Long-Cherished Dream

There are few differences to attract one's attention as the border separating the United States and Canada is crossed; indeed, were it not for the custom houses and their uniformed officials the traveler might well be aware of no change at all. The people look and dress alike, and the language, except in French Canada, is the same. The countryside could as well be on one side of the border as on the other.

Yet each of the two nations takes pride in its uniqueness. Each has its own traditions, its own holidays and its own national character. Canadians love the maple leaf, their country's emblem, as much as the Scots do the thistle. One of the institutions in which many Canadians take special pride is the United Church of Canada. Churches of this denomination will be found in every city, and few villages are so small as to be without at least one. Yet the perceptive traveler will notice that there is a much smaller number of Presbyterian churches and no Methodist and Congregational churches at all. Why this difference?

"The Grand Old Man"

The story behind the United Church of Canada is an interesting one, full of drama and the product of the devoted labors of many people. One of the most influential of its pioneers was the Very Rev. George C. Pidgeon, long affectionately known by fellow United Churchmen as "the grand old man" of their church. Born in Maria Township of Quebec on March 2, 1872, he graduated from the Presbyterian College of Montreal in 1894, and in 1905, was awarded a Doctor of Divinity degree by his alma mater. Then he served as a missionary in some of the rural areas in Quebec and New Brunswick for a few years, and finally had a church in Toronto. In 1909 he joined the faculty of Westminster Hall, a Presbyterian school in Vancouver. Later he served overseas in World War I with the YMCA, and afterwards as minister of another Presbyterian church in Toronto. We shall return to him later.

But the United Church is also greatly in debt to Dr. Dwight Chown, long the General Superintendent of the Methodist Church in Canada, and to Dr. William T. Gunn, who served the Canadian Congregationalists as Secretary-Treasurer from 1906 until the union of the three denominations was finally consummated in 1925. Dr. Gunn later became the third Moderator of the United Church, and it is said, literally wore himself out in its service, dying in 1930.

Early Church Unions

Where does the story of the United Church of Canada begin? There were movements aimed at reunion of divided churches very early in Canadian history. One of the more interesting, and also one of the earliest, concerned two minuscule branches of Presbyterianism in Nova Scotia in the first years of the nineteenth century. These were the Burghers and the Anti-Burghers, who had split in Scotland over an oath required of the citizens ("Burghers") of certain cities. These hardy Highlanders were required to swear, "Here I protest

Portrait of the Very Rev. George C. Pidgeon. (Board of Information and Stewardship, United Church of Canada)

before God, and your Lordships, that I profess and allow with all my heart, the true religion presently professed within this realm, and authorized by the laws thereof: I shall abide thereat, and defend the same to my life's end; renouncing the Roman religion called 'Papistry.' "[1] Some of them demurred because they thought it involved a recognition of the Established Church, which they opposed, so they became Anti-Burghers. Others, who felt no such recognition was involved, became the Burghers. That these differences should have been exported to Canada seems ridiculous to us now, and apparently the two groups came to a like conclusion after a few years, since reunion came in 1817.

A division of another sort involved the Methodists. Canadian Methodism sprang from two roots: some churches were founded by missionaries from the United States and others by British missionaries ("Wesleyans"). The former had bishops, while the latter adopted a presbyterian form of government. The two merged in 1829, but there were dissenters who believed so strongly in government by bishops that they took the matter to the courts and even, it is said, occasionally resorted to violence. They lost their case, but as time went on other Methodist groups arose and final reunion did not occur until 1884.

Presbyterianism had a rather similar history, with nine unions required to ultimately create a single denomination in 1875. Congregationalism fared better, but there were divisions here also, and they did not become a single church until 1907.

"Why Four?"

In many ways the religious history of Canada is like that of the United States. As its great west and north were settled, missionaries followed the pioneers and preaching stations were

---

[1] This, and much of the other material in this chapter is taken from George C. Pidgeon, *The United Church of Canada—The Story of Union* (Toronto, Ryerson Press, 1950). The author is also indebted to S. D. Chown, *The Story of Church Union in Canada*.

established, often visited only occasionally, for rounds had to be made on foot or horseback and there were long distances to be covered. Canada is, indeed, larger than the United States. These missionaries were sent out by all denominations, but the most active were the Methodist, Presbyterian and Congregationalist. Measured in terms of memberships, the first two of the three were the most successful. At the time of union in 1925 the Methodists claimed 407,261 members, the Presbyterians 369,939 and the Congregationalists 12,762. Many Anglican and Baptist churches were also founded, but since both these denominations preferred to keep their own identity they are not considered here. Often two or more of these missionaries, or circuit riders as they were frequently called, found themselves attempting to start churches in a village only big enough for one, while at the same time there were regions not being reached at all for lack of workers. It was not rare to find small villages with several churches but lacking the resources to support even one adequately. The story is told of a Doukhobor[2] who, visiting a prairie town and seeing churches on the four corners of the public square, asked, pointing in succession to each of the four, "Is that a Jesus church?" On being assured that it was, he queried simply, "Why four?" And thus it came to seem to many Canadians.

As long ago as 1875, a committee was appointed by the Presbyterians to investigate the possibilities of union with other churches, and in 1885 the Montreal conference of the Methodist Church appointed a similar committee, with the purpose: "That the consolidation of the forces of our common Protestantism may be effected for more economical and extended prosecution of the work of God among the people residing in those parts of the Dominion where the denominations there represented are not able to support the minister among them."

[2] The Doukhobors are a small religious sect founded about 1750 in Russia. They strongly resemble the Quakers in belief, emphasizing the primacy of love and the equality of all men, and opposing war. Because of their objection to conscription and for other reasons, they were bitterly persecuted in Russia in 1899, and 7,500 of them emigrated to Canada where they have prospered. They are partly communal in practice.

"Far Larger Union"

Nothing came of this, but there were others who foresaw eventual union, among them Dr. John Cook, first Moderator of the then freshly merged Presbyterian Church in Canada. In 1875 he said, "Far larger union is, I trust, in store for the churches of Christ even in Canada than we effect this day." Many years were to pass before his prophecy was to materialize, and much of the most unrelenting opposition came from within his own Church. Some of this opposition persists even to the present day, for about 30 per cent of Canadian Presbyterians chose to remain outside the United Church and there are still some 800,000 Presbyterian members or adherents who maintain their religious separateness.

It seems likely that many of the 70 per cent who did merge would probably not have done so but for the untiring labor and great influence of Dr. George Pidgeon who stood stoutly for union throughout the twenty years before 1925, while the final decision remained in doubt. During these critical years, when the question of whether to merge or not to merge was being intensely and hotly debated, he was minister of the great Bloor Street Presbyterian Church of Toronto, from the pulpit of which his vigorous voice for union was often heard. His brother, Dr. Leslie Pidgeon, was also an ardent unionist and urged union from the pulpits of some important Presbyterian churches. The great services of Dr. George Pidgeon in the cause of merger were recognized by the United Church of Canada when they elected him their first Moderator.

Opposition

Opposition to union was at first small, and it was always chiefly from Presbyterians. It finally reached the point where opponents even went from door to door circulating anti-union literature and soliciting votes for their cause. Some absurd claims were made, such as that the Presbyterian form of gov-

The United Church House, Toronto, Canada. (Board of Information and Stewardship, United Church of Canada. Photo by Herb Nott and Co., Ltd.)

ernment originated with the Israelites in Egypt and was thus God-given and not to be abandoned, and that the Methodist Church was "an apostate church." Methodists were accused of not believing in the atoning death of Christ, or in his infallibility, and that he did not "die for sinners." But the three churches finally voted by large majorities for merger, and on June 10, 1925, in the great Arena in Toronto, almost 7,000 people from all over Canada assembled to celebrate the formation of a United Church of Canada.

Organization and Beliefs

Membership

The United Church is a far-flung Church, with some 3,000 "pastoral charges" and more than 6,000 local churches. These are spread all over Canada; some are so remote that they must even be reached by boat or plane. Its present membership is about 1 million, which makes it the second largest Church in Canada, exceeded only by the Roman Catholic, which owes its predominance chiefly to the great number of Catholics in Quebec, settled originally by French Catholics. Since the United Church had only about 600,000 members in 1925, the year of formation, its growth has been considerable —indeed at a higher rate than that of the general population; it is the only Protestant Church of which this can be said. The total amount of money for all purposes raised in 1960 was $58 million.

Organization

In organization, the United Church is presbyterian, with a system of "courts" extending from the Session of the local congregation through the Presbytery, the Annual Conference, and the General Council. Thus, it has inherited characteristics from each of the founding churches. The Annual Conference, which ordains and "settles" ministers, came from Methodism, and the General Council was originally the Congregational name for its highest "court." Ministers are chosen by the local churches.

Beliefs

In belief, the United Church is strongly evangelical. Its creed was agreed upon only after prolonged consideration by representatives of the three founding churches; each group conceded something. Presbyterians gave up some of their long-cherished beliefs as set forth in the Westminster Confession, thus leading some opponents of union to say that the door was "opened wide to every error." Congregationalists yielded on their traditional objection to requiring any creed. The Methodists, for their part, agreed to a creed emphasizing Divine Sovereignty rather more than it was stressed by John Wesley.

The pattern of worship of the United Church is also little different from that of the merged churches, and is based on a Book of Common Order.

Schools and Colleges

Like other denominations, the United Church maintains a number of schools and universities, as well as eight theological colleges. Among them are Victoria University in Toronto; Mount Allison University in Sackville, New Brunswick; United College in Winnipeg; and Ontario Ladies College in Whitby, Ontario. A recent and interesting venture was the founding, in cooperation with the Jesuits and the Anglicans, of Laurentian University in Sudbury, Ontario. Here (as is also done in some other Canadian universities) each of the cooperating churches will have its own college; that of the United Church will be known as Huntington College.

"For The Common Good"

On the domestic scene, the church maintains a number of hospitals, several institutions for the treatment of alcoholism and seventeen homes for the aged; others are being built. Work for the Indians of Canada is extensive, and 25,000 of them are served by missionaries. Some of these are teachers, nurses and doctors who staff schools and hospitals. Much work of this kind is also done abroad, and the United Church supports schools and hospitals in Africa, India and elsewhere. Nor are immigrants coming to Canada from other nations forgotten. These are helped in various ways to resettle and become at home in the country of their adoption.

It is sometimes said that because people differ so much and in so many ways no one Church can adequately meet their needs. But Dr. Gunn, the former Congregationalist, could write some years after the union, in answer to the question, "Do we really enjoy the new mixed fellowship?"—"Beyond all expectations." The United Church of Canada proves that merger is not only possible but that it works. It exemplifies the great ideal attributed to Jesus by St. John "that they may all be one." Men are being helped to lead better lives in the four corners of the earth.

16. Judaism

Hear, O Israel: The Lord our God is one Lord: And thou shalt love the Lord thy God with all thine heart, and with all thy soul, and with all thy might. (Deut. 6:4, 5)

Thou shalt not hate thy brother in thine heart: . . . Thou shalt not avenge, nor bear any grudge against the children of thy people, but thou shalt love thy neighbor as thyself: I am the Lord. (Lev. 19:17, 18)

Mother of All Churches

The seventieth year of our era has never been forgotten by the Jews of the world. Beginning in April and lasting all through the long hot summer months, the walls of the great city of Jerusalem had been daily battered by the might of Roman battalions. With each succeeding week, the people of the city had been huddled into smaller and smaller quarters. The outer walls of the city had long since been breached. Thousands of homes had become heaps of rubble. Even the walls of the holy temple had been broken down. The uncircumcised Romans had destroyed the holy altars. Thousands of Jerusalem's inhabitants had been killed. Others had died of epidemics and famine. The hardy ones who still survived wept over their dead. Because it was unlawful according to ancient Jewish law, to bury the dead inside the city walls, there were still intrepid spirits who were willing, under cover of darkness, to risk carrying the bodies of their comrades outside the city walls for their final disposal.

Thus on a dark night under the light of a thin crescent

moon, four gaunt and ill-clad men carrying a coffin stole out
one of the city gates. As they walked down the rugged banks
toward the valley, they almost stumbled under their heavy
awkward load. Strangely enough they made their way directly
toward the tents of the sleeping Roman army.

Presently as they neared the enemy line, the men laid
down their coffin, and began talking to a sentinel. They asked
for an interview with the Roman general. As they talked, the
lid of the coffin was opened and, to the sentinel's great astonish-
ment, out jumped a man.

The truth was that the coffin had carried a secret envoy,
none other than a member of the Sanhedrin, Jochanan ben
Zakhaí, the most respected rabbi in all the city.

Jochanan was granted the audience for which he asked,
and this was his message to the Roman general. He and his
fellow citizens well knew that their holy city had been successfully besieged. Even their holy temple had been destroyed.
But their faith in God and the Laws that Moses had given
them, which they had been teaching in their synagogues—
these Jochanan was determined should not be destroyed. All
that Jochanan asked was that he be allowed to start a school
in Jabne on the coast, to which Jewish young men could go
and be taught the Law, and where scholars and teachers might
be trained.

Probably to the Roman general it seemed an inconse-
quential favor to grant; yet what he actually did was to make
it possible for the Jews to retain their religion and their soli-
darity as a people even though they no longer had a temple
and were scattered throughout the known world.

The Growth of Rabbinical Schools

This rabbinical school in Jabne, long directed by Jochanan ben Zakhaí himself, became a famous center of learning
and authority from which scholars were sent forth to every
corner of the Roman empire to establish other schools. Finally
such schools were so plentiful that it became an accepted re-

quirement that every Jewish boy should attend some school. This was no small achievement since there were approximately 8 million Jews distributed in every country in Africa, Europe and Asia. It is estimated that every tenth subject of the Roman Empire was a Jew.

These rabbinical schools performed a significant function during the first few centuries of our Common Era. Not only did they help to keep the Jewish people intelligent regarding their religious heritage, but they also preserved the traditions in written form. These rabbinical scholars collected a large mass of oral laws and teachings that had long been current and that had become almost as binding upon the devout Jew as was the Torah or Law of Moses. This set of volumes of laws, wisdom and lore, which was finally completed about the year 500, is called the Talmud.

Importance of Jews in Christian Movement

In its beginnings Christianity was a Jewish sect. Its new message was preached and the movement was carried forward largely by Jews. Most of the early churches flourished where there were large Jewish settlements and their meeting places were synagogues. In a very real sense, therefore, the synagogue is the mother of all Christian churches. It was not until the third century that any large numbers of pagans joined the movement.

The Wall of Separation

The Jews who did not join the movement and who became wanderers throughout Europe and Asia were faced with a profound conflict. With their country and temple gone, the outward grandeur of their ancient culture had been destroyed. The rabbinical schools and synagogues were all that were left to keep reverence and love of the Torah alive. The Jews knew in their inmost hearts that they had a treasure which the world should not lose. Their greatest prophets had taught a truly monotheistic faith and had called them to the stern virtues of justice and piety and humbleness before God. As long as the Jews retreated into communities exclusively Jewish, they could maintain their special religious customs and ceremonies. Although segregated, they went in and out of the Christian world as artisans, farmers and traders, but they had almost no natural social part in the community life.

In the meantime, when Christianity became a political power, the wall which was at first a voluntary form of protection, became a wall of exclusion. Antagonism on both sides of the wall grew. To Jewish eyes, the Christians belittled the Law even though they included it in the Christian Bible. To Jewish minds, Christians renounced monotheism by their worship of a second God, eternal and co-equal with the Creator. And finally, Christians proclaimed a gospel that condemned the Jews as a people for the death of the Savior of the world. In spite of their Jewish Christ, Christians fostered hatred toward Jews, who refused to accept Christianity. So the wall of separation between Christians and Jews in many countries became a wall of mutual hatred.

The Jewish-Christian Dilemma

Throughout history until the present day, wherever Jews have been treated with tolerance and friendliness by other groups, and where the Jews have been accepted and understood, they have usually responded with equal tolerance, understanding and friendliness. In such communities the walls of separation seem slowly to disintegrate. Jews and Christians intermarry. In some places the two groups are now beginning to work together toward ways of fusing the greatest common values in the two traditions, and hand-in-hand they are seeking to develop a richer common religious culture that will be adapted to a scientific age.

Usually, however, when Jews have abandoned their

special Jewish religion or have definitely entered the Christian ranks, their distinctiveness as Jews has been soon lost. This to many seems tragic. If the Jewish people as a distinct people with a distinctive religion should be lost, would the values of Moses and the prophets also be forgotten? Or might the free-ing of this great Jewish heritage from its national roots release it to flower into a higher and more universal monotheism?

On the other hand, if the glorious monotheistic faith of the prophets is to be preserved as a matter of heritage rather than of conviction, is not the real glory of a universal faith destroyed? By keeping his religious culture for himself, may not the Jew lose the very treasure he most cherishes? This was, and still is, the outstanding Jewish dilemma. Christians, on the other side of the wall of separation, should also realize that their present social and religious attitudes toward Jews are serving as the foundation of this dilemma.

Who Are the Jews?

It is often assumed that the Jews are all one race. This is a mistake. In fact in Palestine in Bible times the Jews were a combination of different peoples and nationalities. For two thousand years the Jews have been living in practically every country in Europe and in the Western Hemisphere, and natu-rally they have become a part of the people among whom they have lived.

Large groups of Jews in America have no institutional religious ties. To these, religion is a personal matter, not a national characteristic. Many have grown discontented with the traditionalism of many Christian denominations as well as with the content of religious instruction offered their children in Jewish synagogues. Yet often such Jews, in their daily lives, follow the teachings of prophetic Judaism. They are active in social movements and concerned for world peace. They find themselves religiously neither Jews nor Christians. Often they are troubled to know just what to call themselves.

Types of Adherents to Judaism

Those Jews who are followers of Judaism differ among themselves just as radically as do the different Christian sects. In general, there are on the one hand the Orthodox Jews, who retain the religion of their fathers very much as it was at the beginning of the present era. They observe the old Mosaic laws and use the Hebrew tongue in all their services. On the other hand, there are the Reform Jewish congregations that correspond to the more liberal denominations among Christians. Although honoring the heritage so remarkably handed down in the Old Testament, they do not feel bound to the past. They are continually creating new expressions for religious sentiments that have a modern appeal. In between these two groups, are the Conservative Jews. These accept the results of Biblical scholarship, yet believe in preserving the traditional forms of worship.

Jewish Holidays

As with all ancient religions, Judaism has many holy days and festivals. Although changing living conditions have brought about some modifications, yet these holy days are still of high importance. The first ten days of the Jewish New Year, which come in the fall, bring the most solemn of all Jewish holidays. Jews who rarely attend divine service will be in their synagogues on New Year's Day. It is called the Day of Judgment, for on this day the individual stands before God, examines his deeds, prays in penitence and solemnly resolves to be more faithful. The entire tenth day, the Day of Atonement, is spent in fasting and prayer in the synagogue. At the final blowing of the ram's horn at sundown, the people return to their homes with a sense of forgiveness and new resolves for the year to come.

The other major holidays that are commonly observed are in commemoration of historical events. Originally they were largely seasonal holidays, related to similar holidays ob-

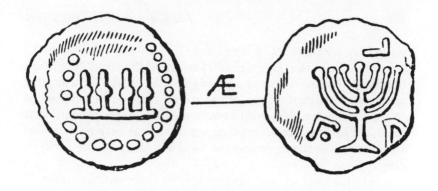

The first historical representation of the Menorah, the holy candelabrum of the Jewish temple, appears on a bronze coin from the reign of Antigonus Mattathias (40-37 B.C.). On one side of the coin are four trees, on the other is the Menorah with its seven candlesticks symbolizing the seven days of creation, seven continents and seven planets. (The Jewish Museum, New York, N.Y., Frank J. Darmstaedter)

served in all lands. The Passover, for instance, is meant to commemorate the freeing of Jewish serfs from Egyptian bondage. Originally it was a spring festival related to a similar spring festival in the land of its origin. Succoth, the Feast of the Tabernacles, meant to commemorate developments that followed release from Egyptian serfdom, was originally a harvest festival of thanksgiving for God's bounty in the form of crops.

Hanukkah, which corresponds in time to Christmas, is meant to commemorate the freeing of the Jews from the Syrian-Greeks by Judas Maccabeus in 165 B.C. It commemorates the successful end of the earliest known struggle for religious liberty. Originally it had the same ancient origin as the Christmas holiday. Both Hanukkah and Christmas are meant to commemorate historical events. Both, however, are festivals of light and owe their origin to ancient annual celebrations that greeted the lengthening day with the end of the winter solstice.

The Jewish Sabbath

With the truly orthodox, the Sabbath is a most solemn religious occasion. No food may be prepared, no money or tool may be handled, no weight may be carried, no journey, not even a long walk, may be taken. The children, of course, may play no games that involve any objects that need to be carried or hurled. The difficulty of observing a Sabbath of this kind under modern conditions may be one of the reasons for the reduction in the numbers of Orthodox Jews. Every male over thirteen is expected to spend the day in religious reading and contemplation. Modern Orthodox Jews vary in the degree of their observance. Most of the members of Conservative congregations observe the day with prayer but perform necessary work.

Synagogue Services

The most prized treasure in any synagogue is its copy of the Torah, or The Five Books of Moses. This is written by hand in Hebrew on a parchment scroll that is rolled about two upright sticks, usually overlaid with silver and elaborately carved and ornamented. This scroll is kept in an ark which also is artistically carved and ornamented with Jewish sacred symbols. Before the ark there hangs a sacred lamp whose flame, never being allowed to go out, symbolizes the eternal.

In all Orthodox and Conservative synagogues and in Reform congregations, this scroll is taken from the ark and portions are read during the service.

Reform congregations conduct their services mainly in English, and in many ways these are similar to those in Protestant Christian churches. These services usually include responsive readings, hymns and a sermon. In Orthodox and Conservative congregations, the services are in Hebrew. The men usually wear the traditional skull caps and prayer shawls. The entire congregation participates in singing the hymns and in reading the prayers, although no effort is made to read in unison. There may or may not be a sermon. The prayer book of the Conservative and Orthodox congregations is similar in form to the Roman Catholic Missal or prayer book, and may have originally served, to some extent, as a model for it.

Jewish Schools in the United States

There are many Jewish religious schools in the United States. Most of these are under the auspices of Orthodox or Conservative congregations, and are usually conducted on weekdays after public school hours. There are a few all-day schools. These make no attempt to produce Jewish scholars, but they do emphasize Jewish history and the Old Testament and teach at least the rudiments of the Hebrew language. In all Jewish religious schools special attention is given to acquainting children with the ceremonies of the Jewish holy days and festivals. As in many Christian Sunday Schools, so much time is often devoted to acquainting children with the heritage from ancient times, that little is left for dealing with problems and interests that directly concern modern children.

Nevertheless, the Jews have always had the highest regard for learning and there have been many noted Jewish scholars, among them Albert Einstein in science, and Justice Louis Brandeis of the Supreme Court. In their honor the Jewish people have established the Albert Einstein School of Medicine and Brandeis University. And in Jerusalem they have also founded the Hebrew University. Their humanitarian interests have also been expressed in the establishment of numerous hospitals of the highest standing. Such a one is the Mt. Sinai Hospital in Baltimore. Colleges and hospitals alike are open to those of all faiths.

The Bar-Mitzvah Ceremony

Those boys who continue faithfully in their Jewish schools until they are approximately thirteen years of age, or until graduation, are dedicated to the Jewish faith by means of the Bar-Mitzvah ceremony. Although related to an older ceremony, the Bar-Mitzvah, as it is now known, is of recent development. It is held in the synagogue. The boy is called to recite certain prayers and to give a talk and sometimes to read from the Torah in Hebrew. The rabbi prays for him. At a home party afterwards, the boy receives congratulatory gifts. In recent years there has developed in some congregations a somewhat similar ceremony for girls who have also completed their studies in the Jewish school.

The Great Tragedy

Until World War II there were about 16 million Jews in the world. Of these about $5\frac{1}{2}$ million now live in the United States and almost 2 million in the new Jewish state of Israel. During World War II the Jews of Europe were overtaken by the greatest group tragedy in history. It is estimated that over $5\frac{1}{2}$ million were slaughtered or starved in Nazi concentration camps. This, however, did not close the story of persecution, for it has continued in less brutal form in much of eastern Europe and even elsewhere. Tradition, extending back through many centuries, dies hard.

A New State

Discrimination and cruelty toward Jews, especially in Austria and France in the 1890s, were largely responsible for the dream of Austrian journalist Theodore Herzl of a Jewish state which should be a refuge for Jewish people from everywhere. This flowered in the Zionist movement, which had its genesis in 1907. But the vision of a Jewish homeland is much older than that. In the United States as early as 1825, it led a wealthy and successful Jewish American, Mordecai M. Noah, to buy Grand Island in the Niagara River as a haven for Jews of the world. Appropriately enough, it was to be called "Ararat." But this scheme never proved attractive and indeed there have always been Jewish people who objected to the formation of any kind of Jewish state. Nevertheless, the Zionist movement culminated, in 1948, in the proclamation of the new state of Israel, though the bitter fighting between Jews and Arabs which preceded its establishment left a heritage of hatred which threatens to long persist.

Despite this and other difficulties the Israelis have proceeded with energy and rare courage to build up their state. A policy of unrestricted immigration has resulted in the admission of more than 1 million Jews from all parts of the world, and there are plans to admit many more, even though Israel's total area is but 7,993 square miles, much of its land is arid, and its natural resources are limited.

Why Persecution?

How was it possible, one must ask, for Hitler to obtain German consent to the massacre of so many human beings? Obviously without general mass consent, such wholesale destruction could not have been possible. Such a phenomenon can be explained only if one assumes certain conditioning factors already in the cultural life of Europe and especially of Germany that encouraged such a response. Yet it is only fair to add that Western Germany has paid reparations of millions of dollars to Israel since its formation, and has thus attempted to make partial amends for the crimes of its predecessor, the Third Reich. Although the value of human lives can never be measured in money, the indemnity from Germany has made possible the establishment of industries and of shipping lines which have given needed employment to many Jewish citizens of the new state.

This terrific human destruction must be seen as a climax of centuries of persecution of the Jewish people. Isolated in ghettos, deprived of citizenship in many countries, lied about, cheated, robbed, and made victims of the cruelest pogroms— the Jews have lived with tragedy from generation to generation.

It was in nominally Christian lands, for the most part, that this long tale of sorrow became history. The Christian peoples of Europe must plead guilty before the nations for the major responsibility for this accumulation of crimes. Nor can Christian America wash her hands of the guilt. Here, too, have been Jew-baiting, anti-Semitic riots and even murder of Jews simply because they were Jews. Such feelings of hate and such acts of violence have a long history. Their roots are deep and widespread.

There is one branch among these roots which it is especially important for Christians to discover; and strange as it seems, this branch grew from the Old Story of Salvation. In that great story the Jewish people were accused of having killed the Son of God. Such an accusing attitude toward the Jewish people is surely not a fitting part of the Christian gospel.

Bibilography

The following is a select list of readable books which may be of interest to readers of this book who are not specialists in the field of church history. Although those marked with an asterisk are out of print, they are of special value and should still be available in public libraries.

ASCH, SHOLEM. *One Destiny: An Epistle to the Christians.* New York, Putnam's, 1945.

BAINTON, ROLAND, H. *Here I Stand.* Mentor, MT 310; New American Library. (Life of Martin Luther.)

————. *Hunted Heretic: The Life and Death of Michael Servetus.* LR2; Boston, Beacon, 1960.

*BELLOC, HILAIRE. *Cranmer.* London, Cassell, 1931.

*BOOTH, EDWIN T. *Martin Luther, Oak of Saxony.* Round Table Press, 1931.

*BOWIE, WALTER RUSSELL. *Men of Fire.* New York, Harper's.

BRODIE, FAWN M. *No Man Knows My History: The Life of Joseph Smith.* New York, Knopf, 1945.

*BRODRICK, JAMES. *The Origin of the Jesuits.* New York, Longmans, 1940.

*BUNYAN, JOHN. *The Pilgrim's Progress and a Life of the Author.* (170 illustrations). Philadelphia, Foster. (There are many other editions in print, none so lavishly illustrated.)

*BURGESS, WILLIAM, H. *Pastor of the Pilgrims: A Biography of John Robinson.* New York, Harcourt, 1920.

CASSARA, ERNEST. *Hosea Ballou.* Boston, Beacon Press, 1961.

*CHADWICK, JOHN WHITE. *William Ellery Channing: Minister of Religion.* Boston, Houghton, 1903.

CHEETHAM, HENRY H. *Unitarianism and Universalism, An Illustrated History.* Boston, Beacon Press, 1962. (Illustrations by Roger Martin.)

CHOWN, S. D. *The Story of Church Union in Canada.* Toronto, Ryerson, 1930.

CLARK, ELMER T. *Small Sects in America.* Nashville, Abingdon, 1937.

*COHON, SAMUEL S. *What We Jews Believe.* Cincinnati, Union of American Hebrew Congregations, 1931.

COLE, ALFRED S. *Our Liberal Heritage.* (Pamphlet.) Boston, Department of Education, Unitarian Universalist Association.

EATON, JEANNETTE. *Lone Journey.* New York, Harcourt, 1944. (Story of Roger Williams.)

EDWARDS, CECILE. *Roger Williams, Defender of Freedom.* Nashville, Abingdon, 1957.

*ERNST, JAMES E. *Roger Williams, the New England Firebrand.* New York, Macmillan, 1932.

FAHS, SOPHIA L. *The Old Story of Salvation.* Boston, Beacon, 1955.

FERM, VIRGILIUS, ed. *Living Schools of Religion.* Patterson, Littlefield, 1956.

*FLEMING, SANDFORD. *Children and Puritanism.* New Haven, Yale, 1933.

*FOX, GEORGE. *George Fox: An Autobiography.* Ed., Rufus Jones. Philadelphia, Ferris and Leach, 1904.

*FRITCHMAN, STEPHEN H. *Men of Liberty.* Boston, Beacon, 1944.

GARRISON, WINFRED H. *American Religious Movement: A Brief History of the Disciples of Christ.* St. Louis, Bethany, 1945.

GOLDBERG, DAVID. *Holidays for American Judaism.* New York, Bookman Associates, 1954.

GRAY, ELIZABETH JANET. *Penn.* New York, Viking, 1938.

HARKNESS, GEORGIA. *John Calvin: The Man and His Ethics.* Nashville, Abingdon, Apex Books (date unknown).

*HARRISON, ELSIE. *Son to Susanna.* Nashville, Abingdon, 1938. (Life of Wesley.)

HAVILAND, VIRGINIA. *William Penn, Founder and Friend.* Nashville, Abingdon, 1952.

HINCKLEY, GORDON B. *What of the Mormons?* (Including a short history of the Church of Jesus Christ of the Latter-day Saints.) Salt Lake City, Church of Jesus Christ of the Latter-day Saints, 5th ed., rev., 1954.

*HODGKIN, L. V. *A Book of Quaker Saints.* New York, Macmillan, 1922.

*HUTCHINSON, PAUL. *Men Who Made the Churches.* Nashville, Abingdon, 1930.

*JONES, RUFUS. *George Fox, Seeker and Friend*. New York, Harper, 1930.

*JOY, JAMES R. *John Wesley's Awakening*. Methodist Book Concern, 1937.

KJELGAARD, JAMES A. *The Coming of the Mormons*. New York, Random House, 1937.

LIFE MAGAZINE, eds. *The World's Great Religions*. New York, Simon and Schuster, 1954.

*LYON, WILLIAM H. *A Study of the Christian Sects*. Boston, Beacon, 1926.

McCONNELL, FRANCIS J. *John Wesley*. Nashville, Abingdon, 1939.

*McGIFFERT, ARTHUR C. *Martin Luther: His Life and. Work*. New York, Century, 1911.

McNEER, MAY. *Martin Luther*. Nashville, Abingdon Press, 1953.

———. *John Wesley*. Nashville, Abingdon Press, 1958.

*MEAD, FRANK S. *See These Banners Go: The Story of the Protestant Churches in America*. Indianapolis, Bobbs- Merrill, 1936.

MOEHLMAN, CONRAD. *The Christian-Jewish Tragedy*. Rochester, Hart, 1933.

PARKE, DAVID B. The Epic of Unitarianism. LR6; Boston, Beacon, 1960.

*PIDGEON, GEORGE C. *The United Church of Canada*. Toronto, Ryerson, 1950.

*POLLARD, ALBERT F. *Thomas Cranmer*. New York, Putnam, 1904.

POWELL, LYMAN P. *Mary Baker Eddy: Life Size Portrait*. Rev. Boston, Christian Science Publishing Society, 1950.

ROSTEN, LEO. *A Guide to the Religions of America*. New York, Simon and Schuster, 1955.

SCHAUSS, HAYYIM. *The Jewish Festivals: From Their Beginnings to Our Day*. Union of American Hebrew Congregations, 1938.

SCOTT, C. ANDERSON. *Romanism and the Gospel*. Philadelphia, Westminster, 1946.

SCOTT, CLINTON LEE. *The Universalist Church of America*. Boston, Universalist Historical Society, 1957.

SKINNER, CLARENCE R. and COLE, ALFRED S. *Hell's Ramparts Fell: The Biography of John Murray*. Boston, Universalist Publishing House, 1931.

SPERRY, WILLARD L.   *Religion in America*. New York, Macmillan, 1946.

*SPRINGER, FLETA CAMPBELL.   *According to the Flesh: The Story of Mary Baker Eddy*. New York, Coward, 1930.

*SWEET, WILLIAM WARREN.   *Religion in Colonial America*. New York, Scribner's, 1942.

TARSHIS, ALLAN.   *Not by Power: The Story of the Growth of Judaism*. New York, Bookman, 1952.

Three Prophets of Religious Liberalism: Channing, Emerson, Parker. LR12; Boston, Beacon Press, 1961.

WILBUR, EARL MORSE.   *A History of Unitarianism*. Cambridge, Harvard, 1946.

————.   *Our Unitarian Heritage*. Boston, Beacon, 1925.

*WILLCOCKS, M. P.   *Bunyan Calling: A Voice from the Seventeenth Century*. London, Allen and Unwin, 1944.

*WILLISON, GEORGE F.   *Saints and Strangers*. New York, Reynal and Hitchcock, 1945.

Index